HUMAN HORIZONS SERIES

BREAKING BARRIERS

Educating people about disability

ROY McCONKEY and BOB McCORMACK

A CONDOR BOOK
SOUVENIR PRESS (E&A) LTD

First published 1983 by
Souvenir Press (Educational & Academic) Ltd,
43 Great Russell Street, London WC1B 3PA
and simultaneously in Canada

ISBN 0 285 64989 2 casebound
ISBN 0 285 64994 9 paperback

Printed in Great Britain by
The Anchor Press, Tiptree

ACKNOWLEDGEMENTS

The content of this book has derived, in the main, from our work on the CARA research project (Community Attitudes to Retarded Adults) which was jointly financed by the Irish Health Education Bureau and St Michael's House Research Fund. In addition a small supplementary grant was received from UNESCO.

However, the views expressed in this book are those of the authors.

Grateful acknowledgements must also be made to the following: Mrs Lynda Chalker, MP, for permission to use part of her statement on handicapped people in society; Geoffrey Chapman, a division of Cassell Ltd., for permission to quote from Louis Batty's article 'The Chatterly Syndrome' published in *Stigma: The Experience of Disability*, edited by Paul Hunt; the Editor and Publishers of *Community Care* for permission to reprint in full the article 'If monkeys did the same work there would be a national outcry' by Peter Beresford and Patience Tuckwell which appeared in a supplement to the journal on August 2nd, 1978; Constable & Co. for permission to quote from *Persons and Places* by George Santayana; The Council for the Exceptional Child, of Reston, Virginia, for allowing us to use extracts from 'Changing attitudes towards handicapped persons: a review and analysis of research' by Joy Donaldson, published in the journal *Exceptional Children*, and also from 'Public Attitudes and Community Acceptance of Mentally Handicapped Persons: A Review' by Allen Sandler and Rick Robinson, published in the journal *Education and Training of the Mentally Retarded*; the Editor and Publishers of *Harvard Educational Review* for permission to quote from Ivan Scheffler's article 'Philosophical Models of Teaching' (*Harvard Educational Review* Vol 36, 1965); the Controller of Her Britannic Majesty's Stationery Office for permission to quote British Crown copyright material from *Report of the Committee on Local Authority and Allied Personal Social Services* (The Seebohm Report), Cmnd 3703, 1968; the Editor and Publisher of *Impact Journal on Mental Handicap* for permission to reproduce extracts from an article on the life-and-death decisions surrounding the birth of a severely handicapped baby; The Irish Health Education Bureau for allowing us to cite the results of their National Opinion Polls on leisure pursuits and on attitudes to disability; Kluwer Academic Publishers Group, Holland, for permission to quote from *Not Made of Stone* by K. Herlingaetal; Ms Francesca Lunström-Roche for permission to quote from her study *Our Lives* published by the Irish National Committee for the International Year of Disabled People; the Editor and Publisher of *New Society* for permission to report on the findings of the Gallup Polls commissioned by *New Society* and the BBC programme *You and Yours* in 1980 and 1981 on the public's perceptions of disabled people, and for allowing us to quote from an article by Norman Dennis published in *New Society* no. 1, 1963; MENCAP (The Royal Society for Mentally Handicapped Children and Adults) for permission to quote from *Public Attitudes towards the Mentally Handicapped*, a research study conducted for MENCAP by Market and Opinion Research International in 1982; The National Fund for Research into Crippling Diseases for permission to quote extensively from *Integrating the Disabled – Evidence to the Snowdon Working Party* (The Snowdon Report); the Editor and Publisher of *Youth Service Scene* for allowing us to quote from an article by Alf Morris published in *Youth Service* Vol 14, no 3, 1974; The Open University Press for permission to quote from *Adults Learning* by Jennifer Rogers (Second Edition, 1977); Penguin Books Ltd. for permission to quote 10 lines from page 32 of *The Politics of Mental Handicap* by Joanna Ryan and Frank Thomas (Pelican Books, 1980), copyright © Joanna Ryan and Frank Thomas 1980; People First of Nebraska for permission to quote from their brochure describing their aims and intentions; A.D. Peters & Co. Ltd., for permission to quote one line from John Mortimer's play *Voyage around My Father*, published by Methuen; Prentice Hall, Inc., for permission to quote from *Stigma: Notes on the management of a spoiled identity* by Erving Goffman (copyright © Erving Goffman 1963); The Press Association for allowing us to use extracts from their reports on the recent case of a Down's Syndrome baby in our sample material 'You the Jury'; Routledge & Kegan Paul Plc for permission to quote two extracts from *Mental Handicap and Community Care – A Study of Mentally Handicapped People in Sheffield* by Michael Bayley; The Russell Sage Foundation, New York, for permission to quote five lines from *The Making of Blind Men* by Robert A. Scott, copyright © Robert A. Scott 1969; Martin Secker & Warburg Ltd. for permission to quote a sentence from Christy Brown's *My Left Foot: The childhood story of Christy Brown*; *The Sunday Times* and Times Newspapers Ltd. for permission to adapt the article by Marjorie Wallace and Linda Melvern published in *The Sunday Times* of 16th August, 1981; The Union of Voluntary Organisations for the Handicapped (UVOH) for permission to quote statements by Peter Moore and Anne

O'Sullivan from *People Like Us: Disability the people and the facts* by Anne Dempsey; The United Nations Secretariat for permission to quote a sentence from United Nations Resolution 3447, December 1975; The United States Department of Health, Education and Welfare for permission to quote from the article 'We Are People First', published in *Mental Retardation: The Leading Edge – Service Programs that Work* (Report to the President: MR78, 1979, US Dept. of Health, Education and Welfare); The University Park Press, Baltimore, for permission to quote two extracts from Richard D. Ashmore's article 'Background consideration in developing strategies for changing attitudes and behaviour towards the mentally handicapped', published in *The Mentally Retarded in Society: A Social Science Perspective*, edited by M.J. Begab and S.A. Richardson, 1975.

THANKS

We have been helped in the preparation of this book by the advice and practical support of many people; to them we would like to say thank you.

* Dr Des O'Byrne of the Health Education Bureau and Dr Barbara Stokes, Chairperson of St Michael's House Research Committee.
* Mary Naughton, former Research Assistant on the CARA project.
* Our colleagues in St Michael's House Research and Training Departments — Jodie Walsh, Francesca Lundström-Roche, David Kenefick and John McEvoy.
* The members of the CARA Project Liaison Committee — Anton Carroll (Chairperson), Eugene Donoghue, Professor John Jackson, Liam McCarthy, Professor Martin McHugh and Aidan O'Connor.
* Our colleagues in St Michael's House and other mental handicap services throughout Ireland, the teachers and tutors who used our programmes and the participants who took part in them.
* Claire Devlin, Librarian, Health Education Bureau.
* Michael Judge for the cartoons and Rita Coyle for the figures.
* Francesca Lundström-Roche and Sue Jones for typing the manuscript.

CONTENTS

PREFACE

Educating people about disability has been variously described as a 'huge task', a 'mammoth undertaking' and the 'uniting of two nations' – enough to deter anyone from trying. Nobody doubts the need, yet few have attempted to discover the wherewithal.

Our aim in this book is to show how community education can become a reality and although it may take many forms, the goal remains the same: the full participation of disabled people in community life.

The book is written primarily for professional staff in services for disabled people. We argue that they are the people who should take most responsibility for educating their fellows as they are unique mediators between the two 'worlds' – living in one yet earning their livelihood in the other. Equally disabled people themselves have become increasingly active in challenging the public's attitudes towards them. We hope that they, their families and friends will find our suggestions helpful.

This is intended to be a practical handbook rather than an academic treatise. We will provide you with ideas, detailed guidelines, sources of information and sample materials so that you can formulate your own programmes on disability. As you will discover, our emphasis is on modest projects dealing with specific disabilities and tailored to selected groups or 'communities'.

In *Section 1* we review the need for community education by highlighting the social isolation of people with disabilities and the misconceptions which the public has of them. We then summarise the findings from research on the best ways of changing attitudes and the implications these have in practice.

Section 2 includes detailed suggestions and practical guidelines on various aspects of community education programmes – such as arranging meetings between disabled and non-disabled people, using video and organising publicity.

Three ready-made educational packages on mental handicap are described in *Section 3*. These have been developed within our research studies in Ireland and can either be used as they stand or taken as examples for your own programmes. Brief descriptions are also given of other educational packages on disability, along with the address of the firm or organisation selling them.

Section 4: Resources includes sample materials which you are

11

welcome to photocopy and use directly. There is also a compilation of useful resources such as films and video-programmes, books, magazines, etc., which you could refer to in devising new programmes. To aid your search, the addresses of many organisations are listed.

We must admit to a deliberate bias in the book. Mentally handicapped adults feature prominently. All our experiences in community education have centred on this group, but if anything this work is even more challenging than dealing with physical impairments. The public is much more confused about mental handicap and appears less willing to have contact with such people. If our methods can work for this group – and they do – then they can be applied with confidence to other disabilities.

Finally, a word about terminology. Throughout the text we, like the public, use the terms 'disability' and 'handicap' interchangeably, and by 'community' we mean people who share common interests and who experience regular social interchange rather than a geographical locality.

We also assume that you, the reader, will be involved in the preparation and implementation of community education programmes. Should you feel that it is not your responsibility, then all we can say is, whose is it?

SECTION 1: THE NEED FOR COMMUNITY EDUCATION

Introduction

INTRODUCTION

> To cement a new friendship especially between foreigners or persons of a different social world, a spark, with which both were secretly charged, must fly from person to person and cut across the accidents of place and time.

> *George Santayana*

Community education about disability is a huge and important task. Its aim is the complete acceptance and integration of disabled people into every facet of daily life – equal opportunities in education; parity in job openings; comparable choices in living accommodation; the same chance of participation in recreational and social activities and similar freedoms to travel – and all this not within a selective, segregated and parallel system, no matter how excellent, but shared with the non-handicapped community.

The separation of handicapped people from normal living is all too apparent today. In part, this is understandable. Ours is a society founded largely on capabilities: primarily the capacity to look after oneself. Disabled people – as the very name implies – are misfits. Instead a plethora of special services have sprung up to cater for them. Admittedly this is a great advance on the days when people with handicaps were neglected or shut away – a situation still prevailing in many third world countries. But our systems are far from perfect; they have colluded with society in labelling and segregating disabled people.

Robert Scott, in his stimulating study, *'The Making of Blind Men[1]*, claimed that agencies for the blind enrol 'people who may not be able to see at all, or they may have serious difficulties with their vision. When they have been rehabilitated, they are all blind men. They have learned the attitudes and behaviour patterns that professional blind workers believe blind people should have.'

In Chapter 1 we shall examine the social and community life of disabled people. For some, this will mean integration at work or in education, but this raises particular difficulties for others. But even if some handicapped people can not learn or work alongside their able-bodied peers, why should this prejudice their participation in recreational activities, their attendance at community events, their membership of social clubs, their chances of making new friends and acquaintances? Indeed a visitor from another

15

planet on studying this data may well conclude that disability is a contagious ailment, requiring quarantine.

Yet advances in training and technology have meant that most disabled people can look after themselves, albeit with special aids or assistance. The elusive goal is their social integration within the local community, mixing freely and comfortably with their neighbours. We prefer to emphasise integration in pubs, discos and sports clubs, rather than at work, and to focus on children mixing in the street or in youth groups, rather than at school. Wherever people come together to relax and enjoy themselves, there disabled people should be accepted as fully and as equally as any other person.

Of course, one consequence of their separate co-existence is predictable – the ignorance of the able-bodied about their disabled peers. Chapter 2 details the public's schizophrenic attitude – pity and sympathy on one hand but a reluctance to meet combined with mistaken stereotypes on the other. As Lynda Chalker, a British Member of Parliament with a long interest in disablement, said, 'I've grown to realise that society has gone down a very strange path for years, not believing that handicapped people would enjoy getting involved in the same sort of things that you and I would enjoy.'

The commitment of disability organisations to community education is often blunted by other demands. Public support for their fund-raising activities is most easily enlisted by emphasising the inadequacies of their handicapped clients. The lack of suitable community facilities has led them to develop specialist services – residential accommodation, social clubs and workshop employment – which only disabled people are entitled to use. But such is the stigma of disability that able-bodied neighbours are unlikely to avail themselves of them in any case, no matter how high the standards of these facilities.

It is not surprising then, that many disability organisations, when faced with the dilemma of inadequate resources to undertake the immense task of public education, concentrate their efforts on producing and distributing literature or providing speakers for local functions. But as we shall examine in Chapter 3, the evidence from research suggests that these methods are largely ineffective. Rarely do they educate the public and worse still, they may even confirm rather than change their stereotypes of disabled people. Take this familiar scenario:

The office phone rings. 'Mr Brown? John Murphy speaking, I'm headmaster here in Hill Street Comprehensive School . . .We'd like you to give a talk to our senior students on the good work your agency is doing with the mentally handicapped . . .Fine, next Tuesday afternoon, 2.30?'

Tuesday arrives, a busy day with little time to spare before lunch; quickly you assemble what you need – the film on mental handicap, some leaflets to leave with the teacher, and your few notes.

You arrive, are received by the headmaster and are escorted to the assembly hall; four senior classes have been brought in; the projector and screen are in place. A sense of occasion pervades. You stand on the raised dais, looking quite at ease, but happy to rest an elbow on the lectern where you have arranged your notes. You are introduced in glowing terms . . .

No matter how brilliant the presentation which follows, there are obvious limitations arising from the "hidden curriculum" of this presentation:

1 Unless you are handicapped yourself, you are speaking on behalf of a group of people, none of whom are present. This implies that they cannot speak for themselves.

2 By your training and work, you are well qualified to give factual information about handicap, but the social and emotional aspects of being handicapped are difficult to convey, and easily overlooked.

3 While your presentation may be memorable, the setting suggests that handicap is a specialized subject with little or no relevance to everyday school life. Handicapped people, it would seem, are a race apart.

Once-off lecture presentations may be good for your ego but they can never achieve the effects you want. Ivan Scheffler, an educational philosopher, distinguishes between information and knowledge. He wrote[2], 'Knowledge requires something more than the receipt and acceptance of true information. It requires that the student earn the right to his assurance of the truth of the information in question. New *information*, in short, can be intelligently conveyed by statements; new *knowledge* cannot.' For too long we have given the public information about disability but we have done little to increase their knowledge of disabled people.

There are ways of increasing knowledge and understanding about disability. In Chapter 3 we shall summarise the essential ingredients to successful education and attitude change. These methods have been used to bring together peoples of differing religion, race and social class. They have proved effective, too, in helping to integrate disabled with non-disabled people and they have worked for us in our efforts to introduce mentally handicapped adults to their neighbours. One word sums up the essence of this approach – *involvement*. People cannot be bullied, pressurised or bribed into changing their attitudes; but they will change if *they* experience a need to change – through meeting disabled people, listening to them talk about themselves, finding out more of the aspects which most interest them, and discussing their reactions and feelings with others.

Such approaches require more time, commitment and personal contacts than do talks, information leaflets and mass media campaigns. They must be carefully planned and tailored to meet the needs of that target audience and they must be used regularly and systematically so that everyone in the community has a chance to participate. In sum, the same methodical approaches we use in the education and training of disabled people have to be applied to the even greater challenge of educating the public.

But whose responsibility is it? The people most obviously affected by negative attitudes and who stand most to gain from community education are disabled people themselves. As more of them shrug off the mantle of helplessness and live full and varied lives within the community, they will challenge the public's presumptions. The frustrations and depressions in doing this are many. Peter Moore[3], a Dublin writer who was a spastic from birth, encapsulated his philosophy with a beautiful anecdote. He tells of the day he met a 'hippie', a great guitarist who didn't believe in organised societies. 'One day we were out for a walk together and we got round to music and he mentioned his stereo; I jumped at him and asked him how he could reconcile using a stereo, a manufactured item, with his rejection of organised societies. But he said, "If I hadn't got my stereo, I could play my guitar and if I couldn't do that, I could clap my hands and if I couldn't clap my hands, I could whistle the tune." He said "If you can't do a thing one way, don't get hung-up about it, try another way," and that was the statement that changed my life.'

Increasingly, people with physical or mental handicaps are beginning to speak for themselves. We hope that this book will give others courage to become active community educators if not in systematic projects, then at least through daily contacts.

But given the tradition and pattern of services for disabled people in western countries, one group more than others must take on the responsibility for community education – the professionals employed in services for disabled people. They are ideal mediators between the two communities – living in one and working amongst the other. Yet so often the bridges are left un-built.

Uppermost in our mind when writing this book have been the professional staff in disability organisations – doctors, social workers, nurses, teachers, psychologists, administrators, care assistants – all whom Erving Goffman[4] describes as the 'wise': 'persons who are normal but whose special situation has made them intimately privy to the secret life of the stigmatised individual and sympathetic with him and who find themselves accorded a measure of acceptance, a measure of courtesy membership of the clan.' We hope this book will encourage and enable more of our colleagues to introduce their disabled friends to their neighbours.

Goffman also mentions a second type of wise person: those related to the stigmatised individual – parents, sisters, brothers, friends. Most of the advances in the care and education of disabled people have sprung from the initiatives of these wise people. We expect that many of them will want to be at the forefront in community education and we trust this book will give them support and suggestions.

Introductions can lead to friendships; friendships to sharing and sharing to change. During the past century our services for disabled people have changed as they have evolved. The evolution must continue. Educating the community may help in the end to bring about the extinction of a species – Homo Sapiens Handicapus. All it needs, as Santayana reminds us, is for a spark to fly.

1 DISABLED PEOPLE AND THE COMMUNITY

Disabled people have the same fundamental rights as their fellow-citizens of the same age; first and foremost, to enjoy a decent life, as normal and full as possible.

United Nations Resolution, 3447,
December, 1975

'There is a glass wall separating the able and the disabled.' So wrote Christy Brown[1], the Irish author, handicapped from birth, who penned his autobiography with his left foot. And such walls are every bit as daunting and difficult to cross as the brick ones which once surrounded cripples' institutes, epileptic colonies and mental subnormality hospitals. The difference today is that disabled people can see what they are missing. Although many live in the community, few are part of it.

But first we need to look at the terms 'community' and 'disability' – at least as we understand them in the context of this book, and you will find that we make frequent reference to them. Secondly, we shall let disabled people tell you of their experiences when attempting to join in community life and we shall supplement this with data from surveys which suggest that these impressions are not peculiar to any one locality or person. Finally we shall argue that public education is the only way to break glass walls, to unite the two nations to which Lord Snowdon[2] referred in his Report and to remove the stigma of second-class citizenship which so many disabled people feel.

Communities

For disabled people the 1960s heralded an era of change in Western countries with a move from models of institutional to community care. The transitions were often erratic and confused. One difficulty – and still a continuing one – was the definition of 'community'. In Britain an Interdepartmental Committee of Government chaired by Sir Frederick Seebohm[3], succinctly summarised the essential feature of a community that could care, when they wrote:

The term 'community' is usually understood to cover both the physical location and the common activity of a group of people. The definition

20

of a community, however, or even of a neighbourhood, is increasingly difficult as Society becomes more mobile and people belong to 'communities' of common interest, influenced by their work, education or social activities, as well as where they live. Thus although traditionally the idea of a community has rested upon the geographical locality – and this remains an important aspect of many communities – today different members of a family may belong to different communities of interest as well as to the local neighbourhood. The notion of a community implies the existence of reciprocal social relationships, which among other things ensure mutual aid and give those who experience it a sense of well-being.

A community is more than a collection of people, houses or streets. Rather it evolves out of personal relationships and is sustained by them. Two phrases in the above definition capture this theme – *'mutual aid'* and *'communities of interest'*.

By defining communities in terms of friendships we bring a new dimension to the expression 'community care'. This implies that there exists not one, but *many communities* who could care. As we have attempted to illustrate below, these can range from the family right up to a nation. The common attributes, which Michael Bayley[4] noted, are 'a sense of belonging, locality and the existence of reciprocal social relationships.' All of which is well typified by children, when they write longer and longer addresses for themselves – 'Copperfield Street, Duncairn, Belfast, N. Ireland, Europe, Northern Hemisphere, Earth', and so on.

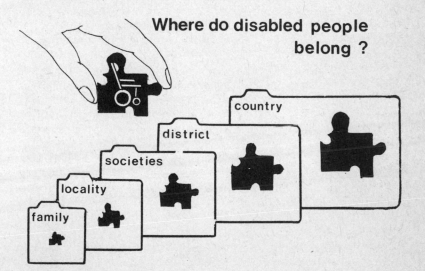

Where do disabled people belong ?

In each of these communities, the disabled person may or may not be a fully participant member. Indeed some would argue that this only occurs within the family and particular social groups, whereas at district or national level, the disabled person is a misfit.

Bayley takes this argument one step further with his proposal that 'care by the community at the small scale level of the intimate face-to-face relationships of the social networks of kin, friends and neighbours can be seen to be the basis on which care at the larger scale level depends.' In short, if your friends and neighbours don't care, your fellow countrymen won't. The lobbying of councillors, civil servants and cabinet ministers will have little effect unless grassroots concern has built up.

What are so perturbing are the pressures operating against the development of neighbourliness in local communities, especially in areas of rehousing. Bayley quotes Norman Dennis:

> On estates the home is well equipped for leisure and the neighbour-hood poorly equipped. Instead of the neighbourhood being 'the rail-waymen's district' or 'the fishermen's district' . . . many occupations are represented . . . The location of the estate in relation to the facilities of the rest of the town reduces the number of occasions on which a woman is likely to come across a particular neighbour as she goes to any one of a number of nearby shopping centres, any one of a number of churches.'

Bayley refuses to be pessimistic. He maintains that social contacts will be forged in neighbourhoods, whether by chance or in response to emergencies. He is convinced that 'mutual aid, social intercourse and friendly help, still happen.' Indeed that is probably the simplest and best summary of what a community is all about.

More than most, disabled people are dependent on others for some help, a little friendly assistance, yet they can reciprocate if given the opportunity. Such sharing leads, as Seebohm noted, to a sense of well-being for all. But if the people in the community don't know how to help, then sharing does not occur and feelings of well-being are not fostered. The result is quite predictable – disabled people are set apart from others. Yet it need not be so. All it requires is for the able and the disabled to be prepared to help each other. A question remains though: who prepares them for giving mutual aid?

The Disabled
'People think we're all the same – but we're not all the same, we're not all the same.' Percipient words spoken by a Dublin lady

who is mentally handicapped when she was interviewed for a television programme. She could have been speaking for all disabled people. Some would stress the differences between various forms of disability – deafness, epilepsy and mental handicap. Others will emphasise the degree of impairment and may even use terms like defect, disability and handicap to mean different things. At other times, the difference between acquired disabilities and those present from birth may be stressed: 'Some people are born handicapped, some have handicap thrust upon them and there are even some who achieve handicap by their own efforts' (P. Phelan giving evidence to the Snowdon Committee).

David Thomas[5], author of the book *The Social Psychology of Childhood Disability*, eschews all these possibilities and proposes instead a social categorisation derived from observations as to how disabled people are received by society:

1 *Highly visible disabilities* – such as the paraplegic in a wheel-chair or the blind woman with her white cane. These signals cue the public to anticipate an 'atypical' person.
2 *Interpersonal communication difficulties* – visual cues about the disability are lacking but problems of reception or expression will occur early in any social encounter. Deafness and speech impediment are typical examples.
3 *Social stigma* – this grouping refers to people who are stigmatised by the connotations which society places on the label given to them – epileptic, mildly mentally handicapped, nervous breakdown – because their behaviour or appearance in daily life are not at all atypical.
4 *Combinations of the above* – this category covers multiply handicapped people such as those with Down's Syndrome, Cerebral Palsy, etc.

Moreover, various research studies[5] suggest that people find certain disabilities more acceptable than others and the ordering used above reflects their preferences. The most liked are people most like themselves.

Thomas's view, that disability is largely in the eye of the beholder, has been echoed by handicapped people themselves. For example, Anne O'Sullivan[6], paraplegic as the result of a car accident: 'I tend to close my mind to what I can't do, and I find I can forget I'm disabled a lot of the time.' Or this, from a Danish contributor to the Snowdon Committee:

I see very clearly that the difficulty lies not really in what the world thinks of the handicapped but what the handicapped *make* the world think about them. You need only remember the late President

Roosevelt . . . he was a person so fascinating that I wonder whether many people realized that he was so severely disabled. It is what the handicapped achieve with the abilities they have left that matters – not what they must do without!

But the ability of handicapped people to shape the public's perceptions of them is limited by their exclusion from community life. Consequently the public not only underestimates the competence of disabled people but does not even appreciate the number of citizens who have disabilities and the many hurdles they face when joining in the simplest of community activities – shopping, eating out, going to a football match and so on.

Disabled People in the Community
Out of every 100 citizens, as many as six will be disabled to some degree, and there will be three under 65 years of age who will have some form of physical, mental or sensory impairment. These are the conclusions from surveys in various European countries[7] and borne out by Amelia Harris[8] and her colleagues during their nation-wide survey of British households.

We cannot give a precise breakdown by the nature of disabilities – accurate national figures are seldom available – but projections from available data[9,10] suggest that in a town or district of 100,000 people there will be:

– 700 people with severe physical impairments (Cerebral Palsy, Multiple Sclerosis, Paraplegia)
– 270 people with visual impairments
– 300 people with severe hearing impairments
– 350 mentally handicapped persons (moderate and severe)
– 250 mildly mentally handicapped persons (in receipt of special services)

The remaining 1,100 or so who are handicapped will have disabilities which do not materially affect their capacity to take care of themselves but do limit their lifestyle.

Lifestyles of physically impaired people
'No one knows what being handicapped is like until they are, and able-bodied people can only have a second-best idea.' That comment came from one of over 300 contributions by disabled people to the committee set up in 1974 by the National Fund for Research into Crippling Diseases and chaired by Lord Snowdon. Its aim was to consider ways in which the 'disabled person may, so far as his personal disabilities permit, have equal opportunities and appropriate facilities as his non-disabled fellows.' The con-

tributors' suggestions for change are much more eloquent than data from survey findings or polemics from experts. Hence, using quotations from evidence given to the Snowdon Working Party[2], this is what disabled people had to say about their lifestyle within the community. Their problems begin as soon as they step out of their front door:

> Many times we don't go out because the effort is too daunting; high and uneven pavements, awkward doors, the list is endless. The preliminaries to a train journey are a nightmare.

> I often wonder why the curbs cannot be ramped at pedestrian crossings . . .it would not only make it easier for us but for the elderly too.

> Why cannot traffic lights be regulated? Evidently the Minister of Transport expects pedestrians to cross the road 'at the double' which is tough on any disabled person.

> Public transport needs to redesign access to their vehicles which many elderly or disabled people find at present impossible to enter because of the height of the steps.

> Having watched how difficult it is for a blind person to find a vacant seat on a bus, it occurs to me that if every bus had a seat 'earmarked' so that it became obligatory for a sighted person to give it up should a blind person enter . . .

> The prevailing trend of turning city centres into pedestrian precincts has sounded the death knell for all disabled shoppers as in most it is no longer possible to park cars anywhere near the areas containing the multiple (and cheaper) shops.

Something as simple as shopping becomes a real chore:

> The disabled eat food, wear clothes and play a part, however restricted, in the consumer society – yet the layout of many shops resembles a military assault course for even the most expert wheelchair pusher.

> Supermarket aisles are too narrow and cluttered with bargain offers piled precariously in unstable bins; the checkouts are too narrow.

> There should be a special fitting room in shops . . .for handicapped people to try on clothes.

> There might be something to be said for all big stores having available an assistant who doubled as 'A Store Hostess'. Their

*duties would be to guide disabled/elderly and frail to the depart-
ment they seek, helping on lifts (possibly organising wheelchairs
on goods lifts if easier) – helping should the person wish to try on
the garment.*

Nor is access to other public facilities – many built with public
money – any easier:

*I am only able to get into one local church of my own
denomination.*

*The Public Library of this town has never been open to the
disabled.*

*I am really annoyed and disappointed that the new swimming
pool has no facilities for the disabled.*

*Many disabled people enjoy swimming and I am no
exception . . .At least one changing cubicle should be built right
beside the pool as they used to be in old fashioned pools. When I
was at school I went swimming alone as I could simply crawl
the yard or two to the water with no help.*

*Very few handicapped people ever attend a Council meeting –
usually the public are in a gallery.*

'Going out for an evening' is not an option open to many disabled
people:

*In the entertainment area the most important issues are for doors
to be wide enough to accommodate wheelchairs and special slots
in cinemas, theatres and football grounds where wheelchairs
can be safely secured.*

*Our town has only one cinema with 3 screens. The disabled are
only allowed in their wheelchairs into one that normally shows X
films. It so happens I usually want to see U films.*

*It is essential there be easy access to public buildings, shops,
places of entertainment etc. I have only visited one cinema during
the past 14 years and the experience was far from enjoyable due to
wheelchair problems.*

But it isn't always because of access problems:

*A paraplegic friend of mine was refused entry to a restaurant on
the grounds that it would upset the other customers. If this was to
happen to any coloured immigrants at least they would have
recourse to the law.*

I have once been asked to leave a public house because of 'upsetting other patrons'.

I personally would attend many more places and events if I knew previously that there was a place to park the car, easy access and that my presence would not make others feel uncomfortable.

Hobbies and holidays – times of relaxing and making new friends – are denied many disabled people:

The disabled should be encouraged to go to evening classes. These present an opportunity for 'normal' people to get to know individuals who have particular disabilities but similar interests. I fear that not many Institutes seek disabled students.

Another problem is that of evening classes. These are usually held in local schools which never seem to have lifts.

A lot of money is spent on disabled sports but not on woodland or riverside walks which some of us would like best. Excellent though sport is for some disabled people, it is not always realized . . . that comparatively few disabled people are able to participate in it. Moreover sport for disabled people means 'segregation' not 'integration' as they are mixing and competing with other disabled people. I would suggest that encouragement be given to disabled people to follow other leisure activities if they wish. In many cases the obstacle is lack of transport.

There must be many disabled people with good voices who would enjoy singing in an ordinary choir. Too often they are relegated to 'disabled choirs and orchestras'.

Wheelchair people need more encouragement to get out of doors. Tent camping is not as lunatic as it seems as everything is on the level and people are always around to help.

I use the trains for long journeys. This means a spell in the guard's van which I am well used to by now, if only it was a little warmer; it is so cold in winter, but at least one is getting out and about.

The idea of leisure holidays for the disabled seems to take on a pattern here that all these kind of people must be herded off like cattle to one place, the same place every year, at the same time, before the Summer begins or when it is over . . . it would appear that freedom of choice goes out when disablement walks in.

A drive to discover and publicise hotels with wide doors – centrally situated lavatories – bed tables – low placed electrical switches – razor plugs – washbasins, etc. – these things make the handicapped less dependent and therefore more integrated on holiday.

There are still many examples of bad planning which could be avoided. For instance a Trust House 'post hotel' with a splendid ramp up to the front door as an alternative to the steps; but in the Gents two right angled bends to be negotiated to get inside, and then lo-and-behold, special facades to the WCs making them too narrow for a wheelchair, or the alternative of wall-fitting urinals out of reach of all but the most cocky of males.

The consequence is isolation and loneliness:

As I become more withdrawn socially I sit at home with my family and, being unable to hear the television, I just sit there thinking what I am missing in life, and this has caused me to suffer from nerves and depression.

I can't blame the man who opts to spend his life chain-smoking in front of the TV at public expense.

From being happy and full of self-confidence, due to deafness I find that I am more reluctant to go out socially with friends and relations because I cannot make conversation with them . . . if they are not answered the first time (they) don't bother again, saying 'forget it' – or that 'it didn't matter'.

I've come to the conclusion that the only thing for me to do is to spend the rest of my life vegetating.

Communities may be built around friendships, but these have to emerge out of meetings. Yet there are so many obstacles preventing disabled people from meeting with others that it is not surprising they remain isolated within their homes or families. All the things we can easily do – walk around the neighbourhood, visit the pub or cinema, shopping trips in town – are much more of a chore for disabled people. But as they have pointed out above, many of these obstacles could be removed with a little foresight and proper planning. The wherewithal is there, it's the will that is lacking.

The lifestyle of mentally handicapped people

In 1980, the Medico–Social Research Board of Ireland[11] carried out a survey of mentally handicapped adults living at home in the city of Dublin. Over 200 parents (or care-givers) were interviewed on the way their sons or daughters – average age 23 years – spent their leisure time. Watching television was the most frequently mentioned pastime for nearly three-quarters of the sample. Around two in five listened to radio or records, went to clubs (mainly for mentally handicapped people) or had a hobby, such as drawing or playing with toys. Less than 1 in 3 took part in any sports and only 1 in 7 in indoor games.

For non-disabled 16–24 year-olds in Irish Society, watching television is also the most frequently cited pastime, according to a poll conducted in 1979 for the Health Education Bureau[12]. But there the similarity ends. Around half of the young people attend dances, go to pub or hotel for drinks or participate in sports; and between one quarter and a third go to the cinema or theatre, have a hobby or attend night classes. All of these pursuits were rarely mentioned for mentally handicapped adults.

Other studies[13] have found that three-quarters of the young people in Dublin regularly share their leisure time with a friend or group of friends. But this doesn't happen for people with mental handicap. As the figure below illustrates, most mentally handi-

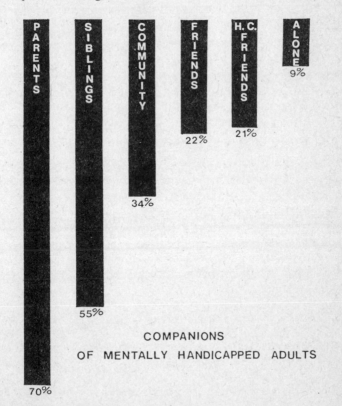

PARENTS
SIBLINGS
COMMUNITY
FRIENDS
H.C. FRIENDS
ALONE

9%

22%   21%

34%

55%

70%

COMPANIONS
OF MENTALLY HANDICAPPED ADULTS

capped adults spend their leisure time with their parents or close family. Only one third join in any community group and even fewer have friends of their own age – whether handicapped or not. Overall 1 in 10 have no companion at all, but this increases to 1 in 5 for those who are most severely handicapped.

Similar findings have been reported for young mentally handicapped adults in other countries – by Sally Cheseldine and Dorothy Jeffree[12] in Manchester, England, by Shunit Reiter and Avraham Levi[15] in Israel and by Beck Ford[16] and colleagues in Canada.

But again, mentally handicapped people can better describe their experiences than any set of figures. The Irish Committee for the International Year of Disabled People commissioned Francesca Lundström-Roche[17] to obtain the views of people attending workshops or training centres in Dublin. The following are some of the comments from the 54 people interviewed (more are given in Section 4).

Ah no, I've no friends at home – no way – I stay in the house every night.

I don't go out – just watch telly . . . I like to look after my mother and make tea for her and myself, and light the fire for her.

I need a friendship; I wish I had a companion, a boy I could have as a companion, I could go out with and chat to. I have nobody and it hurts me.

I have loads of friends. I wish I could get to know a lot more people.

I've nothing really else to do when I get home, just look at television.

I'd go for a long walk if I was let . . .but there is too much traffic on the roads . . . I'd prefer out in the country.

It's boring on Sunday afternoons.

Well, I'd go [to the club] but I felt it wasn't worth it . . . they hadn't got the games that I like . . .they only had Ludo, Snakes and Ladders and it wasn't up to my taste.

They [clubs] are good in one sense and very boring in another; you might get the same record over and over again.

I'd go to the dances but I've such a long way to come, it would be half-eleven again I got home.

I would like to have friends. My mammy wouldn't like friends coming in all the time.

I love my mum . . .sometimes I hate the rest . . .the rest always go out for drinks and dances (sigh). I hate the rest.

It's always the same face, like having one last snap in the camera . . .you keep looking at that one and you can remember all the other times in the past you have done this (attend dances for the mentally handicapped).

The consequent feelings are much the same as for those with physical impairments:

I'd like to go home and let everything start all over again. Start my life all over again.

Thus, the lifestyles of disabled people have much in common. Alf Morris[18], a former Minister for the disabled in Britain summed it up when he said, 'For too long, disabled people have been isolated from the general life of the community. They have been treated as if they were apart from, and not as part of society. This is what must be put right; it is a huge task involving major changes in public attitudes.'

Educating the Community
As contributors to the Snowdon Report noted, bridges between the able and the disabled within our society can be built in many varied ways. Some suggested broad avenues like work and better services for disabled people, whereas others pinpointed more specific paths. All are agreed, though, on the need to educate the public.

Employment

The real secret behind a disabled person living a happy and useful life is simply to work – but if possible, not with other disabled people.

Biggest bugbear in employing disabled people: 1. Ignorance of employers of the subject. 2. Ignorance of Trade Unions.

Work is not just an opportunity for mixing with others; it embues a dignity as a contributor to the community and more practically it provides money for spending.

The daily living expenses of disabled people are high, as they have to employ a handyman to do the small jobs around the house that others do for themselves. Hence money for leisure can be scarce:

> *The biggest complication that arises from one's integration with active, able-bodied people is one of money to stand my corner . . . the knowledge that I cannot stand my corner in the bar is more upsetting to me than my disability.*

Job prospects are not hopeful. The number of disabled people unemployed is two to three times the national average, and for some groups can be even higher. For example, surveys in Scotland and Ireland have found that as many as 70% of people in wheelchairs were unemployed.[19,20]

Better services

Others see the bridge starting from the disabled side and stress the need for more and better services:

> *The more services we can offer disabled persons to encourage them to get around, the better for them and for the general public who will eventually learn to be helpful naturally.*

> *If a suitable motorised wheelchair, which could be used in or out of doors, was available, I could visit neighbours, shops and a park independently.*

But extra services involve extra money. How willing are the public, politicians and prime ministers to divert resources to disabled people? In times of financial stringency must they shoulder a share of the cutbacks?

Changing people's attitudes

Knowing the bridges that have to be built is but a preliminary; the motivation to build is the keystone. This means changing people's attitudes (as Michael Bayley noted) particularly within 'face to face' communities for it is they who will ultimately bring about changes at district or national level.

Equally, disabled people must be motivated to build:

> *At least half of any dialogue between disabled and able-bodied must originate from the disabled themselves . . . We find it so much easier passively to wait for others to come to us all of the time, even when it is possible for us sometimes to go to them.*

And some professionals will have to change their attitudes as well:

> *The disabled will NEVER be accepted into society unless education starts at the top – health and social workers, doctors,*

local councils. Too many of these people look on us as second class citizens.

Changing people's perceptions is a huge task, but not an expensive one. Money doesn't build these bridges, human attributes do. The result – a new lifestyle for disabled people. The Snowdon Committee had this vision:

> *Integration for the disabled means a thousand things. It means the absence of segregation. It means social acceptance. It means being able to be treated like everybody else. It means the right to work, to go to cinemas, to enjoy outdoor sport, to have a family life and a social life and a love life, to contribute materially to the community, to have the usual choices of association, movement and activity, to go on holiday to the usual places, to be educated up to university level with one's peers, to travel without fuss on public transport.*

And this is the wish of a mentally handicapped Dubliner:

> *I feel I'm not as bright as other people might be. But at the same time I think we should be allowed to have the chances the others have in their lives.*

Of course, if this were to come about, it would mean a new lifestyle too for the able-bodied. No longer would they live without disabled people.

2 COMMUNITY PERSPECTIVES OF DISABILITY

> The cripple is an object of Christian charity, a socio-medical problem, a stumbling nuisance, and an embarrassment to the girls he falls in love with. He is a vocation for saints, a livelihood for the manufacturers of wheelchairs, a target for busy-bodies, and a means by which prosperous citizens assuage their consciences . . . He is pitied and ignored, helped and patronized, understood and stared at. But he is hardly ever taken seriously as a *man*.

Louis Batty[1]

Community education must begin with what the public knows and thinks about disability so that they can be led on to new insights. But perceptions of disability change from person-to-person, country-to-country and generation-to-generation. They are never standard and rarely static; they are individual and dynamic responses evolving with experience. The actual defect in body and mind, no matter how accurately and objectively described, is but a trigger for many diverse reactions. People with exactly the same handicap may be perceived by their neighbours in quite different ways. Some will glance and see an odd, unfamiliar, extraordinary stranger, others will look and discover a friend.

This argument has one very important consequence. You cannot generalise from specific instances. This means that your own attitudes to disabled people or those of your friends, may be quite different from those of fellow countrymen. Likewise, the reports from disabled people as to how others react to them – although a rich source of enlightening material – may also be atypical, outdated and culturally specific. Rather you have to get the views of many people in order to build up a picture of the public's reactions. Social researchers have eagerly embarked upon this road, ably assisted by a recent invention – the opinion poll.

Polling opinions

It is wasteful, not to say impossible, to obtain everyone's reactions – even the turn-out at a General Election is less than perfect. Instead a sample of people is interviewed, but great care must be taken to ensure that this smaller group is representative of the population at large. Opinion pollsters have developed many techniques for doing this and despite the politicians' protestations of disbelief, they do usually come up with reliable findings. That is, the same poll with a different sample of people would yield much the same result.

The polls are not perfect. Their commonsense approach of asking people for their reactions has an inherent flaw, namely people's tendency to give different answers to much the same question asked on different days or by different people. Accurate opinion gathering is as much an art as it is a science and it will continue to be so, as long as the focus is on people's reactions rather than their actions. Full-scale studies of the latter would be infinitely more time-consuming, complex and costly than those which rely on the ubiquitous questionnaire.

On balance, though, we find the drawbacks of opinion polls are outweighed by their advantage of providing representative data from the general public. As our focus in this book is on local communities, the bulk of this chapter is devoted to the results of four recent polls.

Opinion Poll Results

Gallup polls[2,3,4]
To mark the start of the International Year of Disabled People, the Gallup organisation was commissioned by *New Society* magazine and the BBC Radio programme *You and Yours* to quota sample 983 people in Great Britain aged 16 years and over, during December, 1980. A similar poll was also undertaken at the end of the International Year in December, 1981.

Irish poll[5]
The Market Research Bureau of Ireland, on behalf of the Health Education Bureau, conducted a national poll within the Irish Republic involving a quota sample of 758 adults aged 15 and over. Fieldwork took place in late October and early November, 1981. Again, the International Year of Disabled People was the stimulant.

Mencap poll[6]
The Royal Society for Mentally Handicapped Children and Adults (Mencap) commissioned a study on British attitudes to the mentally handicapped in February, 1982. This was conducted by Market and Opinion Research International (MORI polls) and was based on two quota samples of adults aged 15 years and over living in Great Britain and involved 1,909 people.

Thus within 15 months of one another, four major polls had sampled the general public's reactions to disabled people, albeit in two different countries. This unique concurrence enables us to draw together for the first time a profile of the public's views on disability and to highlight the implications for community education campaigns in terms of recommendations. (Where appropriate, references will be made to other data).

What do the terms disability and handicap mean to the public?
The answer in a word is wheelchairs. In the Irish poll, just over half mentioned 'people in wheelchairs' in response to the question, 'What type of people do you think of when you think of the disabled or the handicapped?' A further one in five referred to a physical disability or ailment – 'crippled people; multiple sclerosis; people on crutches.' Thus for nearly three-quarters of Irish adults the terms disabled or handicapped conjure up images of physically handicapped people.

As the Figure opposite shows, other disabilities were mentioned by only a minority of people.

Gallup reported a similar ordering among British perceptions, although in this poll fewer people mentioned each disability. For example, in Ireland 1 in 4 people mentioned mental handicap, whereas only 1 in 8 did so in Britain.

Interestingly, Gallup went on to see if people responded differently to the terms 'disabled' and 'handicapped'. They discovered that British adults saw a *disability* in terms of paralysis, loss of mobility, an amputation – with a late onset – whereas the term *handicap* was more likely to elicit congenital defects such as mental handicap, deaf, dumb and blind; although even here, most opted for some form of physical handicap.

In both the British and Irish polls, at least one in five of the people surveyed chose to define disability in terms of people 'who cannot do things for themselves'. A most significant perception.

---

1 *Community educators need to specify the particular disability they are referring to, otherwise people will assume it is physical handicap, and secondly they will need to counteract the 'helpless' image that surrounds disability.*

Confusion between mental handicap and mental illness
The common adjective 'mental' to both these conditions has generated much misunderstanding. In our research into Irish attitudes to mental handicap[7], we found that nearly half of our respondents selected the term 'mental illness' as a suitable

THE PUBLIC'S PERCEPTION OF THE 'DISABLED'

MENTALLY ILL OR DISTURBED   (6%)

PEOPLE WHO CAN'T LOOK AFTER THEMSELVES   (17%)

DEAF AND DUMB PEOPLE   (18%)

BLIND PEOPLE   (27%)

MENTALLY HANDICAPPED   (27%)

PHYSICALLY HANDICAPPED   (71%)

alternative to the term 'mental handicap' and of these fully one quarter went on to pick it as the most suitable alternative in preference to terms such as 'slow learner, retarded, slow developer'.

Mencap's poll explored this confusion in some detail. Half their sample were asked to describe their feelings towards the mentally handicapped and half their feelings for people who are mentally ill. The patterns of answers were so nearly identical that the pollsters concluded that 'they seem to indicate a degree of inability to differentiate between mental handicap and mental illness' (p 7 of report).

They tried another approach. People were asked to judge whether certain characteristics fitted or did not fit their ideas or impressions of the mentally handicapped and likewise of the mentally ill. From a listing of 28 characteristics there were only two on which mentally ill people were clearly distinguished from mentally handicapped people – 'often violent'; 'can be cured' – and merely three unique to mentally handicapped people – 'physically deformed'; 'low intelligence'; 'tend to die young'.

Both groups were rated similarly on 19 other items – including ones such as 'slow-thinking'; 'child-like'; 'problem can start at any age'; 'unpredictable'; 'affectionate'. For both groups a dominant characteristic was the 'need for supervision'; an echo of the results from the other polls.

When the pollsters put the direct question, 'What do you think are the main differences between mental illness and mental handicap?' one in six didn't know or felt there were no differences. The latter were being particularly defiant, as the wording of the question presumes everyone knows there is a difference. The other respondents valiantly struggled to think of differences and the most frequently given answers were that mentally handicapped people usually had physical problems; that they could not be cured and that they were born like that. All of which, incidentally, are only partially true. Thus, at best, only a minority of respondents could clearly distinguish between these two conditions.

---

2 *Community education programmes about mental handi-cap or mental illness should emphasise the essential characteristics of each condition. There is a tremendous gulf between professional and public knowledge in this area.*

Contact with disabled people

Gallup reported that over half their sample (60%) of British adults knew someone who was disabled or handicapped, while in the Mencap survey just under half (47%) knew a person who was mentally handicapped. For one quarter of these people, their contact was with a family member who was disabled (29%) or who was mentally handicapped (23%).

When these figures are applied to the whole population, it suggests that 1 in 7 British families have a disabled member. By contrast nearly half the population do not know any disabled person.

The Irish poll approached this topic in a different way, by ask-ing, 'During the past year, about how frequently have you been in contact with a disabled person?'

As the figures show, around 2 in 5 people were seldom or never in contact with a disabled person; at best only 1 in 8 reported constant contact, and that was with physically disabled people.

Our own research confirms these findings. Whereas nearly all respondents have seen mentally handicapped people around the city or on TV, only about one-third have ever visited a centre for them or shared an activity with them. In short, the public has been

THE PUBLICS CONTACT WITH DISABLED PEOPLE

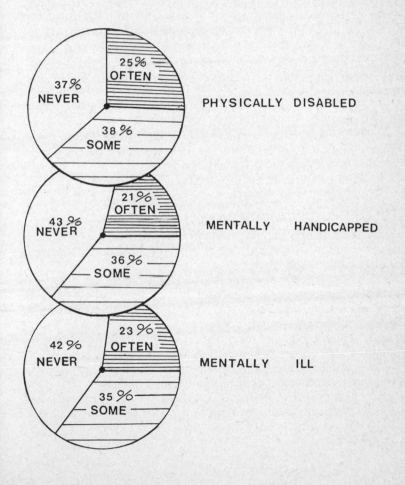

segregated from disabled people. Isolation is the prime breeding ground for myths and stereotypes.

> **3** *Education programmes will need to bring the public into personal contact with disabled people but in a positive and meaningful way.*

Reactions to meeting disabled people

The Irish poll attempted to explore people's feelings when they did meet disabled people by asking, 'When you meet a disabled person do you feel uncomfortable or embarrassed?' Respondents could select from three alternative answers: 'Yes, definitely; Yes, somewhat; and no, not at all'. Over one quarter of the adults said they were embarrassed and this was so for physically disabled (26%), mentally ill (26%) and mentally handicapped people (31%). When asked what would help them to feel less uncomfortable or embarrassed, in all three instances, three-quarters opted for 'knowing how disabled people like to be treated'.

The Mencap poll explored this topic in a different way. First they invited people to select the statements which best described their feelings towards mentally handicapped or mentally ill people. In both instances, the majority went for 'sympathy' (70% – by far the most popular), 'sadness and acceptance' (50%) and 'friendliness and kindness' (43%). However around one third chose items like 'worry about coping with them' and one in six chose items such as 'discomfort' and 'embarrassment'. Only one in five of those who did not know a mentally handicapped person reported feeling 'at ease' or 'confident at coping with them'.

Secondly, Mencap posed the intriguing question, 'If two mentally handicapped adults moved in next door to you, please would you tell me whether you think each of the following would be a major concern, a minor concern or no concern to you at all.' As the Table opposite shows, concern for the handicapped people dominated the replies. Over three-quarters were worried that the local people/children might make fun of them or that they would not get enough professional care, or they would feel isolated. However the most dominant concern among those with little experience of mentally handicapped people was that they would feel awkward in their presence – an item selected by half the respondents.

CONCERNS AT HAVING TWO MENTALLY HANDICAPPED ADULTS LIVING NEXT DOOR

For mentally handicapped people		For themselves or neighbours	
Local people/children might make fun of them	79%	Feeling awkward in their presence	48%
They might not get enough professional care	73%	They might harm local people/children	46%
They might feel isolated	64%	They might cause noise or disturbance	45%
		Might have to help look after them	44%

Source: MORI poll for MENCAP, March 1982

We don't know how to cope with them. We're not used to their ways. It's the same I think, almost as looking after a strange child – you know, you're not sure of what he usually does, so you're sort of groping in the dark a bit. But I think that if they were integrated into society more then we would learn to cope with them, instead of them being shut away in places.

Birmingham woman interviewed in Mencap Poll

Our own findings concur well with these results. When we invite people to select the aspects of mental handicap they would most like to receive further information about, the most popular are its causes, how mentally handicapped people like to be treated and how to act with them. Three-quarters and more pick these three topics.

---

4 *Community educators cannot be content with merely providing information about a disability. People's reluctance to meet – due to their feelings of inadequacy – has to be overcome. The public's disabilities in this regard have to be attended to.*

Views of services
In the British poll by Gallup, a majority of the population were prepared to pay increased rates or taxes for services to the sick/-disabled and handicapped. In the Irish poll, the percentage was

even higher – 66% – the disabled receiving more preferences than did old people (54%), unemployed youth (32%), children (12%), and itinerants (6%). Obviously the high degree of expressed sympathy for disabled people, noted earlier, extended to an apparent willingness to put their money 'where their mouth is.'

In Ireland, there was an overwhelming feeling that services for the disabled should be government financed (80%) rather than have the costs borne by voluntary bodies or disabled people's families. British opinion favoured a single disability benefit being paid to all disabled people, irrespective of the type or cause of their handicap.

As to whether these services should be community based or not, Gallup found an equal number in favour of providing better facilities at home for severely handicapped old people and for more residential centres – one third in each instance. A further quarter wanted both options to be developed equally.

Mencap obtained more clear-cut replies to the care of people who are mentally handicapped. Over three in five people favoured care within ordinary homes in the community and fewer than one in four felt that 'they should be kept apart and cared for in special homes or hospitals.' The remaining 15% could not decide. The sceptic might argue that the addition of the phrase 'kept apart' could have biased the outcome.

There is no doubt about the public's willingness to give money for disabled people. We too found that this was the most popular option when respondents were asked to select the ways they would most like to help mentally handicapped people, with nearly three-quarters in favour of this. By contrast, fewer than one third would be prepared to visit them; less than one quarter would work in services and only one in ten would consider having a mentally handicapped person as a paying guest at home.

---

5 *The challenge for the community educator is to translate public sympathy into deeds as well as donations.*

Community involvement

All the polls included a very similar question, namely whether or or not handicapped children should go to ordinary schools. The actual wording of the question varied and this may well account for the discrepancy in the results obtained, which were:

Percentage of respondents who were in favour of . . .

	GALLUP	IRISH*	MENCAP
. . . physically handicapped children attending ordinary schools	71%	89%	Not asked
. . . mentally handicapped children attending ordinary schools	35%	70%	61%

(*Figures adjusted to take account of those without children)

It is clear that physically handicapped children are looked on more favourably in this regard. What is more puzzling is the difference in results across surveys. Both Mencap and the Irish poll asked the question in terms of how concerned they would be if a handicapped child attended the same school as their child, and provided a 5 or 3 point scale of reply. Gallup, however, asked their sample to indicate whether they agreed or disagreed with a statement that, as far as possible, handicapped children should attend ordinary schools. This is a good example of how hypothetical questions asked in different ways can produce very different results.

The Irish poll further investigated the public's reactions to disabled people in other aspects of community life. The percentages who said they would accept them completely were as follows:

Accept completely, disabled people . . .	Physically Disabled	Mentally Handicapped	Mentally Ill
. . . living in my neighbourhood	95%	89%	85%
. . . joining in my social life	79%	59%	67%
working in my place of work*	78%	56%	61%

(*Figures re-adjusted to take account of those who were not in employment at the time of the survey eg housewives)

Two trends are apparent in this data. First, a preference for distance or chance contact rather than close and regular contact and secondly, fewer preferences for mentally handicapped people.

The Gallup poll in Britain obtained similar data in response to this question: 'If your son or daughter, or close friend, said they were going to marry a disabled person, would it be a good or bad idea if the person were . . . (type of disability inserted).

As the figure shows, mentally handicapped and mentally ill people could expect a cool reception. However, one third of

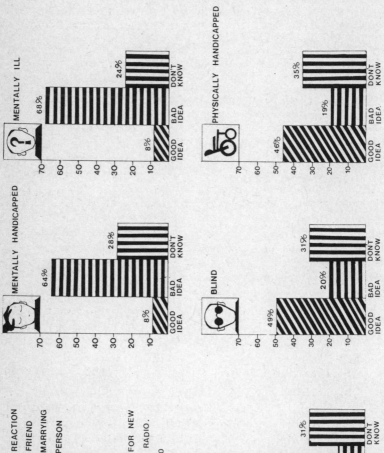

THE PUBLICS' REACTION TO A CLOSE FRIEND OR RELATIVE MARRYING A DISABLED PERSON

SOURCE:
GALLUP POLL FOR NEW SOCIETY/B.B.C. RADIO.
DECEMBER 1980

respondents opted out of dealing with such hypotheticals and wisely gave a 'don't know' response. We are rather sceptical about the value of questions of this type, our reason being that they take no account of people's natural inclination to say 'if'; and hence the replies which people are polite enough to give the pollsters are extremely difficult to interpret. For instance, when asked whether handicapped children should attend schools, one person may think 'if all necessary back-up facilities are provided', decide that they would be and say 'yes', whereas another would decide that it is highly unlikely and say 'no'. Similarly as one lady replied in the Mencap survey:

> Well it would depend upon the degree of their handicap. You know, perhaps the more serious the handicap they would need a special school. You know, like the blind need special schools and the deaf but even so they are part of society, more so than the mentally handicapped.

> (p 30 of report)

It is not at all surprising, then, that questions dealing with generalities and hypothetical situations can yield widely differing outcomes. As we shall see in a later chapter, our advice to community educators is to deal in specifics and with the here and now.

Differences by age, sex and social class

Pollsters frequently report the overall results for their sample and are then tempted to go on and contrast the replies given by the subgroups they used in drawing up their sample, for example, determining whether females gave markedly different answers than males. But these analyses are much less dependable than the overall results and should be treated as suggestive rather than definitive data.

The recent opinion polls on disability imply that the following differences might be present:

AGE

Age – People under 25 years are the most likely to report feeling uncomfortable or embarrassed in the presence of a disabled person, even though they are the group who tend to have a positive image of them, who are most likely to favour opportunities for community integration and who are the most favourably disposed to marriage with a disabled person.

SEX

Sex – Differences by sex are not particularly marked among the adult population, although in our own studies we have found consistent sex differences among 15 and 16 year olds. The Mencap survey – the only one to investigate extensively adults' images of mentally handicapped people – found that females, more than males, imbued them with childlike characteristics: 'needing supervision, affectionate, and happy.'

SOCIAL CLASS

Social class – Again these differences were not particularly marked. There are suggestions that people from professional, managerial or skilled backgrounds ('the middle class') are more knowledgeable about disability and its causes, have more contact with disabled people and are more in favour of community integration. By contrast, persons in manual occupations and the unemployed (ironically termed the 'working class'), are more ready to pay extra taxes.

KNOWING A DIS-ABLED PERSON

Knowing a disabled person – Although this variable was not used in the construction of the sample, not surprisingly it does influence people's perceptions. In particular, those who already know a disabled person are more likely to report knowing how to cope with them and to feel at ease in their company and generally to have a more positive image of them. They are only marginally more willing to pay extra for services and on questions regarding community involvement they respond similarly to people with no prior contact.

Research articles in journals
Alongside opinion poll results, there is a plethora of studies reported in various journals, mostly dated from the mid 1960s onwards. These can provide useful data on the attitudes of specific subgroups, for often they aim systematically to contrast the opinions of males and females, younger and older people, etc. However, the generalisation of these results to other populations is questionable. Most originate in North America; they usually

involve school pupils or college students; the focus is mainly on physical disability and many diverse questionnaire styles have been used. It is hardly surprising that reviewers of this literature regularly lament the unreplicated and contradictory findings they have encountered. Nonetheless, these studies have yielded a rich harvest of techniques for exploring people's attitudes. Examples of useful studies are listed in Section 4: Resources.

The writings of disabled people
A third source of information on the public's reactions to disabled people is to read of their experiences in autobiographies. Usually these accounts are by people with a physical disability – although others with mental illness or mental handicap have started to tell of their encounters. Such data may not be wholly representative, but they are rich in human interest and feeling. Suggested sources are given in Section 4.

Accounting for Public Attitudes
The facts and figures we have looked at are not just snap-shots of public reactions to be catalogued in albums such as this. They are portraits which some should find familiar, other perhaps strange and surprising. But in either case, superficial glances will not do full justice to the people portrayed. Observers need to ponder on the reasons for the expressions.

Sociologists, anthropologists and psychologists have taken eagerly to this task. Sad to say, their efforts have not produced great clarity – jargon proliferates, speculations abound and theories multiply. A balanced review of their collective wisdom falls outside the scope of this book – fortunately. Rather, we will focus on the complexities underlying the question 'why do people react in this way?' and then describe a perspective which we have found insightful.

Are attitudes to disabled people positive or negative?
The best answer is an emphatic 'maybe'. The public are quite ambiguous in their views on disabled people. They are willing to pay more taxes; they favour preferential treatment for handicapped individuals over other needy groups and they are willing to have them join in social and communal activities – all indications of positive attitudes and 'favoured' status. Furthermore, the sympathy and concern they expressed in the polls has been translated into tangible – and expensive – services. It costs the taxpayers three times as much to educate a disabled child.

Yet alongside these sentiments and favours, there co-exist other indicators which cannot be described as 'positive'; whether they merit the adjective 'negative' is debatable. The public's lack of personal contact with disabled people; the confusion in their mind regarding disabilities; their mistaken stereotypes of such people and their apprehensions about meeting them. Or more pertinently, the failure to make public buildings and transport facilities accessible to people in wheelchairs, or the opposition from community groups to the siting of services within their neighbourhood.

In short, it is an over-simplication to describe the public's perceptions as either positive or negative. The reality appears to be that both co-exist.

Yet this ambivalance does not arise with other atypical groups, such as minorities. The reactions to black people from a majority white population would tend to be much more consistent. What we lack, though, is any indication of the public's strength of feeling about disability. If most of them rarely encounter disabled people, their response may well be, 'It's really no concern of mine – but seeing you asked me . . .' Their views are spoken more out of politeness than from conviction. As *New Society* so aptly noted, the best adjective to describe their views is – 'muddled'.

Making muddled images clear

Milton Rokeach, an American psychologist, argues that people's beliefs and values can only be understood by considering the beliefs they hold about themselves. Moreover, he is convinced it is our beliefs about ourselves which determine our attitudes towards others. So what do people believe about themselves vis-a-vis disabled people, and might this clear the picture for us?

'I am able' – In a society which places a high value on ability – and pre-eminently the capacity to look after oneself – it is not surprising that disabled people are seen as different – a 'race' apart. As a clerk from North London explained to the Gallup interviewer, 'A handicapped person is an abnormal person who wants help and attention constantly.' Hardly a description any of us would apply to ourselves, least of all, disabled people.

'I can afford to be generous' – A civilised society is supposed to take care of the weak and unfortunate. It is immoral not to do so. The basis of this morality may spring from religious beliefs, an empathy felt with a fellow human being or a thanksgiving for an affliction averted. Charities have appealed to all of these in their fund raising efforts. Interestingly the public do not expect

disabled people to reciprocate this generosity – they need only be thankful.

'I am incompetent at dealing with disabled people' – Although not often mentioned, this belief lingers close to the surface. It certainly helps to explain the public's reluctance to meet disabled people and indeed it may even be reinforced by the emphasis placed on specialist services and trained personnel. These feelings of inadequacy are usually swamped by a spirit of generosity, giving so that others can help.

'I am afraid of strangers' – The feelings people experience also motivate their reactions to others. For many, physical disfigurement elicits feelings of fear, even repulsion. Labelling these reactions as irrational or unwarranted does not make them any the less real for the person experiencing them. Feelings are part of their reality.

'I have other concerns' – For many, disability rarely impinges on their daily life and hence has little relevance to their concept of themselves; other concerns predominate. Consequently many of the foregoing thoughts are more explicit than the vague connotations usually conjured up in people's minds as they give their reactions to disability. Personal involvement heightens awareness, clarifies thinking and increases the motivation to learn more.

Looked at from this perspective, the public's attitudes are not quite so muddled as first impressions would suggest. For people have cleverly woven their reactions to protect both disabled people and *themselves*. The positive and negative feelings which they express towards disabled people are but reflections of the feelings they have of themselves. We cannot understand their attitudes to others, still less begin to change them, unless we focus on their individual needs, beliefs and concerns. We have to study the singer as well as the song.

3   CHANGING ATTITUDES

Bringing people into more personal contact . . . at least makes them
more aware of the individual character of the disabled child or
adult . . . they will eventually get. . . to see us as people first and as
disabled people second. [Then] they will have begun to see that we are
also the products of our social backgrounds and environment just
like anybody else and not just a disability breed.

Contributor to the Snowdon Report

Everyone concerned with disability – handicapped people, their
families, friends and professional helpers – are agreed on one
thing: community attitudes must be improved. As Joy
Donaldson[2], a noted researcher into community attitudes, put it:
'until disabled persons are seen as individuals who, like all people,
have differing skills, interests and personality traits, the ultimate
outcome of legislation mandating integration and equal
opportunity will be unpredictable – handicapped people will
continue to bear the consequences of unfavourable expectations
and fear on the part of persons who control their life
opportunities.' Likewise, Allen Sandler and Rick Robinson[3],
directors of services for handicapped people, concluded that,
'Attitudes toward mentally retarded persons must be improved if
programmes such as deinstitutionalization are to succeed.'

The need can be clearly stated but not so the wherewithal.
'Changing beliefs and attitudes about the disabled is spoken of
much but little has been done to help understand how change may
be brought about,' wrote Brian Kutner[4], some 10 years ago.
Since then progress has been made, but even today people too
often rely on methods they think, or hope or pray, will work. They
are taking a risk. And the risk is not just that they might fail, but
that in trying they might make matters worse. Jay Gottlieb[5], a
leading American expert in attitudes to the mentally retarded,
concluded that opening the doors of institutions and providing
guided tours for the public, only served to change attitudes
towards the institution – they actually *worsened* the public's
perceptions of the persons living there. As Mark Twain wryly
noted, 'half of the results of a good intention are evil.'

Beyond good intentions
In this chapter, we shall review some of the ways which are known to change the public's attitudes to disability, concentrating on the methods used and pinpointing the aspects which have been successful. In so doing, we shall be drawing heavily on reviews of research written by Richard Ashmore[6], Joy Donaldson[2], Jay Gottlieb[5], Allen Sandler and Rick Robinson[3]. We commend these to interested readers who would like to find out more. Here is a preview of some of their conclusions:

Magazine advertisements and radio and TV programmes . . . have been remarkably unsuccessful in changing attitudes. Contact is not always conducive to reducing prejudice and conflict. In fact contact can often heighten conflict and reinforce prejudice.

The present fad of game-type disability simulations (eg spending time in a wheelchair) may have little effect in helping participants to see handicapped persons in less stereotypic ways.

Educational programmes (eg an academic course, a movie or lecture plus discussion) have been numerous and the reported success/failure ratio is about 2:1.

Use group discussions cautiously, providing guidelines or differential reinforcement to ensure that discussions are based on information rather than biased opinions and emotions.

. . . attitude change is maximised when the instructor believes in or at least understands and accepts the position being advocated and has a positive effective relationship with the students.

Disabled persons are powerful sources of information in that they contradict stereotypes by their own personality.

Carefully structured contact experiences, as opposed to contact per se, are likely to have a positive impact upon attitude.

Where the contact experience has involved greater cooperative activity with roughly equal status and authority support, positive change in attitudes to the retarded have been noted.

Improved attitudes or reduced discomfort can be produced in a relatively brief session.

. . . positive information stressing the strengths and abilities of the mentally retarded should be presented. Care should be taken to avoid attempting to elicit sympathy for the mentally retarded by presenting portrayals of individuals who fit negative stereotypes or who make the audience feel uncomfortable.

. . . those who wish to maximise the effect of brief access to professional or lay groups should provide opportunities through live or media presentations for handicapped persons to convey information about what it is like to be handicapped, who they are as individuals and how they expect non-handicapped persons to relate to them.

Strategies for changing attitudes can be grouped into three broad categories;

1　Contact with handicapped people.
2　Giving information.
3　Experiential learning opportunities, such as role-playing.

We shall deal with each in turn, although any one programme may, and usually does, employ more than one strategy. The final section will attempt to give an explanation as to why people change their attitudes.

Changing Attitudes through Contact with Disabled People

As we saw in Chapter 2, most people either do not know a disabled person or they have met them only occasionally or perhaps not all. Hence the public's impressions of them are not based on first-hand experiences. One of the obvious approaches to community education is to arrange for the public to meet disabled people; they will then realise that their impressions are mistaken and their attitudes will change.

At least that's the theory, and it sounds good; the reality, as research has shown, is not so straightforward. In fact this approach can be rightly described as 'high-risk'. Some contacts between disabled people and the community have actually worsened rather than improved the public's perceptions. Fortunately, enough studies have been undertaken by now to enable the key ingredients to success to be identified. If these are followed, the risk of damaging attitudes is slight and the pay-offs are plentiful.

Ingredients for successful contact
Research to date has identified each of the following factors, given in order of importance, as contributing to success:

Equal status – It should, as far as possible, be a meeting of equals. This means selecting the disabled people to match the characteristics of the non-disabled group. For example, both groups should be of similar ages, and drawn from similar social, educational or vocational backgrounds or share common interests. This means at the very least, matching children with children and adults with adults. Mixing adults and children has been less successful.

This has worked
- Disabled children mixing with able-bodied children of similar ages.
- 15 and 16 year-old school students meeting young mentally handicapped adults[8].

This hasn't worked
- Teachers from ordinary schools meeting handicapped children. (There would have been a better chance of changing their attitudes had they met 'successful' handicapped adults).[9]
- Volunteers working with handicapped children.[10] (This suggests that attitudes to disabled peers may not be influenced by working with handicapped children).

Personal contact – The contact is most successful when it gives disabled and non-disabled people the chance to talk to one another; to share information about themselves and to learn more about each other. Obviously small groups or even one-to-one meetings are best for such personal dialogues. Nonetheless there is also some evidence that watching a video of disabled people talking about themselves can effect attitudinal changes; although not to the same extent as does direct contact.

This has worked
- Blind lady talking comfortably about her disability to a group of students.[11]
- Neighbours invited to dinner in local hostel for mentally handicapped people.[12]

This hasn't worked
- Replaying audiotape discussion by disabled people to college students.[13] (It is harder to build up a visual identity for the person talking).

Sharing joint activities – Merely bringing people together is insufficient. You also need to plan what they will do. Ideally both groups should participate in a common activity during which each can contribute to the overall outcome. At the very least, these co-operative ventures ensure that both parties have something to talk about and should conversation run out, the interactions can still be continued at the non-verbal level. But the benefits can be much greater – an appreciation that disabled people can be valued members of a team.

The activities should be chosen with care. They must not exceed the capabilities of the disabled persons who must be competent in the chosen tasks and should have prior experience of them. Avoid contexts in which disabled people have to depend on help from non-disabled partners in order to participate.

This has worked
- Physical education activities or co-operative games have successfully mixed children or teenagers.[14]
- Table-top games, such as draughts or card games, have been successful with mentally handicapped adults.[8]
- Groups of handicapped and non-handicapped classmates making a film or slide-show.[15]

This hasn't worked
- Disabled student participating in class discussion[16] (no opportunities for contact, interchange or sharing experiences).

Emphasising the positive attributes of the disabled person – People's negative stereotypes of disability can be counteracted by presenting opportunities for disabled people to demonstrate what they can do rather than dwelling on their limitations. In this respect, it is perfectly legitimate to focus on the 'exceptional' rather than the stereotypical handicapped person. Certainly in the case of mentally handicapped adults, our focus initially is on the more able. Otherwise the danger is that the public's tendency to underestimate is reinforced. Strong medicine is needed to counter-act ill effects. Moreover, meetings with people who do not fit exist-ing stereotypes are more likely to bring out the things both groups have in common, rather than the peculiarities of the disability.

This has worked
- Arm-wrestling between handicapped and non-handicapped peers[17].
- Video of disabled workers tackling a complex job, such as weaving.[8]

This hasn't worked
- Tours of institutions.[18]
  (These tend to emphasise what needs to be done for disabled people – the special aids and equipment – rather than emphasising what they can do for themselves).

Reducing the discomfort felt by non-disabled people
Some people openly state that the presence of a disabled person is unnerving for them; it is likely that most feel some form of discomfort. It is vital, then, to put people at their ease. By their very nature, some of the points already mentioned will help to do this, but the following additional features are also worthy of consideration:

1 Provide guidance on how to interact prior to the contact session. This preparation could come from a disabled person, from the 'tutor' of the group or via films or videos of others interacting successfully with handicapped people.
2 People's natural tendency to stare at the unfamiliar creates an extra tension in the context of meeting handicapped people. Some have argued that people need the opportunity to engage in 'sanctioned staring' – looking at photographs or watching films or videos[19].
3 There must be an enjoyable atmosphere to the meeting. It should take place in familiar, even homely, surroundings and preferably those with pleasant connotations – bar, social club, etc.

As against these positive influences, the things which make people uncomfortable are:

1 Being surrounded by more 'strangers' than they can cope with.
2 Meeting them *en masse* rather than individually.
3 Encountering them in strange surroundings.
4 Not knowing how to react to them.
5 Being aware that their 'mistakes' will be noticed by others.

These circumstances are by no means peculiar to meeting disabled people. Think of your first foray abroad; the party where you knew no one; your first day at work, etc. The feelings you experience then are probably akin to those felt by people on a guided tour of the local workshop or school or when they enter the local café and discover a large party of handicapped people occupying most of the tables. In short – they get put off and want to go home!

Is all the work worth it?

It does require a lot more effort to ensure that the meetings are a success – there's no denying that. But relying on chance meetings or hastily arranged visits is not likely to change people's attitudes and the greater risk is that they may make them worse. This is because:

1 People will be unprepared for the meeting and hence will feel uncomfortable and uneasy with the 'forced' contact.
2 The meeting will probably occur in surroundings which are not at all conducive to a friendly chat.
3 The chances are that they will meet (some) disabled people who reinforce their negative images.
4 They will not have the opportunity to get to know an individual person.
5 The disabled people themselves will be going about their own work and may not want to be interrupted; or the circumstances may not permit them to take a break.

All in all, the most damning argument is that this *laissez-faire* approach, the usual one until now, has done little to change people's perceptions of disabled persons.

Planned contact

Change *can* be produced if it is planned; indeed people's attitudes can be shifted dramatically in a very short time – even following half an hour's contact with disabled people.

The educational programme we used with senior pupils in secondary schools[8] included a class period when a group of trainees from a local centre for mentally handicapped adults visited the school and took part in club-like activities with the students – table-top games, music, coffee, etc. This contact session incorporated most of the ingredients noted earlier and it came half-way through the programme. Previously the students had seen videos of mentally handicapped adults and had brief guidelines from the tutors on how they might interact. Initially students were paired with a visitor, but later they mingled more freely around the classroom.

At the beginning of the programme, students completed a range of questionnaires, one of which explored their feelings if a mentally handicapped person of their own age was to visit their home tomorrow. From this, a measure of 'confidence' could be calculated ('know how to react; feel relaxed and know what to say'). On this scale, the maximum score was 21 and as the Figure shows, the students had very low confidence scores for meeting a mentally handicapped person compared to meeting a stranger of their own age.

CONFIDENCE AT MEETING

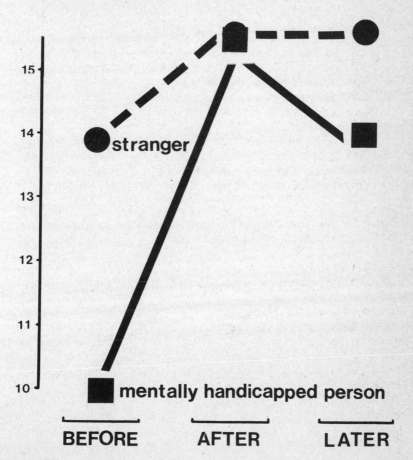

After the programme, however, their scores had improved markedly and were equivalent to those given for meetings with a stranger.

The brief contact they had with handicapped trainees from their locality had therefore brought about a significant change in their confidence. We went back to the schools some four months later to see if these effects were maintained. By and large they were, although there was some falling off – a finding reported by other investigations[29]. This suggests that time can dilute the potency of a once-off contact – short, regular meetings may be necessary to maintain attitude change.

Changing Attitudes by Providing Information
Attempts at changing the public's perceptions of disabled people by advertising campaigns, talks or lectures to community groups, or by distributing leaflets, have been singularly unsuccessful[2]. Nor is this unique to disability, it is equally true in other areas of attitude change – health education, accident prevention,[20] etc. Put bluntly, the conclusion must be that messages don't get across.

We question the wisdom of perpetuating strategies destined to fail, not merely because the organisers become discouraged but worse still, because the community gets a bad name. It is they who are blamed – 'they're not interested/don't care/unconcerned,' etc. Ultimately people may come to see community education as an impossible task. This is not to suggest that we abandon attempts at getting information across to the public; quite the contrary. We need to disseminate accurate and realistic information about disabled people rather than the half-truths and myths which are still prevalent. But social scientists have long made a distinction between information and feelings. It is quite possible for people to remember the facts about disability and still retain the same feelings towards disabled people. Nonetheless, information *can* produce attitude change, but only if it becomes 'personalised' knowledge, to use Scheffler's term.

The information must be useful and relevant to the recipients
People are bombarded daily with a mass of information and only a small proportion ever 'sticks'. Information is much more likely to be attended to and retained if it has relevance for the person at that moment. Few if any of us, store up information in the hope that it will come in useful some day!

In advertising terms, we have to slant our message to the customers' needs. Hence information on causes of mental handicap is much more likely to be heard by 'pre-pregnant' women.

Or advice on interacting with disabled people could be presented in terms of 'helping customers who are disabled' (if you are focussing on sales assistants), or 'meet your new neighbours' (if it is a neighbourhood educational programme).

Credible presenter of information – people are not foolish enough to believe information simply because it is told to them. They need to have some basis for judging its credibility. In this respect, handicapped people themselves[21] are the best equipped to give information on disability and what it is like to be disabled.

When we asked participants in an adult education course[12] whom they would most like to have talking to the group, first preference was invariably a mentally handicapped adult; second, a parent of a handicapped person and lastly a professional worker. It is ironic then that until recently it has been able-bodied people who have been to the fore in community education. Maybe that accounts for the lack of success to date?

Presenters need to have friendly relationships with 'students'[6]. In face-to-face contacts, this is of primary importance. Overly dogmatic, aggressive and down-right 'unpleasant' characters are unlikely to prove good advocates. Hence the job of community educator is not one which can be handed over to anyone who is willing to do it.

Equally, the atmosphere for information exchange is important in written or visual media. The colourful, attractive leaflet is more likely to be picked up and read than is the poorly produced duplicated sheet. The text that engenders an element of humour will help to buoy up flagging spirits.

Positive information is preferred
There is evidence that people attend more to 'good' news, especially when they are forming an opinion or when their commitment to an opinion is low.[22] The implication is that strengths, abilities or potentialities of disabled people should be stressed rather than their shortcomings or their need for help.

For example, information on causes might be given in the context of 'producing a perfect baby'. Notice how health educators have shifted from the threatening 'if you smoke you die' approach to the more positive one: 'stop smoking and your clothes don't smell, you can taste your food, you don't get out of breath.'

Using opinion leaders within a community
This idea, largely untried in the field of disability, is to utilise well-known personalities within a community to help plan and execute

an information campaign. There is considerable evidence from studies of attitude change in other areas[23], that the word-of-mouth support of such leaders is important in gaining acceptance for new ideas. Certainly advertisers use this strategy with good effect and, at the very least, it is a useful way of demonstrating the social acceptability of disabled people.

Keep the message simple
So often, information fails to get across because the message is too complicated. The party game of Chinese whispers is ample demonstration of how misinterpretations can arise. Unfortunately professionals set their standards too high. They want to ensure their message can pass critical comment from fellow profession-als – the 'experts' in the field – as well as informing the 'ignorant'. Often the result is that only the former are satisfied – the public are confused.

Films and video
Finally, the *medium* used to convey information can be crucial. The superiority of audio-visual modalities over the written or spoken word is well attested in education technology.[24] Although there have been fewer studies in the area of attitude change, there is sufficient evidence to suggest that film or video can be an effective way of informing the public. It appears to be most successful if it incorporates some of the ingredients identified earlier under contact with disabled people, namely an emphasis on the positive attributes of the disabled person and an opportunity for them to talk about themselves. Several studies have elicited changes in viewers' attitudes following a visual presentation.[13] Admittedly the differences were not as great as those found with a face-to-face meeting, but video proved decidedly superior to audio-recordings of the same events. Additional advantages of film or video are the opportunities they give the viewer for 'sanctioned staring' and for seeing others interacting with disabled people.[25]

Film has proved *un*successful in changing attitudes when it has taken the form of a factual, educational-type production presented by a non-disabled person.[26] Equally a short film, narrated by an adult, of handicapped children in wheelchairs participating in physical education and classroom activities with non-handicapped children, made little impression on 10 year-olds.[27] The invest-igator concluded that, 'film alone does not appear to be sufficient to handle all the questions that a non-handicapped child might have about a handicapped peer and its effect does not appear to be permanent.' They go on to recommend that film be used in conjunction with other experiences such as listening to handicapped speakers and participating in discussion sessions.

Much of the above will seem like common sense and so it is – once you begin to think about it. Sadly people still make the naive assumption that if they talk, people will listen.

Changing Attitudes through Experiential Learning

There are other ways of learning besides hearing and reading; people can learn through doing. These methods gained credence in primary education but they are in their infancy with adults. We shall focus on two promising techniques – role playing and project work. A common feature to both is the opportunity for participants to share their feelings and reactions through discussions.

Role playing

Blindfolding people, plugging their ears or confining them to wheelchairs are just some of the ways used to disable the able, so that they can experience the role of the handicapped person. Research suggests that these simulations are only successful under certain conditions.[28] Above all, the role players must get a realistic impression of the disability and a chance to experience the reactions of strangers as they portray the disabled person. For example, making a journey in a wheelchair around a busy neighbourhood will be much more beneficial than playing a game of blind man's buff in a classroom. After all, the scarf tells everyone that the person is not really handicapped. Opaque contact lenses worn as the person shopped in a local supermarket would be a more realistic experience.

Investigators have shown that realistic simulations, involving contact with strangers, were effective in producing attitude changes which were maintained up to four months later.[29] Moreover, a partner who followed the role-player, at a distance but close enough to observe, also changed to the same extent.

Another role-playing technique, used more in research with racial minorities, has involved participants in writing an essay or making a speech which espoused a strongly positive attitude.[6] Two factors – searching out the supportive data and presenting it publicly – are thought to account for the success of these methods. However, to date they have been little used in disability research although they are readily applicable, for instance making a case for positive discrimination in the employment of disabled people.

Projects

Personal involvement in the learning process can be elicited in other ways. Participants can be assigned tasks which involve seeking out information and making use of it. In one study, pupils assembled dossiers on creative Americans who were disabled and presented them to their peers,[30] while in another, students prepared and administered questionnaires for comparing the life-styles of students and young handicapped adults.[31]

The results of these projects are usually presented to the group for discussion. But a word of caution must be noted. The consensus from social science research is that discussions generally tend to strengthen the opinions held by members beforehand.[32] Group leaders must ensure that the discussions are based on factual information and that biased opinions and emotions do not go unchallenged. Ideally, members of the group should take responsibility for doing this and the project work should prepare them for it. Nevertheless, there are reports in the literature of negative effects resulting from unstructured group discussions.[16]

New Approaches

The foregoing review is not exhaustive. New methods may yet be discovered. Richard Ashmore[6] speculates on three possible developments:

Self-insight training – in which participants are challenged on their use of irrational defence mechanisms in coping with atypical peers.

Special orientations during childhood – and the need for educational curricula which make children more aware of and comfortable with differences, so that non-normality should not be anxiety arousing or thought of as bad.

Tokenism – may have to be tackled. The characteristics and behaviour patterns of those who espouse 'positive' attitudes should be scrutinised more closely. It may be that some of this group engage in token acts of integration which will reduce their commitments to more significant steps towards better inter-group relations.

Accounting for Change

There are as many theories of attitude change as there are effective methods, because investigators tend to account for their successes in differing ways. Yet, the value of a theory is not only in explaining all the available data; it provides a framework for deriving possible courses of action in the future. Unfortunately this is an area in which the criteria of success or failure are rarely stated explicitly – what is a positive or negative attitude? – and the measures used are so varied in both content and format that it is impossible here to review and evaluate the possible theories in any succinct or systematic way. (Those eager to embark on this can consult the original sources listed in the references).

The alternative we have chosen is to present one conceptualisation – theory would be too strong a word – that we have found useful. The basic premise is that attitude change is preceded by modifications in people's beliefs about themselves. Milton Rokeach[33] has pinpointed two triggers for changing people's self-concepts – perceived incompetence and perceived immorality. The data obtained in the studies reviewed earlier would then be interpreted as follows:

> 'Forcing' people to meet a disabled person is a challenge to their self-concept in that it creates feelings of incompetence – 'I don't know how to react to disabled people.' If, however, the meeting takes place in a familiar and enjoyable setting and involves personal interchanges, then people are likely to discover that they can cope; their concepts of themselves are modified to 'I know how to cope with disabled people.' From these positive feelings about themselves will flow more positive attitudes to disabled people. Alternatively, if the 'forced' contact is too threatening to the people's feelings of competence – as might be experienced during a tour of an unfamiliar institution – then the reverse result would be predicted and has indeed been found: 'Aren't the staff wonderful – I could never work there.' The negative feelings they have towards themselves only reinforce existing attitudes towards the disabled people they saw. The second trigger is perceived immorality and for this people need to be challenged on moral grounds. The opportunity to hear at first hand of people's lifestyles and to appreciate their positive attributes can cause people to identify with finding solutions; whereas, if the emphasis is on the anonymous group called the disabled, the responsibility for any immorality falls upon an equally vague group – society.

There may well be other ways of modifying people's images of themselves. Other theorists dwell more on emotional and affective triggers; nevertheless the recurring theme is still one of changing people so that people's attitudes can change. This means that it is not enough for the public to learn about disabled people, but rather that in so doing, they have to learn more about themselves. We have to change the singer, not the song.

4   STRATEGIES FOR COMMUNITY EDUCATION

> First the target group for a particular programme must be carefully identified and the programme specifically geared for this group.
>
> *Richard Ashmore*

Chapters 1 and 2 illustrated the need for change in public attitudes and Chapter 3 outlined ways of bringing it about. We now consider how you could change the attitudes of your own community.

Forget 'the disabled' – More than anything else, you have to throw out the notion of *the disabled*. As a term it is no better at describing human characteristics than is 'the blue eyed' or the 'red heads', yet it implies that these people are distinct, a race apart.

At the very least, this means presenting each disabling condition separately. It is so easy for the public to presume that people in wheelchairs are also deaf, mentally handicapped or prone to fits and that people with mental handicap are likely to have physical deformities. We need programmes which educate the public about the distinct effects of each disability.

But even when the focus is on people with a common handicap, their individuality as persons must be emphasised.

Forget 'the public' – There is an Italian proverb which runs, 'he who builds on the mob, builds on sand.' Attempts to educate *the public* will continue to fail. It is no use pitching your message at some vague, anonymous mass of people in the hope that some – you know not who – will listen.

Rather your target should be *communities* of people. As we saw in Chapter 1, these exist at many levels, but the most pertinent are the smaller groups who can offer disabled people mutual aid, social intercourse and friendly help. These are the people we need to influence and if changes can be effected at this level, it is bound to produce results at district or national level. Shops, cinemas and sports centres will become accessible to people with disabilities once the people employed there and other users appreciate the obstacles that buildings present to their disabled friends. Attempts to legislate from the top have not been successful. The alternative of working from the bottom up must be tried.

Unfortunately, as this is a general text written for a wide

audience, we shall have to continue using terms like 'public' and 'disabled' – please translate these to your particular situation.

Forget the 'overnight success' – People can't change overnight; community education must be an ongoing process. There will be new people joining communities and new communities to contact. Moreover, research suggests that the positive results of an educational programme tend to wane over time and some 'topping up' will need to be done. As long as our efforts to educate the community are done on a part-time, occasional and random basis we will continue to have confused communities. We need regular, country-wide programmes on disability aimed at specific communities within our nation.

Obstacles to Community Education
We are confident that the means to bring this about are there; we are less sure about the will. It strikes us that there are two major obstacles – disagreements on perceptions of disability and a failure to identify who is responsible for community education.

Perceptions of disability
Marked differences exist in philosophies of caring for the disabled. No one denies their need for special services, but some see these being provided in designated centres whereas others feel they should be available in ordinary settings.

A second debate concerns the people best suited to help. Some would argue that only trained, professional staff can give a dependable and reliable service, whereas others see help coming from networks of personal contacts.

Then there are varying concepts of disability. Some view it as a permanent illness and handle their 'patients' in much the same way as those with physical ailments. Others see disability as a socio-educational challenge and try to nurture the person's abilities and autonomous decision-making.

These and other disagreements are highlighted most starkly in the provision of residential care. These issues are graphically described in studies by Eric Miller and Geraldine Gwynne[1] with people who are physically handicapped and by Pauline Morris[2] with those who are mentally handicapped.

A major consequence of these internal disputes is a failure to give the public a coherent message on disability. One moment they are requested to view disabled people as deserving causes, objects of charity and in need of special help; the next they are presented as capable of independent living and competing for open employment. No wonder the public become confused.

Recently, there have been signs that some of the disputes are being resolved, aided by the following developments:

Disabled people are beginning to speak for themselves – This self-advocacy has been slow to develop, largely because disabled people have been receivers of services with a learned dependency on the non-handicapped providers. Yet it is they who are most affected by public prejudice and misunderstanding and who stand to gain most by greater community support. The growing trend in Western countries for disabled people to band together in arguing their case will do much to fuel community education. This is just as true for mentally as well as physically disabled people.[3]

Habilitation programmes are a feature of most services – The increased resources which have been made available to disability agencies in recent years has enabled them to move beyond basic physical care into the development of training programmes in work, social and independent living skills, thereby equipping disabled people for community life. The next logical step is to extend this ethos to the training of people in the community who provide 'normal' services such as shops, police, transport, so that they can deliver them more effectively to the handicapped people they encounter.

Individuality is respected – The emphasis has shifted from the *'disabled'* as a group to *'people'* with disabilities; each with unique needs and remedies. Likewise community education can focus on personality rather than policies.

Who does the telling?

There may be a growing concensus on what to tell the public, but there remains the thorny issue as to whose responsibility it is. One thing we can be sure of, people are not clamouring to take it on.

To date, most community education has been done by staff employed in disability organisations both in the voluntary and state sector and for the foreseeable future we would envisage this continuing. They are unique mediators between the world of the able and the disabled. What is needed, though, are explicit commitments by these organisations to community education, so that it becomes an essential part of their service.

Too often community education is an adjunct to PR for the organisation and a preliminary for fund-raising, or else it is done sporadically in response to requests for speakers or for information. Serious efforts at evolving coherent educational programmes have been few, largely because the personnel have not been made available to produce them.

This is not a plea for yet more specialist staff – 'community educators' – although that would be one solution. Rather, responsibility could be devolved among those employed in other roles – social workers, instructors, care assistants. But the organisation must write this task into their employees' job descriptions and provide them with the necessary resources to fulfil this obligation, just as they provide facilities for them to carry out their other tasks. Expecting staff to squeeze this in among other commitments or to do it after working hours is hardly evidence of a committed organisation.

Initiatives don't just come from the top; they can equally well emerge as 'demands' from front-line staff to their managers. Indeed this might be preferable, for it shows that the energy to do the job is present.

Organisations concerned with disablement have to be challenged on their commitment to community education. This can come from disabled people, their families and the staff. And it can come from you. The fact that you are reading this book, suggests you are interested. If it isn't your responsibility to educate your community – then whose is it?

Systematic Approaches to Community Education
It is easier to identify problems than create solutions, but optimistically we believe that they can be resolved; although the ways of doing this will be many and varied. We shall assume that you have surmounted the obstacles and go on to examine strategies for making community education a reality in your area.

We begin by emphasising the need to direct your message to specific groups within the community. We shall describe how you might identify appropriate targets and find out what they would like to know about disability. We shall then suggest ways of ensuring that your programme is used regularly and how it could be made available in other parts of the country so that ultimately it might be used nationally. Finally, for the less ambitious, we outline how you might maximise the many other opportunities which arise for educating the public.

Target groups
Community education has to be translated from a chance and random occurrence into one which is available regularly to all. Quite an undertaking but not impossible, especially if the

population is subdivided into smaller groups and you focus on the most relevant targets.

School children are a frequently suggested group. If education about disability were to become part of the school curriculum this would be a way of ensuring that ultimately everyone in our society knew something about disability. This argument persuaded us to produce an educational programme on mental handicap for use in secondary schools, particularly with fifth year students (see Section 3). There is scope for many others – dealing with different disabilities or geared to other age groups. A programme for nine year-olds in primary schools would need to be different from that devised for 13 or 17 year-olds.

Thus one of your first considerations could be a programme on disability for use by the schools in your locality.

In some ways, this strategy is more of a long-term investment; what about the adults of today? Again there is an existing system which you might use: evening classes in adult education centres. Have you thought of organising a course in your local centre? This strategy was successfully used in West Germany[4] as part of a larger health education campaign on disability and we ourselves have had some success in Dublin with an evening class on mentally handi-capped adults. These classes tend to attract people with some interest in disability – which is not to decry their importance but to point out the need for alternatives to make people interested in attending.

You can't afford to wait for people to come to you, you will have to go to them. You might begin by identifying people in the community who could be of assistance to disabled people – such as neighbours in the vicinity of a group home or a day centre, the police, organisers of youth clubs, the clergy or members of sports clubs. Your programme might well open doors in your area and these groups are likely to appreciate the help you are offering them. It is best to devise a programme specifically for each as you will want to relate your information to their experiences and needs. However, these courses on disability can be quite short – a morning or an evening might suffice. A specific example would be to approach staff of the police training college for your area, suggesting a short input on how the police could deal with a mentally handicapped person, eg when questioning them.

There is a third strategy you might use to identify target groups, namely enquiring from disabled people the sorts of people they are most likely to come into contact with around their neighbourhood or town. We did this with over 160 adults – average age 23 years – attending day workshops for people with mental handicap.[5] The

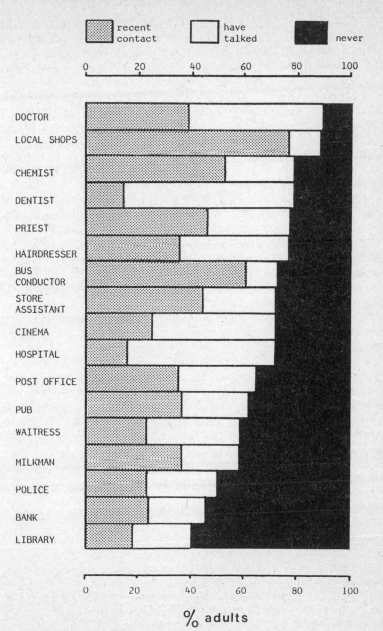

CONTACT WITH PEOPLE IN THE COMMUNITY

staff questioned them individually about the people they had talked to around the community and about how recently this had occurred. The Figure below illustrates the results obtained. Local shop keepers, bus conductors, chemists, sales assistants in city centre stores and clergy were the most frequently mentioned.

Armed with similar data from the disabled people in your area, you could identify pertinent groups. For example, you might devise a short input for sales staff in clothing departments of city stores on how to help customers who are physically disabled.

Indentify what the group wants to know
It is worth finding out in advance from your target group the amount of contact they have had with disabled people; their feelings towards them and the aspects they would like to know more about. This can be done quite informally through discussions with some representatives, or more systematically by interviewing a sample or having them complete a questionnaire. In Chapter 10 we shall outline possible questions, but to whet your appetite, here are the results we obtained when we asked students, young adults and 'friends' of mentally handicapped people (mostly paid and voluntary staff in services) the information they would like to have on mental handicap.

PERCENTAGE IN EACH GROUP WANTING INFORMATION

INFORMATION ON	STUDENTS	ADULTS	FRIENDS
CAUSES	83	77	83
HOW THEY LIKE TO BE TREATED	80	78	90
HOW I SHOULD ACT WITH THEM	78	73	80
WHAT MENTAL HANDICAP MEANS	67	64	81
HOW TO TEACH THEM	45	41	85
VOLUNTARY WORK I COULD DO	40	29	61

The most popular topics were to do with meeting disabled people and the cause of their handicap. As any newspaper editor will tell you, people are more interested in the human angle rather than abstract issues.

Regular usage

Once-off attempts at community education are of limited value, as the recent International Year of Disabled People illustrated.[6] Having devised a successful programme for your target group – a theme we will explore in detail in the next Section of the book – you have to ensure that it is used with all the people you want to reach. For example, will you present it regularly in all the neighbourhood schools, and if not who will?

There are a number of options open to you:

Colleagues – You can recruit a team of colleagues to carry on the work. The only prerequisite is first-hand experience of disability: either they themselves are disabled or they have worked closely with people who are. It helps, though, if they relate easily with others and are enthusiastic about this type of work.

You will need to guide them on what they should do with the group and make available to them the necessary resource materials – videos, handouts, etc.

At least this means the work load is spread and it is less serious if a person leaves the area; others can carry on. But somebody is still needed to co-ordinate their efforts.

Using community resources – Another approach is to do yourself out of a job by handing over your programme to people who are regularly involved with your target group, such as school teachers, training personnel in shops and businesses, community development officers working with youth groups or staff in further education colleges. This means that no extra manpower is needed for the programme and, better still, it will now appear as part of the everyday routine rather than as a special event. This is a most attractive option except for one big drawback: your 'target' presenters may have little or no experience of disability. But you may be able to remedy that. Firstly, they could experience the programme as a participant; secondly, you could give them extra training in using the programme – a vital step for building up their confidence and changing their attitudes; and thirdly, you could provide them with ready-prepared materials for use with their groups. Hence, their role becomes one of presenter and facilitator rather than an 'expert' on disability.

Regional and national usage – This is ambitious but not wildly so. Teacher's kits are a well established feature, particularly in special education. If there were a similar range of ready-made kits in community education, with resource materials such as video programmes, posters and discussion triggers, along with detailed guidance for their use, more people could become involved as educators since the job would be so much easier.

One step toward this utopia would be for people to share with others the programmes they have devised for their locality. National or regional organisations concerned with disability might sponsor the production costs which, incidentally, could be recouped through sales to prospective users.

However, two factors are crucial to making these kits a success. Firstly, the programme must be of proven effectiveness, otherwise the costs of production could be wasted. Secondly, the users need a personal introduction to the programme. Many an excellent teaching package lies on the shelf because the staff have not been properly introduced to it. Prospective users might participate in a training workshop so that they could gain first-hand experience in using the package. We have found this a feasible and productive strategy in Ireland. There need to be many more opportunities for people to develop their expertise as community educators – resource kits and training schemes would help a lot. Examples of ready-made packages are given in Section 3.

Utilising Existing Opportunities

If all we have written in this chapter is beyond your ambition and resources, a word of reassurance. You can start by simply re-appraising your current activities in the community, so that you incorporate into them more of the ingredients identified in Chapter 3 that are essential for attitude change. Here are some examples of what we mean.

Guest speakers

Most organisations receive invitations or requests to supply speakers for clubs, groups and associations. Here is a captive audience and one interested enough to approach you, but you need to maximise this opportunity to change their perceptions by utilising some of the techniques noted earlier.

As the speaker will be aware of the group's common interest, he or she can slant the presentation accordingly; Lion's club members might be interested in the work-skills of disabled people while a Ladies group could be interested in befriending families. There is a chance for personal contact, albeit with one person, and at least the audience can interact through questions, comments and discussion. Moreover, a handicapped colleague might share the presentation; together they might decide to show excerpts from a video, film or slide programme or play extracts from a tape-recording. They could make their points through a case-study, an informational overview or with a documentary type presentation. Alternatively they could provide short trigger material to stimulate discussion, or they might decide to employ involvement techniques such as simulation, role-playing, buzz groups or quizzes. Printed material could be distributed – fact sheets, articles, results of surveys, and so on. Thus careful preparation can turn a dull speech into a vibrant learning experience for both you and the audience.

Public events
Most organisations for disabled people try to attract the public to certain events such as sales of work, open days, concerts, etc. Most are an opportunity to raise funds but that need not preclude community education. With foresight and ingenuity, some effective change techniques can be incorporated into these events. For example, disabled people can demonstrate their skills at pottery making, weaving, etc., and even instruct the visitors in these tasks. Short videos, or slide/tape presentations can be shown, focussing on some of the personalities who attend the centre. Attractive informational displays can be mounted with take-away leaflets provided as reminders. There should be opportunities for disabled people to mingle with the visitors.

For these events you could send out invitations to groups you particularly want to make contact with. Incentives, such as the free use of your swimming pool, may boost attendances. Advertising through personal contacts, posters and handbills is vital. Once again, you can transform an existing event into an opportunity to educate the public.

Mass media
Many disability organisations have developed good working relations with the local media, press, radio and television. News releases and material for articles and interviews are regularly supplied and press attendance at functions and events encouraged.

Often, however, in the absence of positive direction, media coverage merely reflects a condescending, outdated view of disabled people, which will at least partially undermine the best-laid educational attempts[7]. But given more positive direction, the media can become a powerful educational tool, and while the final shape of published material is in the hands of reporters, photographers and sub-editors, they will generally take their cue from you, the 'expert'.

Stories which stress the successes of disabled people in 'open' rather than special competition or of them participating in unusual events – rock-climbing, sailing – combined with photographs of them joining in activities with able-bodied people, can go some way to counteracting the public's misconceptions.

Information leaflets

It might be worth examining the leaflets produced by your organisation to see if they might be more effective in educating the community. Are they attractively produced and easy to read? Leaflets which are drab and boring may transfer these associations to disabled people.

Do they contain the information the public wants to have? In our experience, knowing how to act with a handicapped person and the causes of the disability, are the most popular topics by far.

Do the leaflets give handicapped people a platform to express their views? Are there any photographs of disabled people in them?

Are any attempts made to involve the readers? A simple quiz of the 'do you know' type might help to highlight the differences between their impressions and reality. Are there any suggestions made as to what people can do to help the disabled people in their area – other than give them money?

How are the leaflets distributed? Are they available in public libraries, health clinics, community information offices? Is there a case for mailing or distributing them door-to-door?

In short, there are many possibilities to be explored. However, leaflets on their own are not likely to be very effective. Personal contact with a disabled person is lacking and there is no opportunity for having questions answered. Nevertheless, they can provide a useful back-up resource with other approaches such as open days and talks to community groups.

Self-Advocacy

Finally, a rather different strategy can be tried, that of putting your resources into encouraging disabled people to speak up for themselves.

The aura of charity still pervades many of our services for disabled people and little attempt has been made to obtain consumers' reactions, the justification being that 'they should be grateful for what they are given'. But so long as this attitude remains, disabled people will never become full participants in the community. In democracies, minorities have to argue for, even demand, their rights.

Although the primary goal of most rehabilitation programmes is to help disabled people to look after themselves, too often this aim is confined only to their physical needs. Surely the time has come to extend it to other skills, such as practice at formulating realistic requests for services; at stating their case to others and identifying various strategies for obtaining their goal. In recent years more and more disabled people have proved themselves to be able advocates. With encouragement and training many more could do likewise – and this includes the mentally, as well as physically, disabled.

As the President's Committee on Mental Retardation[8] reported, 'A gentle protest can now be heard throughout the nation from mentally retarded persons who are tired of being over-protected; they have begun to object when professionals . . . make decisions for them when, with a little time and patience, they could have decided and spoken for themselves.'

One example given by the Committee is of an organisation in the USA called *People First* which has held conventions attended by upwards of 1,000 delegates, all of whom were mentally retarded. They discussed topics such as 'How to get people to meetings' and 'How to get more service from service workers'. Similar conferences on a smaller scale have been organised in Britain by the Campaign for Mentally Handicapped People.[9] Encouraging disabled people to have a say in the running of their services is but the first step. The second – that of telling the community about themselves – will follow naturally. As the brochure for *People First* notes, 'We are teaching communities that we can learn and that we have an idea of what's going on around us. We can vote, learn to ride a bus, get married and do many other things.'

Helping disabled people to become advocates for themselves will bring a new dimension to our services. Training packages are now available for professional workers to use with disabled people[10] and no doubt more will be produced in the future. Our focus in this book, however, will remain on direct community education, although we cannot help feeling that a service's willingness to encourage self-advocacy among its clients will reflect its commitment to community education and integration.

Care by the Community

Community education can never be a single entity or an end in itself. It must occur on many different fronts, each a catalyst effecting change in the community, in disabled people and most significantly of all, in the professional services provided for them. Up to now these have evolved from care *out* of the community to care *in* the community. Another step remains – care *by* the community. That can only come about when community education is no longer seen as extra work, done occasionally by specialist staff. Rather must it be an integral part of every service caring for disabled people. The time has come to give the community a chance to care.

SECTION 2: FORMULATING COMMUNITY EDUCATION PROGRAMMES

Introduction

INTRODUCTION

In Section 1 we looked at the need for community education and at ways of positively influencing the community's perceptions of its disabled members. But how do we translate these findings into actual community education programmes? In this section we will focus in detail on the most important elements in bringing about change:

1. Basic information about the disability (this was usually the most over developed element in past programmes).
2. Guidelines for participants on relating to a disabled person (recently this has become a more common feature).
3. The experience of meeting disabled people on a personal basis (this is usually overlooked – too much trouble in arranging it).

These objectives must be achieved in an interesting and stimulating way – using audio-visual aids to impart information; giving the participants an active role in the programme, and keeping the main emphasis on *people*, rather than on abstract issues. Like a newspaper reporter, you are looking for the human angle.

Our aim in this section of the book is to give you practical guidance and suggestions on how to construct new community education programmes or how to make your existing events more effective.

Contact with disabled people is the most significant form of participant involvement and it is *potentially* the most effective way of changing public attitudes to handicapped people – we say *potentially* because the effect depends on how we present handicapped people to the public. If we confirm the old stereotypes of helplessness, of 'deserving causes,' of people without full rights, we have given the non-handicapped public no reason to change their views of handicapped people. Rather they need to meet on equal terms as people with shared interests and common feeling.

In Chapter 5 we shall describe how you can make this happen. We shall concentrate on how you can allay the public's fears and apprehensions by giving accurate information about the handicap and its practical implications, eg how it effects communication; by familiarizing them with the aids and physical effects (if any) of the disability; by stressing the abilities and skills of the handicapped person (instead of the *dis*abilities); and by offering practical guidelines – rules of thumb – relating to a handicapped person.

Chapter 6 focusses on other ways of *encouraging participant involvement*. Educationalists have stressed that we learn most effectively by doing, by *participating* in the learning process. The greater the variety and scope for involvement the more likely your participants are to be committed and satisfied. Involvement may range from questions and discussion through to role-playing, projects and group-work.

In Chapter 7, we deal with *Presenting Information*, especially on topics of interest to your participants. But pure information is often boring, hence we suggest that you:

- have variety in you presentations – audio-visual aids, such as slides, tapes, overhead projectors, can be effective.
- avoid too much detail – it will smother your most important points.
- use information-giving sparingly – as it is the least effective way of changing people's attitudes.

In general, facts and figures should only be given in small doses; what is more important is that the recipients explore their significance.

Chapter 8, *Using Video*, introduces a most effective resource for community educators. It is an ideal medium for disabled people to introduce themselves, to present their point of view, and to say how they like others to relate to them. It also allows them to demonstrate their communication and work skills as well as their leisure interests. Although ready-made video programmes are available commercially, you can make programmes yourself for the specific group in question – and what they lack in professional finish will be compensated for by their immediacy and their local interest and, more important, these videotapes can be easily copied and made available to others.

Video has replaced films as an educational tool but there are films available for hire which could prove useful. But do be selective. The high expense involved in producing a film means that they are made to appeal to as wide an audience as possible; the result is a very generalised view which may be of limited use in programmes for specific groups. Also there has been a tendency in films on disability to rely on comment from non-disabled presenters and to view, but not interview, severely disabled people. However, you may find a 10-minute sequence which makes just the point you need.

The remaining three chapters are devoted to topics which are relevant to certain programmes but not to all.

Chapter 9 deals with *Publicity* and suggests ways of informing people about your courses. This is especially important if the people you aim to attract are not members of an existing group, eg adult education classes.

Consumer Reactions is the theme of Chapter 10. Here we describe ways of finding out the public's past contact with disabled people, their feelings towards them and the aspects they are most interested in knowing more about. These measures can be used also to assess more objectively whether the programme brought about any changes in participants' views. We also explain ways of obtaining reactions to the content and format of your programme.

The final topic, *Working with Others* (Chapter 11), should give some comfort to the overwhelmed. Here we explore ideas for team-work, for gaining access to your target groups and for the sharing of programmes with others.

Finally, a summary of the steps involved in devising a new educational programme on disability:

1 *Personal commitments.* How much time and what resources can you devote to it? Can you recruit helpers? How much time can they give? The answers will determine the scope of your programme.

2 *Target audience.* Who are you aiming the programme at?

What do they need to know; what do they want to know? How do you gain access?

3 *Existing resources*. Disabled people are your greatest resource – consult with them and the staff in services. Establish ways of arranging contact between disabled people and your target group.
   Are there video programmes, films or slide/tape presentations you could use?
   Can you find suitable written material for distribution to your group?

4 *Commission new resources*. Make, or arrange to have made, your own video-programmes, etc., and produce any written materials you may feel are necessary to inform and involve participants. Enlist help from other agencies, eg students in third level colleges.

5 *Trial run*.Test the programme so that you can identify any difficulties – topics which need more time; materials which were not as effective as you had hoped. Obtain participants' reactions. Restructure the programme as necessary.

6 *Sharing with others*. Package the elements of your programme so that it can readily be used again, either by yourself or by colleagues. Train others in its use.

At this point new issues arise, such as integrating your package with other programmes available on different disabilities, ensuring the programme continues to be used regularly, or devising a follow-up so that participants can keep in touch with disabled people. But these are best left until you have established your programme.

5 MEETING DISABLED PEOPLE

> We were learning about a new thing completely. It's not like English and learning about Shakespeare, because we'd heard about him! We were learning about new people, that they were among us all the time, and they were just around the corner going to this Adult Care Unit which none of us had heard of before.

Above are a 16 year-old girl's comments on visiting a local day centre for mentally handicapped adults. It was as if we had all taken part in a conspiracy to hide severely disabled people from the local community, not just in institutions but even in local day centres. As a result the *public* have been disabled – they feel awkward and inadequate when they meet a handicapped person. The Mencap poll referred to in Chapter 2 found that of the respondents who did *not* know a mentally handicapped person only one in five felt at ease in their presence.

From this, the solution would seem obvious; encourage the public to see more of disabled people and their embarrassment will disappear. The reality is not quite so simple.

The guided tour
In their attempts to make the local community more aware of their services, many handicap centres offer open days and guided

tours, and in general, visitors are encouraged. The effect of this form of contact between disabled and non-disabled can be dramatic, but not in the way intended:

> My first vivid impression of the ward itself was of the smell. An unpleasant mixture of urine and faeces . . . I was led down the side of the ward – huge, old-fashioned beige radiators, beige walls . . . A woman was furiously mopping the floor, staring at us as we walked over it . . . Through the next door was the H-shaped dormitory. Uniformity was not in it: the only concessions to individuality were the dark brown lockers and the 'personalized' nylon bedspreads. There was nothing on the walls, the whole scene an abstract pattern of brown wood, pastel nylon, green floor, beige walls. Hiding in one corner, muttering incessantly, was Derek, an older patient.

This was Frank Thomas's[1] introduction to the local mental handicap hospital where he was about to begin working. This was a 'soft option' ward in what he describes as a typical hospital.

There are almost 50,000 people in mental handicap hospitals in Britain[2] and many people with other disabilities are being cared for in similar large institutions. In these settings visitors may well admire the 'dedication' of the staff, but their perceptions of the disabled people will be very negative and research suggests that the public comes away with worse rather than better attitudes towards them.[3] On reflection, it is not hard to see why. Any tour – be it of a school, day centre, group home or whatever – shows off the facilities, is usually done at speed and rarely offers the visitors the opportunity of joining in with the activities. Surely we could do better than this.

A Better Way of Meeting

In fact, it is not difficult to improve on Frank Thomas's introduction to disabled people. Here are some points to keep in mind, building on those mentioned in Chapter 3.

Meeting people – Learning about a disability should mean getting to know disabled people, not inspecting premises. The emphasis should be on meeting not viewing.

Equal status – Those meeting should be of much the same age and equally competent at whatever activities are to be shared; there should be no scope for condescension. If the meeting is not taking place in a 'neutral' venue, whoever is host should act as such, ie. if someone is invited to the centre, then the handicapped person should show them around, offer them a cup of tea and generally cater for his or her visitor.

A purpose in mind – There should be a reason for getting together, even if it's only to share a cup of coffee. Bringing strangers together is, at best, embarrassing as this student's comment shows:

> *We were sort of looking at them and they were looking at us, as if we were visiting the zoo; and they didn't understand why we were coming into their classroom, as if we were intruding.*

Places to meet – Normally we meet people at parties or for a drink, to go to a film, to shop together, to go swimming or to play badminton . . . anything in fact that we prefer not to do alone. But when we think of handicapped and non-handicapped getting together, it's easy to forget about these normal activities. In fact, meeting a disabled person in a 'special' facility only reinforces their differences, a constant reminder of their handicap.

Enjoying the experience – All of these social activities are enjoyable and, because of that, we are likely to go on doing these things. Meeting handicapped people should be a pleasure – for both parties.

Having a choice – An able-bodied person has the choice of meeting or avoiding a disabled person, yet in our enthusiasm for bringing them together, sometimes we fail to offer disabled people the same right.

Provide activity – People meeting for the first time usually find it easier if there is an activity to share – it relieves the pressure to keep talking, supplies an immediate topic for conversation and helps them relax. Indeed it gives people a reason for meeting in the first place.

Being able – Snooker, chess or crosswords would be quite frustrating if you could never pot a ball, capture a piece or think of the right solution. Yet disabled people are often put in the position of having to join in activities where they are disadvantaged. When organizing activities which will bring handicapped and non-handicapped together, we should consider the former's talents. The range of activities in which disabled people excel are increasing – people in wheelchairs completing marathons and winning archery competitions; mentally handicapped people who do well in swimming and gymnastics. Then there are those activities in which participation is all that counts: camping, horse riding, sailing.

Sharing common interests – Friendships are usually based on common interests or experiences; this is a good basis for disabled and non-disabled to get together. It presupposes, however, that handicapped people are encouraged to develop their personal interests, whereas, due to their social isolation, they are often unaware of local organizations or clubs, or may feel too shy to approach them without an introduction or some encouragement.

Being of service – Disabled people have many abilities which they can put to the service of others who may need them, thus reversing their usual dependency role. Looking after an old person's pet while the owner is sick, helping with gardening or with preparing food or serving tea, are all things a mentally handicapped person can do easily.

These general points can be applied to any situation in which you are arranging to facilitate contact between handicapped and non-handicapped individuals. What is important is that people have an opportunity to get to know an *individual* – or several individuals – in a meaningful way. This means a person-to-person chat so that they get to know something about each other's interests and personal concerns.

Sometimes the meetings need not be arranged or held in special venues. There are many places in the community where people congregate, so use them. Being in the community gives the disabled person opportunities to experience, to develop and to practise the social skills they need to be more accepted by the non-disabled world. If that world can become more accustomed to disabled people in restaurants, in pubs, on buses, then they will have overcome *their disability* and with it their feelings of embarrassment and inadequacy.

Preparing for Contact

The prospect of meeting strangers will be less daunting if people are given some preparation beforehand. Indeed, in our experience, the public invariably mention this when asked about the information they would like to have on disability – 'tell me how they like to be treated.' The chances for a successful meeting are much increased if you can give your participants some preliminary coaching in social skills. This can be done in a variety of ways:

Letting participants see disabled people – It is natural for people to be curious about another's disabilities and to want to stare at them. It may be rude to do it in his or her presence, but not when the person is on television. Videoprogrammes will allow them to see whether handicapped people do look different; whether they have difficulties in articulation, are overweight or of low stature, or have poor coordination.

Above all, it will reassure them as to the limits of the disability.

Letting participants hear disabled people – It can be a useful experience to listen to disabled people talking about themselves, either on a videoprogramme or from an audio-recording. More effective again would be to have a disabled person address a group of participants; but this may not always be possible.

As they listen, your participants will get some indication of the disabled person's communicative skills and level of language sophistication – most pertinent with people who are mentally handicapped. These recordings will also provide an insight into their lives and give ideas for topics to talk about when they meet a disabled person.

Giving them 'rules of thumb' – In our experience, most participants welcome explicit guidance on what they should or should not do when meeting a disabled person. Obviously these must vary from one disability to another, and according to the contexts in which the participants are likely to meet. But as an indication of the sort of rules we have in mind, here are a few which we have provided to participants on our courses before they met a mentally handicapped person:

Be yourself: React in the normal way; introduce yourself, find out his name and use it as you talk to him.

Share your thoughts: Tell him about yourself and what you do. Don't always ask questions and don't be afraid of silences. It is easier to chat with someone if you are engaged in an activity together.

If you don't understand what the person is saying, ask him to repeat it, to say it another way, to show you what he is referring to; get the help of a friend of his or take a guess at what he means and check it with him. It is important that you try to follow what he is saying. You will quickly acclimatise to the person's way of talking just as you do when listening to a foreigner. It takes a bit more concentration at first, that's all.

Use simple language – a person who is mentally handicapped does not have the same wide vocabulary as you. Use the same level of language as your partner.

Don't be surprised by their spontaneity – some mentally handicapped people show their feelings more readily than we do and their behaviour at times may be unconventional. They stand too close, shake your hand too enthusiastically, talk loudly or put their arms around you. They do this because they lack practice in meeting people or else they are unaware of the social rules we observe in our society. In other cultures it is perfectly natural for men to embrace.

If you feel uncomfortable when, for example, someone keeps his arm about you, then remove it without fuss and carry on with the conversation.

People differ – and this is just as true for those with mental handicap. Like you, they have their likes and dislikes; some will be shy, others outgoing – you just take them as you find them.

You may feel that guidelines of this type are unnecessary or too detailed for your participants. They may suggest difficulties where none exist. If this is the case, you might consider having a question and answer session where participants can raise any points which concern them so that reassurance – and relevant suggestions – can be given to them.

Suggestions for Meetings

In this section we shall make some specific suggestions about organising meetings between disabled people and community groups. We shall take three examples: teenagers in secondary schools, participants taking an adult education course and shop assistants in a city centre store.

Teenage students

There is evidence that teenagers have greater difficulty than do older people relating to unfamiliar, atypical groups.

In our programme with 15–17 year-old students this was particularly evident. Few of them had experience of severely disabled people and none had come through integrated schools:

We were really looking forward to this [meeting in the school] . . . but when the day actually arrived, we were very nervous about it and felt really uneasy. And when the mentally handicapped people arrived at the school it was very funny because they made us feel at ease.

The students reported feeling even more nervous when they went to visit a day centre and unexpectedly came across a person who was severely handicapped:

We were there sort of looking at her, and we started to giggle and get nervous, and that sort of made the division because we were giggling at this thing that was walking towards us. And I'm sure she felt: 'God, who are these fools standing in the corner there?'

And she came over towards us, and we all backed off even further. And then we all sort of walked away, one by one, trying not to make as if we were scared of her, but we were all terrified – and it put a lot of girls off.

Not only does this scene show how sheltered some students have been from handicapped people, but how important it is to *prepare* for contact. It suggests, too, that students need quite specific guidelines and that you should pay particular attention to the initial meeting they have with disabled people.

We were all gathered in the lunch room and we just saw them come down the corridor. We were all standing there. And Michael – Michael was the friendliest of them all – and he sort of made it easier on us because he was talking to us; and from then on we got into our little groups and we got to know the – the people, and the barriers were broken down between us and them, and it made it much easier.

Many handicapped people like Michael have the happy knack of putting others at ease, although not all will have had the opportunity to develop this skill, and here the students may have to take the initiative.

Contact between groups is always a more difficult thing to organise satisfactorily than bringing individuals together. Consequently many community educators are wary of undertaking any large-scale contact element, and yet they have neither the time nor the resources to arrange person-to-person contacts.

With foresight it is possible to make it a good experience for both groups; and it gives all young people – not just the 'volunteers' – a chance to meet and talk to at least one disabled person.

We suggest hat the initial meeting takes place, not in a handicap centre, but in a school – though preferably not the classroom. It is the students who need to be on familiar territory and it provides many mentally handicapped people with their first opportunity to see inside an ordinary school. A successful 'contact' session will be:

A team effort – The staff of school and centre should work closely together in the planning stages.

Of similar age – Broadly speaking, students would do better to meet handicapped people of their own age. This ensures interests in common and a more equal relationship between them. Hence we choose the younger trainees from an Adult Training Centre or the senior classes in a Special School to visit secondary schools. The slight age advantage of the mentally handicapped participants is a bonus.

Adequately prepared for – The students should have 'seen' some handicapped people beforehand (eg a short video programme); perhaps had a chance to meet and chat to a staff person from the centre and been given some practical 'rules of thumb' to help them cope with any communication difficulties.

The class teacher should have visited the centre and met both the staff and some of the trainees who have chosen to visit the school.

The handicapped students or trainees also need to be prepared for the visit. Ideally their involvement with the school would form part of an ongoing programme for them, eg 'learning-about-the-community' which might include a visit to other public services such as the post office, a bank, the police station, etc. However the school session will be a more personal experience and they should by given the option of coming or staying.

We suggest that a group of 10–15 should visit the school – a ratio of one to two students; and that they are accompanied by a familiar member of staff who could help with the introductions.

As individual as possible – Rather than having one large group, break it down into threes – two students and one handicapped person; in this way students will get to know at least one person by the end of the visit.

Structured – What happens during the meeting should be planned even if these plans are not strictly followed. This is particularly important during the 'breaking-the-ice' period at the beginning of the session. Suggested activities are: two students take a handicapped person on a tour of the school (or those parts of it that are accessible!); a selection of suitable recreational activities (table-tennis, pool, darts . . .); a cup of tea or other refreshments; or a friendly competition in which handicapped and non-handicapped are integrated and work as a team (five-a-side soccer; netball).

Of benefit to both – For the handicapped person it will be a break in routine, an enjoyable outing, a chance to meet peers and share interests and activities.

For the students too, it is a chance to gain new experiences, to overcome their fears, to form friendships and have an enjoyable time. Students are not doing handicapped peers a 'favour' and should be discouraged from thinking they are.

Continuing contact – Bringing together handicapped and non-handicapped people in this way is designed to create more positive attitudes; but a once-off event will not have an everlasting effect. Students need opportunities and encouragement to continue meeting disabled people – though they can not be *forced* to do so. The handicapped pupils or trainees might invite students to pay a return visit to their school or centre, returning the compliment as it were; and arrangements might be made for future contacts such as friendly matches or outings.

Individual initiatives should also be encouraged. For example, a group of senior girls (or boys?) might undertake to give some simple cookery demonstrations-cum-lessons in the centre; or to coach handicapped students in a particular sport which interests them; or arrange to meet when attending local soccer matches. Equally, handicapped students might be made 'honorary members' of school clubs (eg swimming) to encourage them to visit and join in if they felt like it.

Getting it all together
In approaching schools you will need to be aware of the time and organisational constraints under which they operate. In the very initial stages, we suggest that the class teacher and agency staff work closely in planning and implementing the programme on disability. In some instances teachers will prefer you to take the complete programme with the class, while in others they will do it themselves but might require a staff member from the local centre to be available for a discussion and a question-and-answer session, or to facilitate the contact. The balance of the teamwork will alter in individual circumstances, but many teachers will not feel sufficiently knowledgeable about handicapped people to undertake a programme without considerable support and resources. If you can offer teachers a detailed plan of approach and adequate resource materials, you will have greatly increased the chances of your programme being repeatedly used, with the minimum of facilitation on your part. This is what you should work towards and is a theme we will come back to in Chapter 11.

We have included further details of our programme on mental handicap in Section 3.

Programme for adult groups
Many of the points made in relation to teenagers can be applied to adults: they should be matched in age, have some interests in common, or be introduced as individuals. Obviously they should never be 'put-on-show' in any way.

On a local basis, contact can sometimes be encouraged informally, particularly in the case of handicapped people living at home
or in community group homes. Both parties may agree to meet in a
pub or to go to some event together, or to visit one another's home
for a cup of tea and a chat.

The local pub is a good possibility for small groups of 6–8 to
meet. If it is a popular spot, someone (the organiser?) will have to
get there early to reserve some space. Transport to the pub might
have to be organised for the disabled people. Arrange for someone who knows both groups to be there first – this saves the
embarrassment of strangers having to introduce themselves.

The local leisure centre is also a possibility and some sports,
like 10-pin bowling, can be fun for a group.

There are several other options for adult courses: they might
organize their own club, party or disco at the adult education
centre and invite handicapped people along; or they could join
in with existing social outlets for handicapped people such as a visit
to *their* club (on invitation of course).

Finally, one of the group might invite people to come for tea at
her home; and an invitation could also be extended to some
disabled people. Equally, disabled people might reciprocate or
even initiate these invitations. For our evening course, some
mentally handicapped people residing in a group home invited
participants to their house for dinner.

As with students, further contact should be encouraged; one
meeting with a handicapped person will have broken the ice, but
not very much more.

Course attenders' own interests may offer opportunities for

further involvement: a handicapped person who is interested in photography, football or films would enjoy meeting a kindred spirit, and vice versa. This may lead to the handicapped person being introduced to local hobby or social clubs.

Your aim, as we see it, is to provide acquaintances rather than friends. The public has to become acquainted with its disabled members; but it is impossible for you to arrange friendships. At best you can only present opportunities for friendships to develop; you cannot assure disabled people that your programme will result in new friendships for them. You can only increase the likelihood of it happening.

Programme for occupational groups

We turn now to people who earn their livelihood by providing services to the community, such as the police, the clergy, shop assistants, etc. As disabled people become more integrated into the community their use of these services will increase. Hence it is particularly important that these service-providers are not apprehensive of disabled people but are confident of coping with them and adapting their service as required.

In educational programmes aimed at such groups, contact with disabled people should again feature. Ideally this contact should take place in the service setting. For example, in our programme with sales assistants in a city centre store, we arranged for a group of trainees, participating in a social skills training programme that included a 'shopping' exercise, to be at the store around lunchtime and have a snack with the sales staff in the store's restaurant. Afterwards the staff took them in ones and twos on a quick tour of the store. Similarly, contact with the police might include a familiarization tour of the station and its procedures. This form of contact becomes a valuable learning experience for mentally handicapped people, as well as introducing them to a friendly person whom they may later call upon when in difficulty.

Access to these service groups may be difficult and the time available very restricted, but we maintain that the contact element should be a major aspect of any such programme, as it offers service providers a practical opportunity to adapt their skills to the particular needs of disabled people. In fact, this theme should be to the fore in any occupational programme. Section 3 includes further details of the programme we used with sales assistants.

Local community programmes

It may be that your programme is based around the immediate neighbourhood of a disability service – workshop, hostel, training centre – with the intention of bringing handicapped and non-handicapped neighbours together. Ideally any contact you arrange should help the handicapped person integrate into existing community activities, eg local clubs, choirs, social events, and to use local facilities more – shops, recreation centre, etc.

You might start by showing the contribution which disabled people make to the local community. This might take the form of an exhibition and sale of their work with disabled people welcoming people as they arrive, selling items, serving coffee, etc., or it could be an entertainment – trainees might present a display of gymnastics, of art-work, or some form of concert to which neighbours are invited. They might serve tea or coffee at the interval or organize a raffle themselves. Trainees might do some community service work for the old people locally – keeping their gardens tidy, minding pets, helping with spring cleaning. Or they could charge for a local service they provide for the residents in their area – garden-work, window-cleaning, chimney-sweeping, car washing, etc. Mentally handicapped adults are quite capable of doing these jobs with supervision.

Each of these activities highlights their abilities and the emphasis is not on raising money but rather on the people of the neighbourhood getting used to seeing and relating to disabled people. It is so easy to bemoan the lack of visitors to a handicap centre while doing nothing to entice them in.

Meeting again
This chapter has focussed on ways of *introducing* disabled people to the community. We have no doubt that, given the right environment, disabled people will undermine the public's fears and apprehensions, and replace embarrassment with confidence.

As with any skill, the public's new social competences need practice. Otherwise their confidence will wane, old habits are reinstated and those who are disabled will return to their social isolation. On every occasion we need to highlight for participants the opportunities which exist locally for on-going contact, especially through disabled people's participation in local social networks – clubs, organizations and activities. It won't happen by chance, it requires an effort by all concerned.

Further Information
Does he take sugar in his tea? A guide to meeting disabled people, Action Research for the Crippled Child.

6 PARTICIPANT INVOLVEMENT

I hear and I forget,
I see, and I remember,
I do and I understand.

This Chinese proverb sums up all we want to say in this chapter: quite simply, people learn more effectively if they are actively involved.

Of course primary schools have known and practised this under a variety of titles for a long time – activity or discovery learning, child-centred education. But perhaps this style of learning has become too identified with children and is considered 'childish' in the context of adult education. University-style lectures, with or without demonstrations, still predominate.

> The first night of the pottery class we didn't do anything at all, we just sat there while he gave us the whole history of clay. This wasn't what I wanted at all. Once I'd set eyes on the clay, I wanted to get going. He just talked and talked and talked. When it came to 'question time' we were all so exhausted we couldn't think of anything to ask.

(Jennifer Rogers *Adults Learning*, p.118)

While this lecture tradition has a venerable past, it is not the best approach to adult learning. Research has show that:

1   Involvement learning is as effective for adults as it is for children. The activity approach is not a mere concession to the shorter attention span of the child; it has proved to be the best way to internalise concepts.

2   The adult's short-term memory is poorer than the child's, and so the adult is less likely to retain the facts and figures which are so often prominent in the lecture-approach.

3   Attitudes are related to emotions as much as to rational thought. For this reason learner involvement is especially important in programmes on disability. It is easier to revise your views on the basis of what you have discovered or experienced for yourself, than on the basis of second-hand evidence.

4   Unlike children, adult course attenders have a wealth of personal experience; some will have relatives and friends who are disabled. Not to draw on such experience is to ignore a valuable resource.

Of course not all adult learning has espoused the 'academic' approach. Industrial training and leisure 'craft' classes are situations where 'active' learning has always been primary, and the challenge and satisfaction of 'hands-on' experience are hard to equal. The practical element in a pottery class is obvious, but what about a programme on disability? Where is the scope for active involvement? Aside from the obvious one of meeting disabled people – dealt with in the previous chapter – there are plenty of other opportunities.

Scope for Involvement

Involvement is an *approach* which can be applied to any programme; it determines *how* you use the resources available to you, more than it determines the content of the programme. For example, if you wanted the course participants to become aware of the services for disabled people in their area, you might ask a group of participants to assemble the information and present it to the rest of the group in whatever way they felt was most effective, instead of you gathering it yourself and handing it out to them in a way that suited you best.

Similarly, if we were looking at the mobility problems of wheelchair-bound people, participants might survey the area for hazardous obstacles, or better still, they might interview disabled people about the problems of mobility they experience – thus including the personal angle – or they might even push each other around in a wheelchair. That's real discovery learning.

Although people will not decry the theory, not everyone favours this sort of active involvement by participants. The common objections are:

It's too time-consuming – That is, you won't 'get through' enough! The belief that information alone will change people's attitudes – and the more information, the greater the change – unfortunately is not true. As we indicated in Chapter 3, attitude change is more complex than that, and information giving is the least important element in it.

Requires too much organising – Admittedly it may do, but the time spent in preparation can mean less work during the actual meeting. After all, the participants will be doing the work. This can be a real bonus for inexperienced tutors.

Adults would rather not – Especially if you don't encourage them! In fact, adults usually find any sort of new course intimidating, and are wary of being 'exposed' before their peer group. Anxiety and stress are very real, particularly before participants have got to know each other or the tutor – hence the importance of the initial meeting.

The First Meeting
Here the tone of the whole programme is set, since first impressions are lasting and can be difficult to alter later. The atmosphere of this first contact is most important and will be influenced by:

Venue – Is it comfortable and relaxing in terms of heating, ventilation and seating? Is it a 'normal setting' where participants will feel at home? Avoid special clinics or units for the meeting place – your message is that disabled people are part of *ordinary* life. If you have a choice in room-size, small is beautiful; a room which is too large for the group is intimidating and discourages involvement.

Seating arrangements – Rows of chairs facing the front of the room means you are ready for a lecture or sermon. A circle of chairs suggests open discussion and equal involvement, aided by proximity and good eye contact. Each person has equal prominence and an equal opportunity to contribute. Thus the seating arrangements will indicate the level of involvement you anticipate.

Participants – Find out something of the background of your new group – why have they come on the course; what prior experience have they of disability; what are they expecting from the course? This kind of background information may be gleaned from prior 'consumer research' (see Chapter 4), or obtained in the opening minutes through asking questions.

Host – Consider this your primary role at the initial meeting. Arrive early so that you can meet participants as they arrive; making them feel welcome and ensuring they know each other's first names. Try to make the participants feel at ease with each other. You might consider some kind of 'party game' – something as simple as getting each participant to introduce the person beside them. Or you might include a 'mini-group' activity early on in the course, to help participants get to know each other within smaller groups.

Incidental arrangements – Such incidentals as a coffee break or a visit to the local pub afterwards are good opportunities to develop social contacts, resulting in greater group support and initiative.

Previewing the course – At the initial meeting you should give the group an overview of the programme and, in general terms, how you intend going about it. But, unlike the pottery class above, you should be brief. Participants will be keen to get started.

Tutor
The traditional role of instructor-cum-lecturer is not what we have in mind at all. When your aim is to involve participants your role has to be more varied, hence the title 'tutor'. You are the *facilitator*, encouraging participation and interaction within the group, and you are the group *leader* and organizer, supplying direction and exploiting the resources and talent within the group. At other times in the programme your role is one of *presenter*, introducing learning situations and resources – video programmes, disabled individuals, information sheets – and finally acting as a general *resource person* for the course. Indeed you might even give them a short talk.

In more personal terms, the ideal tutor is not only efficient in organizing people, but has a warm accepting personality, good social skills, an ability to incorporate participants' ideas and to radiate enthusiasm. But don't be alarmed – we all have room for improvement.

Handling People
Practice undoubtedly improves a tutor's skills at handling a group

of people. It's no harm being forearmed though. Here are some suggestions.

1   Participant expectations. Older participants in particular may feel disgruntled that the 'lectures' which they have anticipated have turned into something rather directionless and 'woolly'. 'You are the one who is supposed to have the answers,' they comment, 'why are you asking us; that's your job!' Indeed in the involvement approach, the tutor often appears to be doing very little.

You should make your approach clear from the beginning, starting with your course publicity. If discussion, group work and projects will be a prominent feature, then mention this as one of the special attractions. The seating arrangements, the introduction and the overview of the course will reinforce this. However, you should be sensitive to the participants' apprehensions, stressing that this approach will be enjoyable and not unduly demanding. We are all a little afraid of the unknown.

2   A supportive atmosphere. While it is unlikely that anyone will dismiss a suggestion outright ('That's nonsense!'), this can happen more subtly, eg a suggestion is ignored or given little consideration. Any criticism should be constructive – an alternative suggestion, for example – and built upon the person's comment.

Involvement takes time to develop, so allow a generous pause, and avoid the ritual, 'Any questions? No. Right then, we'll go straight to . . . ' Participants will not make suggestions if it's clear that you'd rather they didn't! This is particularly true of the shy person in the group. Do try to draw them out – an issue 'sent round' the circle for comment may help to break the ice; or they may feel more comfortable commenting in a mini-group or in an 'official' capacity, eg reporting back on a discussion.

3   *The long contributor.* Some lectures become intoxicated with the sound of their own voices – and occasionally some participants do, too. And if you are bored or losing track of the argument, then it is likely that the group members are as well. Sometimes the group will solve the problem for you – they can afford to be more direct than you can! The chance of this occurring can be minimized by asking for a comment from everyone, or by breaking up into mini-groups for discussion. Alternatively, the over-long contributor can be given an organisational role in the group – summarising discussions, taking notes – or be given some real scope for his or her energy by undertaking an investigation, mini-project or topic. Such a person may then become a real bonus to the group.

4   *The 'expert'.* Sometimes a tutor is tempted to establish particular rapport with the more experienced participants, directing comments and questions in their direction. This will quickly undermine involvement. However, participants with experience of disabled people can be an invaluable resource, able to speak from personal experience or to give another perspective. For example, the parent of a handicapped child may become the resource person for an improvisation project on the handicapped person at home, or on the reactions of neighbours and friends to the birth of a handicapped child. More generally, try to see all participants as a resource in their own way and to use their particular expertise within the overall framework of the course. Hence, it is worth spending time getting to know your group.

5   *Correcting mistakes.* How should you react when a participant makes a mistake? Ignore it? Pounce on it? Leave it until later to correct? Adults don't enjoy being corrected and generally it is better to anticipate and avoid pitfalls as far as possible. If the mistake is an important one, then it should be corrected, but tactfully. Otherwise it can wait.

6   *Handling criticism.* Very occasionally a participant may be

directly critical of your approach. For example, a participant might unexpectedly turn to you and say: 'I don't think this is a good idea at all.' In this case your first reaction should be to have him elaborate – does he object to the approach, or does he consider the topic irrelevant? Has he any alternative suggestions? How do the group feel about it?

Misunderstanding can arise when you fail adequately to explain the rationale for a particular approach or topic which an individual may find difficult or irrelevant (eg role-playing a handicapped person).

Such direct comment is a valuable form of feedback; and a compromise or change of approach may well be called for.

Planning for Involvement
Involvement can occur spontaneously but equally, like the proverbial well, it can quickly run dry. It must be planned if you want to ensure it occurs and lasts. You may need to prepare 'trigger' material to get a discussion going: devise tasks for small groups to work on, obtain resource material for people doing projects or bring along equipment needed for improvisations.

All this amounts to quite detailed programme planning, as the examples given later in Section 3 indicate. We recommend this level of detail because the amount of time participants are available to you is very short indeed, and you need to make the most of it. The result should be a sense of direction to the sessions and a feeling of achievement at the end. Nor is spontaneity excluded by preparatory planning; what is scheduled should always be scrapped in favour of something better – a good impromptu discussion, an unforeseen opportunity to follow-up on an item, an unexpected chance for further contact with disabled peers. In other words, programme outlines are your guide, not a strait-jacket.

Two final points in relation to planning. First, we are not suggesting that you set out to pack into your programme as many opportunities for involving participants as you possibly can. There are other important elements, but many of the issues and topics you will want to cover in a community programme on disability will lend themselves naturally to this basic approach. Secondly, in planning your programme *content*, keep the human element to the fore and present issues and topics positively. Overall, your programme should concentrate more on the capabilities, the potential and the normality of handicapped people, rather than reinforce their disabilities and abnormalities.

Ways of Involving People
1 *Discussion*
First, a word of caution. This is frequently an over-used technique; good discussions are both rare and memorable, for they combine a genuine concern for the topic with a willingness to contribute freely and to revise one's views in the light of the evidence which emerges. This combination can be difficult to achieve. But, at the very least, discussion gives participants a chance to exchange ideas and comments. In this latter sense, discussions can arise in different ways:

Buzz group – in which two to three people very briefly tease out a dilemma or point of view. Usually lasts 2 – 3 minutes and it allows participants to clarify their thinking on a point or to come up with suggestions.

Brain-storming session – in which participants contribute ideas almost at random into the 'melting-pot'. From the pot-pourri the group rescues the most useful suggestions. An excellent way of arriving at novel solutions and an enjoyable approach to difficult problems.

Impromptu discussion – the unplanned discussion which develops as a result of some comment or incident (eg news item, a TV programme or following on from a group project or topic). There should always be room for such spontaneous developments, as they usually reflect keen interest on the part of the participants. Be sensitive to their wishes and, as leader, be prepared to follow. The rest of the programme may be adjusted accordingly.

Organised discussion – a good discussion rarely emerges unless some 'trigger' material is used to get it started. Trigger material should be provocative and challenging, highlighting a dilemma or situation which will evoke varied responses and solutions. In common with the overall programme approach, it should have a strong human dimension, eg the decision to operate on a severely handicapped newborn, the right of a mentally handicapped couple to marry. Various forms of trigger material can be used – a short film or video-programme; a case study; an article presenting critical or conflicting evidence (some examples are included in Section 4).

Facilitating planned discussion – it helps to appoint a discussion leader who will clearly state the issue at the beginning and encourage participation by all.

Small groups are better (4–8 participants) as everyone can

contribute. Besides being 'triggered', the discussion should have a stated *conclusion*; eg this may be a summary of the main points, a degree of consensus or a response to the specific questions posed at the start. The group should be told how long they have for discussion – but be prepared to be lenient in practice as discussions can take a few minutes to warm up. The group might appoint a spokesperson to report back to the 'plenary' group at the end.

2 *Task groups*
This is a development of the discussion approach, but in this case a small group of participants (4 – 8 people) have a specific task to work on. Examples of tasks are:

a To work out the practical implications of information presented earlier; eg after a presentation on the work-potential of disabled individuals, the group might list the kinds of jobs they could manage, and how managers/employers might be persuaded to employ them. The task might result in a list of recommendations on changing employers' attitudes, etc. This encourages an 'advocate' role to attitude change (see page 61).

b To research a report on an area of concern, eg current employment prospects in the areas handicapped people are being trained for; the causes of disability and ways of preventing it. The necessary reference material should be provided and participants encouraged to present their findings to the whole group, perhaps preparing simple visual aids. Finding out information for themselves means it is more likely to be remembered.

c An *action* task. The group might visit and interview people in connection with a report on a topic, for example the types of leisure opportunities available locally to handicapped people. A task of this extent may require more time than a short programme can allow for. It might be feasible, however, if each individual is given a single task to perform, the results being collated at the next meeting. The great advantage here is that participants actually make contact with disabled people and their meeting has a purpose – they want to find out from those who know.

3 *Simulation – Improvisation*
It is very difficult to simulate realistically the effects of disability.

At best you can put people into wheelchairs, but even here the game element can still dominate. Nevertheless the experience of being wheelchair-bound usefully brings home to participants just how inaccessible buildings are and how the public reacts. This entails going outside and encountering strangers, an essential feature if the simulation is to be successful (see Chapter 3). However, a lot of time and/or a lot of wheelchairs are required. And what of other disabilities? How do you simulate mental handicap?

The alternative is improvisation. Here two or three people role-play characters in a given situation. Let's say one is a 20 year-old person who is mentally handicapped travelling on the bus into the city-centre; a second person sits beside him or her; the bus conductor is collecting the fares. The three participants each assume roles and improvise what will happen. They decide on the main story-line, then act it out – each portraying how they think the person, whose role they are taking, would react in that situation. There is no script as such; no worked out conclusion, simply their ideas being expressed in actions and words.

It is worth encouraging participants to go through the scene for a second time – they'll be more tuned-in and less inhibited.

Following this, participants discuss what happened and why. How did they identify the person was handicapped? How did he feel (confused, frustrated, happy)? What sort of assumptions did the others make and were they valid?

Improvisations of this kind can be a powerful stimulus for discussion. It is particularly effective for examining assumptions and prejudice in a 'real' context, and for explaining emotional responses to handicap.

To many participants, however, improvisation is a new experience and, for adults, may be a little frightening! Where participants do not already know each other, it might be used later rather than earlier in the programme. It is a good idea for all participants to be involved in (different) improvisations at the same time, so that no one feels 'on stage' or unduly inhibited by the thought of spectators.

Another vital role for improvisation is to give participants an opportunity to practise new 'skills'. For example, in our programme with sales assistants, after we had discussed ways of helping customers who were mentally handicapped, we divided the group into pairs and asked each person to role-play a scene in the store with one as the sales assistant, the other as the customer who could be quite awkward! This started off light-heartedly, but participants did go on to practise the 'rules' identified earlier for helping customers who are mentally handicapped.

Finally, improvisations, as we hinted above, can be an emotional release for the participants themselves. In our schools' programme with senior pupils we begin the programme by dividing into small groups and acting out a scene in which one person is mentally handicapped. The embarrassment, mickey-taking, giggling, etc., at the thought of facing up to this new, and for some, threatening subject can be dispensed with straight away. We contrast immediately their impressions with a videotape of mentally handicapped people talking about themselves.

4 Individual involvement

Our preference is to involve people within groups – that way the work-load is shared and no one should feel 'on the spot'. However, this need not preclude individual contributions. For example, if a person has previous experience with disabled people, he or she might speak briefly about it to others, eg a mother of a disabled child. This can be a useful way of exploring feelings.

Another approach which we incorporated into our Adult Education Courses was the *Topic Spot*. Each evening one or two participants undertook to address the group for 3–5 minutes – no longer – on an aspect in which they were particularly interested. Tutors did have to do some coaxing, but the necessary resource materials such as fact sheets were provided and, once some people had volunteered, the others followed. Most found it a useful and informative experience which helped to build morale within the group.

Involvement is an Attitude of Mind

With foresight and ingenuity you will discover many different ways of involving people as active participants rather than passive listeners. Ultimately, however, involvement depends more on an attitude of mind than a collection of methods. If you adopt the attitude of 'expert on handicaps and missionary to the masses', then it is unlikely that you will spend much time listening to others – you'll be too busy talking! If your attitude is one of sharing, mediating and indeed compromising, then involvement will come naturally to you.

Further Reading

John Heron (1977), *Dimensions of Facilitator Style*, published by British Postgraduate Medical Federation, University of London, 33 Millman Street, London WC1N 3EJ.

7 PRESENTING INFORMATION

This is the chapter we were tempted to omit. Information-giving is the aspect of public education which has accrued considerable resources and expertise over the years, resulting in an array of pamphlets, leaflets, books and films. The causes of handicap, its prevention or amelioration, the recent scientific advances and new developments in specialist equipment and services, have all received extensive treatment. A large part of the finance available for public education has been devoted to developing these informational resources, with the result that they are both comprehensive and of a high standard.

But perhaps information-giving has been *too* prominent in educational programmes on disability. The materials developed have tended to focus attention on the *facts*, not the *personalities*; and when people are discussed it is often their *dis*ability, their handicap, which receives most attention. Moreover, these resources have been developed as self-contained items without reference to each other, and with little follow-up. Rarely are they part of an overall planned approach.

As a community educator, you know the key facts which you most want to convey to the public. You are probably well aware of common misconceptions and prejudices, some deep-rooted. The use of disabilities as terms of abuse is embedded in everyday language, and used even by handicapped people. As the blind barrister in John Mortimer's play *Voyage Around my Father* angrily upbraids his wife and son: 'Am I totally surrounded by fools and cretins?'

Being aware of what the public *needs* to know is one thing; it is equally important to discover what they *want* to know. As with any area of learning, readiness is a key factor.

The 'public' consists of many communities based on shared interests or common occupations, or around the social networks of work or home. The information about disabled people of most interest to a policeman will differ from what might concern a local housewife or a youth club leader. Hence in selecting information we should respond to their needs as well as to our priorities.

Nor is it possible to convey all the information we might like to, in short community programmes. We should perhaps concentrate on whetting the public's appetite for more, rather than presenting a surfeit of information. Yet, this needs a strong will – there is a temptation to give more rather than less detail, but the result is a confused message. For example, detailed percentages on the incidence of handicap and the factors influencing it, may be factually correct but nothing like as memorable as the bold statement 'one in ten is disabled', used by the Northern Ireland Committee for the International Year of Disabled People and illustrated by a pair of hands with one finger missing.

Think of your programmes as an *introduction*. Be satisfied to cover only the most basic information on the disability in question. And it should be introductory in the getting-to-know-you sense also. The main purpose of your programme is to bring handicapped and non-handicapped people into contact with each other – a basic step towards integration. Achieving regular and sustained contact entails resources and expertise beyond the scope of the community educator. Nonetheless this aim of integration has implications for the kind of information you present, i.e. effects of disability on the human personality. This is a dimension often overlooked in public education, to the cost of disabled people themselves:

> Nobody imagines that a girl in a wheelchair is pining for love. People say that I am not unattractive and that I have an affectionate nature . . . I am longing for love, how can I keep it to myself?

> (K. Herlingaetal: *Not Made of Stone*)

Nobody imagines that she has ordinary feelings because we have neglected to tell them. We have overlooked showing the public that the effects of a disability are *limited*. Their emotions, their aspirations, their intelligence have not been affected – except by our expectations.

Ironically it is the human dimensions which most appeal to the public, not because of morbid curiosity, but rather to know how to react when they meet people with a disability.

Guidelines for Presenting Information

Perhaps it is worth summarizing all the considerations we have mentioned into more specific guidelines to bear in mind when planning the informational content of your programme.

1 *Keep it short.* Information giving may seem the most productive use of programme time, but research studies suggest otherwise. Do allow time for involvement by participants – discussion, comments, questions.

2 *Be positive.* The public should hear of the abilities and potential of disabled people more often than of their limitations.

3 *Avoid jargon.* Use only the very minimum of medical terms. What has become second language to you, may be Greek to your listeners. Even a phrase like 'open employment' can confuse the uninitiated.

4 *Be practical.* Make the information more understandable by giving practical examples. 'Poor social skills' means 'difficulty in handling money, using buses, shopping, and dealing with strangers'. This helps to translate specialist concepts into ordinary and understandable terms.

5 *Their interests.* When planning your course, find out what the course attenders want to know more about – do some 'consumer research'.

6 *Their backgrounds.* Be aware of the occupations and interests of the group members and link the presentation of information to these interests. Shop assistants, for example, will be most interested in ways of assisting disabled people with their shopping.

7 *'Available on request'.* Although you will have limited your time to priority information, you should make available further details to interested participants, by supplying, for example, a set of topic-based Fact Sheets (see later), leaflets or books, which they can read in their own time.

8 *Their contributions.* Participants themselves can becomes an informational resource for the group either because of their past experiences or when they express an interest in a particular topic, read up on it, and summarize their findings for the group in a 'Topic Spot'.

9 *Be interesting.* Facts are dry stuff! Enliven your material by using cartoons, illustrations, anecdotes and practical examples. In particular, use visual aids to stimulate interest and to high-light important points.

These general points should prove useful no matter what medium or level of sophistication is involved in your presentation of information. In the latter part of this chapter we shall describe the various media you could use in conveying information, but first, here is a brief overview of the possible methods of presenting information.

Sharing Information

There are many ways of sharing information with a group of people. It may take the form of:

A *'talk'*, but the impact of simply speaking to the group will depend very much on the personality of the speaker and the freshness of what he or she has to say.

A *'talk'* combined with a hand-out, which summarizes the main points. If distributed at the end, it is a good aid to memory and is easily available for later reference.

Use of illustrative materials to complement the spoken word. Visuals (poster, wallcharts, transparencies, slides, photo-graphs) can effectively emphasise the main points, and create interest and variety.

A *pre-recorded presentation*, eg slide-tape combination, video programme or instructional film. The preparation in this case is more demanding, but once assembled it can be used by any number of people again and again.

A *question-and-answer* session. This works best if partici-pants are given some prior notice and is more successful towards the end of a programme or after a short presentation.

A *'quiz'* is a fun version of a question and answer session, which may be an enjoyable way of ending the programme. We suggest grouping the participants in teams and allowing them to consult before answering.

A *group presentation.* You could involve participants in assembling and presenting the information for themselves. Mini-groups of three or four people might select different topics and, having researched them, present the main findings to the others using charts or other visual aids that they have prepared themselves. The technical standards may be low, but the participant involvement and satisfaction will be greater.

As involvement techniques have already been discussed in Chapter 6, we shall concentrate here on the use of written, visual or audio-visual methods in presenting information. We shall look in particular at two media: the *Overhead projector*, a common and versatile visual aid, for which it is comparatively easy to prepare excellent material; and the *Slide-Tape combination*, a more demanding but most useful medium in that the presentation can be completely prepared in advance.

Aids to Presenting Information

Leaflets

These are so common that we shall devote little space to this medium of communication. The guidelines given earlier should be rigorously followed when preparing 'give-away' material. Plenty of illustrations – cartoons, diagrams, photographs – clear layout and attractive presentation will increase the likelihood of people picking up a leaflet and scanning it. Getting them to read and take in the information is a much bigger hurdle and this probably explains why people fail to learn from written materials.

Leaflets are best used as a supplement to another presentation. eg summarising the main points of a talk.

Fact Sheets

Pertinent facts on disability are often dispersed among different sources – books, articles, reports, etc. It may be daunting for a beginner to track these down. Fact sheets are an aid to them in that the relevant facts about a topic can be summarised on one sheet of paper and be read in five minutes or so. A collection of sheets could be assembled, each dealing with a separate theme, such as causes and prevention, professional and support services in the locality, ideas for helping disabled people. Each sheet should be clearly labelled and/or printed on different coloured paper.

These information packs form a useful resource for participants engaged on project work. Alternatively, certain sheets could be copied and circulated following a presentation. Participants might be tempted to 'dip into' them, once the programme has ended.

Samples of fact sheets on mental handicap which we prepared for our programmes are given in Section 4 (p 214).

Posters

If there is a single theme or slogan which is central to your community education programme, then poster treatment is ideal. For example, in a programme for employers, you might want to say: 'Handicapped workers are reliable' against a background picture of a disabled worker clocking in on time. Equally the poster might portray a feature that is central to your programme, like the idea of meeting handicapped people individually. We took this theme in our programmes and the poster simply showed close-up photographs of disabled people's faces. Ideally, it would be useful to have a series of posters highlighting key points, but with limited resources, a single theme poster may be all you can afford.

Nevertheless, it is possible to produce cheap posters using a little ingenuity. Most photocopiers now have enlarging facilities, so that it is possible to magnify good quality material (ie. illustrations with strong contrast and good definition) to poster size, by combining two A3 size sheets; a very economical way of making posters.

It is also possible to enlarge material using the overhead projector. First make a transparency of your mastercopy and then pin up a large sheet of paper in place of the screen and copy the projected image using felt-tipped markers. More useful for cartoons and diagrams than for photographs or print.

Posters are a good way of gaining people's attention, of providing a talking point for participants and giving them a reminder of your message.

Wall Charts

These can convey more information than a poster while retaining many of the poster's advantages. People may be tempted to linger over a wall chart before or after a meeting, especially one placed at eye-level in a convenient but prominent location.

However, wall charts rely very much on good design for their effectiveness – well-laid-out headings, diagrams and illustrations, brief lucid text and colour printing.

Although you could prepare a wall chart as a once-off aid, it is worth considering having a few 'core' charts printed. One colour printing on tinted paper is a minimum requirement for a poster to be effective. They can be further enlivened by the addition of colour photographs or illustrations. These charts could cover most of the basic information you want to impart and might prove useful in a variety of programmes. They can easily be made available to others.

Wall charts are particularly useful for open days, exhibitions, etc., as part of an attractive display. They can take the form of a short quiz with spectators pressing buttons to see whether they answered correctly. This might help to ensure that they take note of information.

The old reliable method of telling people the news you want them to hear must also feature. It has obvious advantages – less preparation, low cost, no reading – but it has severe limitations.

What if the people don't listen? The guidelines noted earlier should help get your message across. Another strategy is to get them listening with their eyes as well as their ears.

Visual aids

The use of visual aids can transform a talk. It is essential that they are seen by everyone, so make use of a projector – either a slide projector or an overhead projector. The latter is our favourite as it is so much more versatile. Transparencies for this projector can be quickly and easily prepared and they are an excellent way of summarising information. It can be used as easily by the participants as by the tutor. But in our experience the overhead projector rarely gets used to its full extent.

Slides take longer and are more costly to prepare. For this reason we feel it is better to go the whole way and make a total presentation by recording an audio commentary to accompany the slides. The result is a slide/tape package which can be readily used by others.

Alternatively it is possible to buy or hire slide/tape programmes on various aspects of disability (see Section 4).

We shall now consider the use of the overhead projector and slide/tape presentations in more detail.

Overhead Projector

The advantage of this projector is that the room does not have to be darkened; it allows you to stand facing your audience while showing or pointing to the illustration, so that eye-contact can be maintained with the audience and their questions or discussion can be easily slotted into the presentation.

For those unfamiliar with this projector it is basically a box with a strong bulb in the bottom of it, magnifying glass across the top of it, and a mirror held at an angle over the box to reflect the light on to a screen or white wall. The box also houses an electric fan to keep both the bulb and glass surface from overheating. To focus the 'picture' you raise or lower the mirror by twisting a knob on the supporting arm. To adjust the picture on the screen you tilt the mirror. The screen should be set tilting forward to ensure the picture is square and not wedge-shaped. This can happen if the projector is too low down.

Transparencies – The illustrations you want to project must be copied on to transparent material rather like tough celophane – referred to as transparencies or acetates. This is available in three forms: as a roll which is wound across the top of the projector; as single square sheets or as special transparencies for use with photocopying machines. The single sheets of acetate are also sold in various colours.

Making your own transparencies

Although it is possible to have transparencies commercially made, it is easier and cheaper to make your own. All you need is acetate and special felt-tipped pens (ordinary markers do not work). Projector pens come in either permanent or water-based inks and there is a wide range of colours. Only those colours which contrast strongly with a white screen are most effective – black, blue, red or green. Yellow should only be used for shading.

With the pens you can write or draw whatever you want. But a more professional finish can be obtained by using:

Rub-off lettering – eg Letraset, to give a printed text. There are also sheets of press-on shading and shapes (dots, arrows, lines) for making diagrams.

Stick-on paper shapes – packets of these are sold in most stationers. They come in a variety of shapes and sizes and stick well to acetate. They appear on the screen as strong black shapes very useful when drawing graphs.

Tracing – with acetate, tracing is very simple – just place it over the illustration and mark out what you want to highlight. Different colours of ink can be used to emphasise different aspects.

Cut-out illustrations in paper or card can be stuck onto the acetate or placed directly on to the glass surface of the projector and moved about to illustrate stages in a process.

Coloured acetate – can be cut to shape and stuck on to the illustration to give a solid colouring effect. It is especially effective for drawing attention to particular features – headlines, bar graphs, etc.

Photocopier – The marvels of science now mean that you can produce black and white transparencies with a photocopier. Special acetate sheets (labelled 'for photocopying') are loaded into the machine instead of paper and the original – photograph, cartoon, diagram or table – is transferred on to it. Ordinary type-script or news print is much too small for photocopying – this should be enlarged at least four times before putting it on to acetate.

With the help of a photocopier and some of the other suggestions made above, you should be able to produce transparencies of quality and clarity. The latter is probably the more important. Make sure the print is large and any hand-writing is clear and bold. Don't cram too many words on to the transparency – use head-ings, key words. Avoid large empty spaces but don't go too near the edge, otherwise it will not be projected. A touch of colour in text or illustrations can work wonders.

Presenting transparencies
There is a variety of techniques to choose from when using this projector.

On the spot writing – the projector is used instead of a blackboard or white board with the advantage that you can continue to face the audience; and you can remain seated – useful for people in wheelchairs. Used in this way, it can project the points emerging from group discussion or for recording decisions.

You can also add details to a prepared transparency. This can be done repeatedly if the outline is drawn in permanent marker and the additions made with water-based pens.

Revealing by stages – The prepared transparency is covered with a piece of paper or card which can be gradually moved to reveal the section to which the speaker is referring.

Add/overlay further details – the first transparency may show the broad outline; then a second transparency is placed on top of the first adding further detail, and several more may be added to complete the picture.

Using an indicator – to draw attention to a particular part of the transparency, place your pen on the glass, with the nib indicating the point in question. *Do not hold the pen in your hand* as any shaking on the screen will be magnified. Alternatively, you may cut out a small arrow in card to place on the transparency. Remember there is no need to point at the actual screen and hence turn your back on the audience.

Common faults in presenting transparencies

1 *The writing or print is too small.* You must take into account the size of your audience, how far from the screen they will be, and the amount of magnification (ie. how far is the overhead projector from the screen). Better err towards large print as it is frustrating to listen to someone referring at length to something you can't see.

2 *The transparency is continually trembling.* This will happen if you continue to hold the transparency after putting it on the overhead projector, or if you insist on continually re-adjusting it, or use your finger to indicate points on it. Remember you cannot see the screen and it is very easy to develop nervous habits which will be magnified by the overhead projector and distract your audience. You should also avoid waving your hand over the transparency as you might over a wall-chart: you will only blot out the whole screen.!

3 *The projector distracts* – switch it off when it is not in use. A brightly lit screen is a distraction and it is confusing to leave a transparency on view when a different point is being discussed.

If the fan of the projector is too noisy try oiling it or tighten the screw which holds it in place.

Taking care of transparencies

Transparencies which you use frequently should be framed – cardboard frames are commercially available – and these will prevent the edges from splitting or curling and help to ensure that you place them the correct way up on the projector. You can even write your notes on the frame.

When storing transparencies, lay them flat with tissue paper between them.

Slide Tape Presentations

Much of the foregoing section is equally applicable to the making and use of slides. However, we have chosen to focus more on linking slides with a prerecorded commentary to give what is usually called a slide/tape presentation. These are available commercially (see Section 4) but it is possible to produce your own.

The necessary equipment consists of a slide projector (preferably of the carousel or magazine type) and an audiotape recorder. An optional extra is a synchroniser unit which will automatically change the slides. Alternatively you can purchase a complete unit incorporating all three – looking rather like a portable television.

If you plan to produce your own programmes, a good camera, with close-up-lens is an asset.

Slide-tape presentations are most useful for summarising information. Unlike film or video, the viewer has a chance to grasp the significance of illustrations or to read the text; for there are few distractions. These programmes are ideal when information has to be presented repeatedly – say at an exhibition or when an 'expert' talker is not available.

Making your own programmes

Some of the first decisions you must make are about the aim of the programme (to inform, or trigger discussion) its style (humorous, factual or indignant?) and its length. A ten minute presentation will require around 60–70 slides and about 1,500 words of commentary. As you will discover, you can say a lot in ten minutes.

You might also think where and when it will be shown. Presentations for exhibitions should rely mainly on the pictures to get the message across with little or no commentary, mainly background music.

It is a matter of opinion whether it is better to record the sound track first, or to decide on and prepare the visual materials in the first instance. If you plan to include interviews with disabled people, then these should certainly be completed before selecting the slides, but in general it is the visual material which is the more difficult to locate and as the visual is the more powerful in terms of impact, we suggest the following approach:

1   Decide on the three or four main points that you will make and sketch out possible visuals to illustrate these. Allow around ten slides for each theme.
2   Write rough soundtrack to go with each set. Are you happy

with the effect? If not, you should review your plans and make any necessary adjustments.

3   When you have polished these sequences you can now 'top and tail' your programme and write a detailed script for the presentation.
4   Prepare and assemble the required slides (always shoot more than you plan to use). A slide should be shown for around ten seconds – not less than five and never more than 30 seconds.
5   Assemble the soundtrack – commentary, music, sound effects.
6   Edit the soundtrack to match the slides (two tape recorders are needed at this stage).
7   Synchronise the slides with commentary by:
    (a)   Noting on a copy of the script when the slides should be changed.
    (b)   Adding a bleep sound on to the tape so that the operator knows when to advance the picture.
    (c)   If using a synchroniser unit (relatively cheap and very useful) then you add a 'silent' bleep to the soundtrack which automatically signals the projector to change the slide.

Copies of the slide/tape presentations can be easily and cheaply produced with no loss of quality.

Given the number of tasks involved in producing this type of programme, it is worth enlisting the help of a team of people to help – a colleague with an interest in photography, another who likes drawing cartoons or diagrams and someone with technical know-how when it comes to editing the soundtrack. Indeed you might consider approaching students at a local college to see if they would be interested in taking it on as a project.

Finally, if all this fails and you still want to use a slide/tape presentation – you can hire or buy existing sets and adapt them to suit your purposes.

You can do it
We hope that we have convinced you that it is possible to produce interesting, informative and novel resource materials for use in educating people about disability. Our listing is by no means exhaustive; we have not dealt with audio recordings, for example. We live in an age when there are more and more aids to communication. Yet people's fear of technology often forces them back to written or spoken words, whereas we need to enlist the help of the modern equivalents of the pen and the voice. Indeed we now move on to consider the most novel and powerful medium of all – video.

Suggested Reading

Stephen Lewis, *Slide Tape for Classroom and Community*, published by the Directory of Social Change, 14 Saltram Crescent, London W9.

Richard Need, *An Introduction to A.V.*, published by British Industrial and Scientific Film Association, 27 D'Arblay Street, London W1V 3FH.

8 USING VIDEO

Video will revolutionise community education. It can convey much richer images and deeper meanings than will any lecturer. It presents information more clearly and vividly than books ever could. It is a particular boon to people with difficulty in reading or who can't be bothered to read. Moreover, video is so much more convenient and easier to use than its nearest rival – movie film. Quite simply, it is the most effective and efficient form of communication yet devised.

Fortunately, it is no longer a technology for specialists. The advent of home video-systems and the recent drop in prices means that recorders are now as cheap as colour televisions and will soon be nearly as common.

For the community educator, video is not a luxury; it is a necessity. It has certainly been a key element in the success of our own education programmes on mental handicap. Hence this chapter describes the role of video and outlines how best it can be used. For those wary of gadgetry, a word of reassurance. If you follow the basic steps described in the manual supplied with the recorder, you will not damage the equipment and you'll quickly discover that it is even less likely to damage you.

What Video Can Do

It lets the public see and hear disabled people
When it is not convenient or easy for your group to meet with disabled people, video is the next best thing. In some circumstances it may be an advantage.

There is a natural inclination for people to stare at the unusual or unfamiliar. Langer[1] has argued that, when the public meets disabled people, this desire conflicts with the social convention that it is rude to stare, thereby creating a tension which causes people to avoid contact. His research rather bears this out. The solution, he argues, is to give them opportunities for 'sanctioned staring' – so that the public become accustomed to the unfamiliar. Video provides an excellent opportunity for this, without causing embarrassment to either party.

A second finding from research on attitude change is the potent effects of hearing disabled people talking about themselves, their feelings and their difficulties. It is not easy to do this in front of a live audience but with video a person can be recorded in the privacy of his or her own home.

Video also lets the public see disabled people in everyday situations, illustrating how they have learnt to cope and giving an insight into their lifestyle and daily routines.

Video can highlight issues for discussions
Participant involvement is the prelude to attitude change and must feature in all our educational programmes. Video is an excellent way of triggering discussion and encouraging people to share their feelings and make known their attitudes. In this respect, television plays featuring disabled people are especially useful as they highlight the issues both vividly and personally.

Obtaining Video Programmes

The crucial element in video, is of course the programmes you show; the equipment is useless otherwise. So where can you get hold of video programmes?

Hiring and buying
Various companies specialise in hiring or selling 'educational' video programmes – their names and addresses are given in Section 4 along with details of programmes on disability that we particularly recommend.

Most of these programmes have been made by the national television companies and their technical standards are therefore high. However, the programme's content may not be entirely suitable for your needs – titles can mislead. Catalogues, obtainable from the companies, usually give a brief description but you are advised to preview any programme before purchasing. In the future there is likely to be a wider choice of programmes on disability available commercially.

Recording programmes 'off-the-air'

A video recorder enables you to record programmes as they are broadcast on television. Recently there have been several excellent programmes on disability (see p 239) and they are ideal for use in community education projects. Unfortunately you do not get advance notice of when suitable programmes will appear. You have to keep an eye on the television schedules and record likely programmes. If they prove unsuitable, nothing is lost as the tapes can always be re-used.

There are copyright laws regarding the showing of programmes you have recorded. Strictly speaking, these recordings are for your personal use and should only be replayed on the equipment and in the location where the programme was recorded. However, the use of recordings for educational purposes is treated more leniently. But you must never charge admission to view a programme or sell copies of it to other people.

Making your own programmes

This is the ultimate advantage of video – you can produce your own television programmes. Admittedly, the outcome will be nothing like the high quality you are accustomed to from national television; but what they lack in sophistication is more than compensated for by their content.

1. *Local appeal* – People are much more impressed and intrigued by seeing people and places from their local community on television. This rarely happens on broadcast programmes or on those which are commercially available. Rural communities in particular seem to lose out, as so many productions reflect city life.
2. *Topicality* – Programmes you make for yourself can reflect what is happening NOW and they can be updated easily if things change. Not so with broadcast programmes which are sometimes recorded months in advance of their actual transmission and will be out of date in a few years.
3. *Relevance* – your programme can focus on issues that are particularly relevant to your area and community. No longer need you say 'It's all right for them, but what about us?' In short, video

lets you decide on the content and style of the programme. The critic can become the director.

If you can get hold of a video-camera and recorder, we urge you to start making your own recordings for inclusion in your educational projects. It only takes about 20 minutes to master the basic steps involved in using a video-camera and, as we will see later in this Chapter, a programme can be assembled with relative ease.

Video Equipment
At its simplest, a basic video set consists of four things – a television, a recorder, an RF lead and a tape.

(a)   *Television* – a familiar object now that nearly every home has one. You may hear this referred to as a monitor. Strictly speaking, this word describes a special type of television that cannot receive broadcast signals but which has been specially designed to monitor the pictures from video cameras or recorders.

(b)   *Recorder* – you should think of this as a large tape-recorder. It is a machine which can record events – in both sound and vision – for later playback. Most recorders have many of the features of a sound tape-recorder – there is a range of buttons which made the tape go forward, reverse, pause or stop. But unlike audio tape recorders, different manufacturers have produced machines of various formats. The significant feature, from the user's point of view, is that each format requires a different type of tape cassette – they are not interchangeable. The most common video formats are:

> *VHS.* This format (Video Home System) is now the market leader over most of the world. Originally invented by a Japanese company, called JVC, VHS machines are also marketed by Akai, National Panasonic, Ferguson, Mitsubishi, Hitachi and Sharp.
> *Betamax.* Invented by Sony, another Japanese company, this format is also used by Sanyo and Toshiba.
> *Video 2000.* This is Europe's answer to the home video system. Originally developed by Phillips and Grundig, this system is far less popular with purchasers. Video 2000 machines are also marketed by ITT and Pye.
> *U-matic.* The distinguishing feature of this format is that it uses ¾ inch tape instead of the ½ inch tape used in the other formats. The quality of recordings is therefore much better but, needless to say, these machines are more expensive. They are used mainly by colleges, industry and in recording studios.
> There are other video formats – EIAJ and Phillips 1500/1700 – but

these are now remnants of video history. It is both difficult and expensive to buy tapes in these formats.

(c) *Lead (wire) to connect recorder to the television* – It may be stating the obvious, but video recorders are useless without a television set and this lead. It is frequently referred to as an RF (radio frequency) lead or cable. It is the same type of lead that connects a television to its aerial. One end of the cable fits into the aerial socket of your TV, the other end slots into a socket on the recorder. This is usually labelled 'RF out'.

(d) *Tape cassette* – Finally you need a cassette to put into the recorder. These come in four different formats and they cannot be interchanged. When purchasing or borrowing tapes, make sure you get cassettes of the same format as your recorder.

With this basic set of video equipment you will be able to:
- Play back pre-recorded programmes such as those sold commercially or hired by video companies.
- Record a programme as it is broadcast. Some recorders will do this automatically if you pre-set them. Moreover, you can even watch one channel while the machine records a programme on another – that's technology for you!

If you want to make your own programmes, you will need at least one other piece of equipment:

Video camera – Although similar in appearance to the old home movie camera, these operate in an entirely different way. For a start, there is no film in this camera. Rather it converts photo-graphic images into electrical signals which pass down a cable into the video recorder where they are stored on the tape for later playback. Alternatively the recorder can pass the signals through to a television set – which decodes them and recreates them as pictures. Note that video cameras must always be connected by leads to recorders or televisions. Only recognised television services can broadcast their signals. That is why video is sometimes know as closed-circuit television.

The pictures recorded on video-tapes do not have to be developed. The recorder can immediately play back the images it has recorded. Moreover, some recorders will allow you to do this in slow motion and to freeze the picture at selected points.

The tapes are also re-usable. If your don't want to keep a recording you simply film over it. With up to three hours recording time on each tape, the cost of filming on video is very low. However video cameras are expensive and more costly than recorders.

How to Get Hold of Video Equipment

There are several options open to you, depending on how often you use the equipment and what you plan to do with it:

Borrowing – from a friend, local school or higher education college, or from a friendly TV rental or video dealer. Naturally, some people may be reluctant to trust their valuable equipment to another person, so be prepared for a refusal. Nonetheless, it is worth a try, especially for a recorder or camera that you need very occasionally.

Hiring – specialist video dealers will rent out equipment by the day or weekly. It can be expensive, although it is only a fraction of the costs involved in buying video equipment. Hiring is especially useful for little-used accessories, such as camera and lights, or for obtaining a second video recorder if you want to copy programmes. The telephone directory will list local dealers.

Rental – You can now rent a video recorder from most TV rental companies who make a monthly charge. An advantage is that they will cover the cost of breakdowns. But over two years you will have paid out more than the cost of the recorder, and yet it won't by yours. However, one major British rental company (Radio Rentals) will now rent a camera and accessories on a weekly basis to their customers. This may encourage other rental firms to do likewise.

Buying – This is becoming the most attractive option as the prices of recorders are coming down fast. Do shop around – you can obtain sizeable discounts; but beware of retailers who do not offer an after-sales service.

As regards choice of models, you will have to decide on the *standard* of recorder (home or industrial) you need and the *format* which best suits your purposes (i.e. VHS, Betamax, Video 2000 or U-matic). The books listed at the end of the Chapter may help.

Selecting or Making Video Programmes

You have video equipment, you know how it works – but what type of programmes should you use in your community education courses? The content of the programme will be decided by the aims of your course and the target audience you have in mind. But perhaps more crucial to the changing of attitudes are the production techniques employed. Past research has identified the following as crucial elements in making video an effective agent for changing the public's perceptions. You should keep these in mind when selecting ready-made programmes or when making your own.

(a) *Disabled people talking* – The bulk of the programme should be given over to disabled people – this is much more effective than having able-bodied 'experts' talking. For example, a disabled person might provide the commentary for the programme. However, it is essential that the participants speak reasonably clearly – an unsympathetic audience may not be bothered to listen attentively. The sensitive use of subtitles can help.

(b) *Close-ups of disabled people* – Facial close-ups in particular will help to emphasise the person and his or her feelings. They also give opportunities for 'sanctioned staring'.

(c) *Positive images* – The public's expectations of disabled people are generally so low that the balance of the programme should be more towards their abilities than their disabilities; otherwise their misconceptions may be confirmed.

Programmes designed to highlight the need for more or better services frequently project *dis*abilities and do little to boost the morale of disabled people themselves or of their families.

(d) *Individuality* – You need to convey the individuality of each person, even though they have a common disability. This can be achieved by featuring individuals from different backgrounds, or by giving them opportunities to talk about their likes and dislikes and even to disagree with each other.

(e) *Appropriate settings* – Programmes which reflect the everyday experiences of your target audience are more effective; for instance, American produced programmes may well jar or be dismissed as irrelevant in Europe, and vice versa. The more the programme reflects the audience's everyday experiences, the better chance there is of getting the message across.

(f) *Mixing with non-disabled* – The programme should include shots of disabled and non-disabled conversing and sharing activities, either within the family or better still in work or social settings. This helps to reinforce the normality of disabled people joining with others and gives the audience some tips as to how they might interact.

(g) *Unusual settings* – Disabled people are generally filmed in highly predictable settings – at home, in hospital or doing handicrafts. Scenes of them coping with potential dangers make much more interesting and informative viewing: the blind person crossing a busy street unaided; a person in a wheelchair travelling alone by train; the mentally handicapped teenager mastering a complex work skill.

Video programmes which incorporate these techniques will give your audience an effective introduction to people who are disabled. Sadly, many of the commercially available programmes do not measure up well to these criteria, usually because they were made with other aims in mind – describing available services or lack of them; giving information on prevention. You need programmes which emphasise *people*. If that means making your own – then so be it.

Assembling Your Own Video Programme
There's more to making a television programme than simply recording events with a camera. The finished programmes we see on television are the end-products of a complex and lengthy process. Those of us outside the video business will never achieve their techincal standards, but often our products win hands down on content.

First, though, you have to decide on the type of programme you want to produce. The choice is between two basic types; although they can be inter-mixed.

Information programmes – typified in television documentaries such as *Horizon*, these should convey new insights to the viewer – for example, the activities which go on in a workshop or in a group home for mentally handicapped people.

A second type of informational programme involves people talking about themselves or expressing their opinions. *Interview* programmes are relatively easy to produce and can make compelling viewing, especially when the interviewees are disabled people or their parents. It is a good idea to insert pictures of the activities to which they refer.

Instructional programmes – these attempt to give specific information for the viewer to put into practice. Video is an ideal teaching medium as it easily integrates various potent teaching techniques – explanation, demonstration, replay and analysis, summary captions. These programmes are best augmented by providing a written summary of the main points for distribution after viewing. Ideally, this sort of programme requires 'studio' facilities – albeit improvised ones – although it is possible to struggle through without them.

Making a programme

A programme is essentially an ordering of various recordings into a viewable and logical sequence. Merely playing back to an audience all the recordings you made – mistakes and all – is worse than nothing. So how can you assemble the best of your recordings into a programme? We shall outline four levels of sophistication in programme making.

Level 1: Selected excerpts. This is the most basic, in that it consists merely of a selection of recordings, replayed to an audience. First you preview all the recordings you have made and select those which are most suitable. Second, using the number counter on the recorder, identify the beginning and ending of the sequences you want to show. Third, decide on the order in which you will present each sequence. Finally, after showing each sequence you run the tape fast forward or rewind, ready for the next sequence.

Although not a programme in the strict sense of the term – rather it is a series of illustrations – this is very simple to produce. It entails no editing and any mistakes made while filming can easily be omitted. With this sort of production you are presenting life as the camera saw it – warts and all!

Such programmes can be very effective but they do have one big disadvantage – the distraction and inconvenience of winding the tape between sequences.

Level 2:   Edited excerpts. In this case your selected excerpts are joined together so that they can be replayed without interruption. But for this you need to have a second video recorder available.

Unlike film, videotape cannot be cut and re-assembled – you are dealing with electrical signals. What you can do is make a *copy* of these signals in a new order. You use the second machine to re-record your original pictures in the new order in which you want them to appear. This operation, referred to as *editing*, can be quickly done if you have only a few sequences to assemble. The more sequences you have, the longer it takes. Unfortunately, between each sequence on the copied tape, you are likely to get a flash of interference. This is caused by the electrical signals being 'crashed' together on the new recording. Some of the newer recorders have ways of eliminating this – they are fitted with a facility called 'back-space editing'. If you can't get rid of the interference, don't worry. Viewers find it much less distracting than the stopping and starting of the tape described in Level 1.

In these programmes you can also interlink excerpts taken from other recordings, for example, an off-the-air recording.

Most video recorders are fitted with an 'audio-dub' facility. This enables you to record music or a commentary on to your programme without interfering with the picture but you do lose any sounds already on the tape, although sometimes this can be a positive advantage!

Music is a most useful way of signalling the beginning and end of the programme; it can be added to give atmosphere or variety during a programme and it might be used to mask poor sound recordings.

A commentary is most useful to set the scene for viewers or to provide further explanations. It could well be done by a disabled person.

Beware of these common pitfalls when writing the commentator's script:

(a) Don't tell the viewer about things they can see for themselves – 'Here we see . . .'

(b) Don't let your commentary over-run into the next picture sequence, eg the commentary about work should stop before the workshop sequence ends. However, you can start talking about the next sequence a second or two before it appears. This is a good bridging technique.

(c) Keep the commentary brief and direct. People are too busy looking at the pictures to concentrate on what you are saying as well. If you really want them to listen, freeze the picture or use a caption which summarises the point.

It is a common fault with the inexperienced programme maker to include too much commentary. Let your pictures do the talking.

Level 3: Scripted programmes – camera edited. This level of programme involves a great deal more pre-planning than hitherto. Previously you could have recorded a variety of sequences and afterwards selected among them, but now we are dealing with a programme in which the sequences must be recorded in the order you want them to appear. This means preparing a fairly detailed 'shot list' of all the scenes you want to record and in the order they are to be recorded. This is a useful exercise for any programme maker to do. Most of the cameras and recorders sold today enable you to stop and re-start the recording without causing interference at the point where the picture changes. Furthermore, if the sequence does not work out as you intended, it can be re-shot (again and again, if necessary) before moving on to the next sequence.

Also you can begin to approximate more to a polished programme by having opening credits or using captions during the programmes – simply record these with the camera at appropriate points. These are best made with rub-off lettering to give a printed effect. Black lettering on pale coloured card is best (avoid white backgrounds with monochrome cameras). Keep the captions brief and fill most of the available space on screen; ie. form the wording into three lines rather than having one long line.

Music and commentary can be added at the end of the programme using the 'audio-dub' facility described earlier.

This type of programme is easiest to make when you are recording events that fall into a pre-set sequence, such as assembly tasks or ones which can be easily repeated if necessary, eg an interview. However, it is much more difficult to use this approach to capture spontaneous and unpredictable behaviour, such as children's play actions.

We must confess that it is not our preferred way of making programmes – we prefer to use editing procedures. However, if you cannot get hold of a second recorder, this is the approach you will have to use.

Level 4: Scripted programmes – 'studio' edited. At this point, you will be attempting to emulate the professional television producer, albeit with less sophisticated equipment and facilities. The core requirement at this level is yet another piece of equipment – referred to in the jargon as an 'editor'. This electronically joins the differing electrical signals from the two sequences into a unitary signal on the copy tape. This means that the picture joins smoothly with no interference.

An editor gives you great flexibility in selecting whatever sequences you want from your recordings – long or short – and re-assembling them in any order you wish. Furthermore, additional material such as captions can be easily inserted into the programme, and music or commentary can be dubbed over the pictures. The result can be a programme that is similar in style to those broadcast on television.

However, such sophistication is not only expensive in terms of equipment; it is also time-consuming. We reckon that on average it takes us one hour to edit one minute of the final programme. Thus a 30 minute programme may take 30 hours to edit. An editor is also costly to hire and not worth buying unless you plan to make programmes regularly.

But don't despair – it may be possible to get the editing done for you:

(a) *Third level institutions* – such as Universities or Higher Education Colleges have their own television and audio-visual departments. The staff may well be prepared to edit your programme on their equipment. You will still have to make the recordings and select the excerpts you want to show, but they will do the technical production for you.

(b) *Students* – may be taking courses in video as part of their training – in education, communications or art and design.

They may be willing to produce a programme for you as one of their practical assignments. As they will have access to the full range of video facilities in the college, they may even take on the recording as well as the editing.

(c) *Video-production companies* – are beginning to spring up in the major cities. They earn their livelihood from making television commercials or commissioned programmes for industry, but they may be responsive to a plea for help from you – a gift in kind. Of course if you are willing to pay, they are unlikely to say no. The telephone directory should yield their addresses.

Copying Video-Programmes

It is possible to make a copy of a video-programme by recording the signals from one machine on to another. This simple task is most useful:

1   You can store your 'original' (master) tape and only use the copy for lending or replaying. Any accidents – such as pressing

the record button by mistake or losing the tape – won't matter. You can make another copy from the master. It is well worth doing this, both for programmes you make yourself and with commercially produced tapes you have bought.

2   It enables you to give (or sell) copies of your programmes to other people.

3   You can make a copy of your programme on tape of a differing format. For example, you have made your programme with a Betamax recorder. By connecting your recorder to a VHS recorder you will produce a copy of your programme on VHS tape.

4   All the programmes you need for a course can be assembled on to the one video cassette.

Unfortunately a copy is never as good as the original recording, due to a loss of signal strength in the transfer; a copy of a copy is even worse. Hence you should always copy directly from the 'master' programme to ensure the best standard.

You need two video recorders in order to make a copy of programmes (the second could be borrowed or hired). These are best connected by using the 'video in/out' and 'audio in/out' sockets on the recorders, rather than the usual 'RF connections'. Unfortunately these sockets come in various shapes and sizes, but the video dealers will be able to provide suitable leads and/or socket adaptors.

Video: The medium of the future
If you are unfamiliar with video, much of the fore-going will seem perplexing and daunting. The only cure for such feelings is the experience of using video. We hope we have given you the courage and stimulation to try. Video, without doubt, will transform your attempts at community education with its insights into the life of disabled people in your locality. Talks, booklets, slides and films have all become second best.

Further Information
This chapter is only a brief introduction to the fast-expanding world of video. If you want to learn more, you will find the following books helpful. You might also consider enrolling for a short course on video – enquire locally – or enlist the help of other people.

Recommended book
David Owen and Mark Dunton, *The Complete Handbook of Video*, published by Penguin Books, Middlesex, 1982.

Other books
Richard Robinson, *The Video Primer: Equipment, Production and Concepts*, published by Quick Fox, New York, 1978.
G. Foss, *How To Make Your Own Video Programmes*, published by Elm Tree/Hamish Hamilton, London, 1982.
Michael Murray, *The Video Tape Book*, published by Bantam Books.
Tony Dowmunt, *Video With Young People*, published by Inter-action, 15 Wilkin Street, London NW5 3NG.
How To Use Video published by Sony U.K., Consumer Products Division, 134 Regent Street, London WC1

Training and Help
Grapevine, BBC TV, London W12 8QT, have free leaflets on both *Video* and *Community arts – where to get support and useful contacts* in which they list groups and organisations around Britain that give free advice on the use of video equipment. There may well be one near you. Send a large SAE with your request.

9   PUBLICITY

'What if nobody turns up?'
All your high ambitions; all the hours spent planning; all the arrangements made – and what if nobody turns up? A question to strike fear into the heart of any course organiser. But only the pessimist will spend time finding an answer; the realist will ensure people do turn up.

Publicity – Every course or event must be publicised. Even if you take the easier option of going for a 'captive' group such as school children, students, a ladies' group or whoever, you will still have to sell your course to the teachers or group leaders, and extra publicity should make the participants all the more eager to attend.
   Publicity achieves two important goals:

1   It informs and

2   It embues a status.

The first is the more obvious. People need to know where and when the course is being held; what it will be covering and the special attractions you have on offer – if any. But the second aim may ultimately be more important. At least advertisers see it that way. Much of their publicity is designed to create an 'image' for their product. They do this by implication and association. Cigarette advertisers use sports and outdoor scenes to project an image of health; or the factory-produced, 'home-made' biscuits will be publicised by older people in rustic settings, reminiscing about old times.

You may consider these practices deceitful or unethical. But they are trading on a human failing – that of jumping to conclusions. Give people a little information and their minds start to race ahead. All they need is a small clue. For example, a muddled leaflet or poster, messily printed on cheap paper may suggest a lack of planning, amateurism (in its worst sense) and general insignificance. This is not to suggest that you go to the other extreme and project yourselves as something other than you are. But too often our advertising undersells our product. As the song says, 'It's not what you say, it's the way that you say it . . . that's what gets results!'

Aims of Publicity

One feature of most publicity is that it will be seen or heard by many more people than will turn up to your meeting. Hence you have to consider the general effect as well as the more specific messages which you might wish to convey. Although these two aspects are inter-related, we shall consider them separately within this chapter. In the first part, we shall outline the various ways in which you can publicise a course; the main aim being to stimulate public interest to the extent that they will want to attend, or if they are a captive audience, to make them eager and attentive to your message.

In the second part of the chapter our focus will be on more general use of the media to create awareness of disabled people and to project a more positive image of them within the community. This is a longer term undertaking but an essential element in overall community education.

Publicising Your Course

The extent of your publicity – both in terms of the number of people covered and the different methods used – will vary according to the target audience you have in mind. Attracting people to evening classes in various locations around a city requires wider publicity than for a neighbourhood meeting in a suburb. Similarly, certain types of publicity are more likely to reach your potential audience than others – a mention on a radio chat-show, broadcast mid-morning, will be heard mainly by housewives rather than by teenagers at school. Fortunately there are plenty of methods to choose from and you should be able to find more than one way to contact all groups.

Word of mouth
The original and the best. The only problem is the amount of time involved in face-to-face contact. This approach works best if the people issuing the invitations are known to the recipients and if they are likely to meet them regularly. For example it is much easier to say 'No, thank you' to a stranger than to someone you meet every day.

Door-to-door calls are the best way of achieving blanket coverage of a neighbourhood and person-to-person contacts are best when looking for volunteers in a factory or store, etc.

These personal contacts give you the chance to highlight your message, to answer any questions and to elicit a reaction, possibly even a promise to attend. Indeed you may change your approach in the light of people's responses. This time-honoured method – much loved by politicians at election time – can be very effective, at least for those with a credible message to convey.

Time your calls when people are most likely to be at home and when they have time to talk to you. Best times are between seven and ten in the evening, and on Saturday and Sunday afternoons.

Alternatively you can save some time by meeting people when they come together, for example, in shopping centres, canteens, arriving for church, cinemas. This is best done in conjunction with leaflets.

Announcements
Informing people when they are together as a group is a time-saving but less effective strategy. Some of the possibilities are:

Church announcements – write to the priest or minister asking him to announce details of your community course at services. Alternatively, you could volunteer to be present and speak.

Supermarkets – the manager might be persuaded to play short taped announcements over the public address system to publicise neighbourhood courses.

Factory announcements – 'in-house' or neighbourhood courses could be announced in factories, stores, etc.

School Assembly – a friendly Head Teacher may well announce courses of interest to the pupils or their families.

It is worth providing posters to which people can refer for further information if they miss the details contained in the announcement. Also you might ask for the announcement to be printed in the magazines or newsletters produced by churches, schools, factories, etc.

Make sure your Adult Education courses on disability are listed in the brochure of evening classes produced by local authorities. In our experience this is not sufficient publicity to ensure an audience, but it does help.

Handbills/Posters
The same basic principles apply to the design and layout of both:

Brevity – don't clutter your poster with too many details.
Highlight – Use bolder print to pinpoint the essential details and smaller print for supplementary information.
Eye-catching – try to include a feature that will attract people's attention. It could be a photograph, a witty heading or a highlighted word such as 'NEW' or 'SPECIAL'.

Style – The layout of the leaflet and the print style you choose also convey a message. For example, compare the sample leaflets

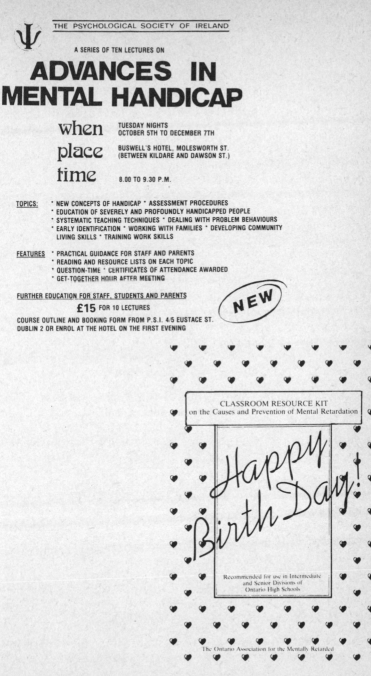

THE PSYCHOLOGICAL SOCIETY OF IRELAND

A SERIES OF TEN LECTURES ON

ADVANCES IN MENTAL HANDICAP

when   TUESDAY NIGHTS
          OCTOBER 5TH TO DECEMBER 7TH

place BUSWELL'S HOTEL, MOLESWORTH ST.
          (BETWEEN KILDARE AND DAWSON ST.)

time   8.00 TO 9.30 P.M.

TOPICS: * NEW CONCEPTS OF HANDICAP * ASSESSMENT PROCEDURES
          * EDUCATION OF SEVERELY AND PROFOUNDLY HANDICAPPED PEOPLE
          * SYSTEMATIC TEACHING TECHNIQUES * DEALING WITH PROBLEM BEHAVIOURS
          * EARLY IDENTIFICATION * WORKING WITH FAMILIES * DEVELOPING COMMUNITY
          LIVING SKILLS * TRAINING WORK SKILLS

FEATURES * PRACTICAL GUIDANCE FOR STAFF AND PARENTS
          * READING AND RESOURCE LISTS ON EACH TOPIC
          * QUESTION-TIME * CERTIFICATES OF ATTENDANCE AWARDED
          * GET-TOGETHER HOUR AFTER MEETING

FURTHER EDUCATION FOR STAFF, STUDENTS AND PARENTS

£15 FOR 10 LECTURES

COURSE OUTLINE AND BOOKING FORM FROM P.S.I. 4/5 EUSTACE ST.
DUBLIN 2 OR ENROL AT THE HOTEL ON THE FIRST EVENING

NEW

CLASSROOM RESOURCE KIT
on the Causes and Prevention of Mental Retardation

Happy Birth Day!

Recommended for use in Intermediate
and Senior Divisions of
Ontario High Schools

The Ontario Association for the Mentally Retarded

shown. The first – for the lecture course – is rather staid and serious, whereas the second attempts to suggest more informality and fun.

Preparing posters

The old-fashioned way of creating posters by hand, using paints or felt markers, is still possible provided only a few copies are needed and that you have a talented artist who can produce good quality lettering. Otherwise you run the risk of conveying the wrong hidden message!

1   *Photocopied posters.* Almost anyone can produce a reasonable black-and-white poster with the help of a typewriter, the rub-on lettering available in most stationers (eg Letraset) and a photo-copying machine.

Prepare your 'artwork' on a standard A4 sheet of paper. Multiple copies can then be run off on the photocopier. Indeed many of these machines can enlarge your original to twice its size – (A3) a good size for posters – or they will reduce it by half (A5) to make handbills. Furthermore, your copies can be done on coloured paper to give a more attractive appearance, and indeed coloured photocopiers have now arrived in some areas.

This method of producing posters is particularly economical if you have access to a photocopier rather than paying commercial rates, or if your quantities do not exceed one hundred copies.

2   *Lithograph copies.* You can take your 'artwork' along to a lithographic printer and he will produce good quality copies in poster or leaflet size. The cheapest jobs involve one colour print-ing but litho enables you to combine different coloured inks and paper. This method is best for large quantities.

3   *Multi-colour printing.* Much more expensive but very attractive and eye catching. This is a most professional product and your artwork will need to be of an equally high standard.

However, the extra money spent is no guarantee of greater effectiveness. You will have to weigh up the pros and cons for yourself.

Obtaining help – Students from Colleges of Art and Design, Poly-technics or Technical Colleges, may help with the design of posters. Frequently they are looking for projects and the possibility of having their design printed is a great incentive.

Printers will also handle the design work for you – but make sure you see the final copy before it is printed, and if you are unhappy about it, insist on it being changed.

For both printing and design work, you should obtain quotations from several firms – prices can vary greatly and sometimes bear no relation to the quality of product.

Displaying posters – Ideally they should be placed at eye-level, in places where people are likely to *stop* – doors, shop windows, lifts – and *clearly displayed* – not buried among lots of other posters; a disadvantage of notice boards!

Try to select the location of posters yourself and check occasionally to ensure that they remain displayed and not thrown away or covered by others. Don't forget to remove them when out of date.

Posters for outdoor display should be pasted on to strong card or board and varnished to ensure durability.

Handbills – These can be a most effective means of communication. Avoid stencils and ink duplicators; the quality of finish is so poor that we would resort to them only if we couldn't afford any better. For small quantities photocopies on coloured papers are much more attractive and reasonably economical, whereas for larger numbers lithograph printing can be used.

The leaflet can be done as a miniature poster, or you can make it more personal, for example in the style of an invitation or a letter.

Handbills are most effective when distributed personally rather than just posted into letter boxes or stuck on windows of parked cars. Hand them out at times when people are likely to read them – at bus stops, going into church, cinema queues, canteens, cafés, etc. Though it is expensive, they can be posted out to target groups or individuals. This is best done as an invitation card with the names of recipients written in.

Media Announcements
You can frequently use the media – free of charge – to publicise community events.

Newspapers – Write a letter to the editor, outlining details of your event and why you are doing it. They frequently espouse good causes.

Some papers also have a 'What's On' column in which they list details of forthcoming events. Send a separate notice for this.

Local Radio – Radio stations frequently set aside time for public service announcements – rather like commercials – this is their way of filling unsold advertising time. These spots last for 30 or 60 seconds maximum, so your message has to be short and to the point. Unfortunately you have no control over when and how often the announcement is made.

All local radio stations and some regional television services also have a slot in their schedules for 'what's on' announcements. You should find out the name of the person who is responsible for compiling these and send written details of your event.

Phone-in programmes are another easy way of making your voice heard. Choose your radio station and type of programme according to your target audience. For example, pop programmes on commercial stations will have a much younger audience.

Alternatively with music or request programmes, you could drop your favourite DJ or programme presenter a flattering postcard asking for a mention. Finally, you could send details of your event to the *producer* (not the presenter) of a magazine or current affairs programme. Frequently they are looking for people to interview and this can be an ideal way of getting as much as five minutes free publicity.

In all these instances of dealing with the media, remember to:

1   Use headed notepaper when writing.
2   Give an address or phone number at which they can contact you for further information.
3   Always include in your announcement or letter an address or phone number for the public to obtain further information.
4   Try to have this repeated within the announcement.

News Stories
The other 'free' use of the media is for you to make the 'news'. Here is how you can go about doing this.

Press Release – This is a brief – one page maximum – account of who you are, what you are doing or plan to do, and why. Preferably it should be typed on headed paper or with your organisation's name clearly stated at the beginning. Always end by giving the name or names of people who could be contacted for further information, along with their telephone numbers.

Other supplementary information such as copies of leaflets, reports, etc., can be attached.

Media people – It is best to send your release to a named reporter in a newspaper or to a particular correspondent in radio or TV news, so check whether they have a correspondent who covers social affairs or education. Often they are on the look-out for stories; it's their bread and butter after all.

In any case, you should always send a copy of your release to the 'News Editor'. Other possible recipients are the producers of current affairs or magazine programmes on local radio or television.

A follow-up phone call within a day or two will check that they received your press release and may persuade them to use the story. Alternatively, you could receive a call from the reporter asking for further details. Answer the questions clearly and succinctly but beware of being indiscreet. Unless you say that your replies are 'off-the-record', the reporter may quote some of your comments verbatim – much to your later embarrassment. Radio and TV reporters may use a telephone call to assess the likelihood of getting a worthwhile interview. That's a chance to sell yourself, so don't be afraid of adding a touch of colour, a humorous anecdote, the 'sacrifices' made in making it successful, etc, etc.

Newsworthiness – The media is inundated daily with 'news' items – that's what public relations officers of firms, local councils and businesses are paid to do. Hence your story has to compete for space. Being realistic, your chances of making the news are much better with community newspapers – such as the give-away advertisers – or with the local weekly or evening newspapers. It is much more difficult with the regional or national press. However, there are some steps you can take to increase the likelihood of any paper using your item.

News angle – You need to play up what is new about your event. Moreover, you might provide a particular slant or angle which the media could use. A lively imagination is helpful here, but don't sacrifice accuracy for sensationalism.

Some possible angles are, 'the first of its kind'; a contribution to 'disability week'; building on the results of a local survey; link with the success of a previous course; or devising a special attraction (see later).

Visuals – The press often appreciate having a good photograph to go with a story. Indeed, it is frequently harder for them to find usable pictures than words. You could send them several glossy black and white prints (8 × 6 inches).

Alternatively, you could note on your press release some suggestions for pictures which their own photographer might take.

Finally, you stand much greater chance of television coverage if you can offer some visual input – probably an 'action-packed' event or 'personalities' to be interviewed.

Pick your time – There are times when the media have a surfeit of stories and other occasions when they are eager for news. Avoid sending out your press release at a time when news abounds – such as during national or local elections.

You can also maximise your chances of publication if:

1   you submit an unembargoed release – that is, the editor can use it whenever he wishes (embargoed releases state at the beginning that they cannot be used before, say, 12 noon on October 5th. This is a long-established media convention but it can be restrictive).

2   you do not tie your story to a particular day. For example the opening of your course by a personality is only newsworthy on the day it happened, whereas having his or her endorsement means the story could be used at any time.

3   Sundays are a good day to deliver releases to the daily papers, as there is less news available over the weekend.

Finally, a word of warning. You have no control over the final wording or headline given to the story. Keep your fingers crossed that they give the facts as clearly to the public as you did to them. If they make a hash of it, a polite correction from you may be called for.

Paid publicity

All of the foregoing is frequently called 'free' publicity, yet it is bought at the price of your time. However, if you have the money, other people are only too willing to take on the publicity job for you, although our experience is that these methods do not give value for money:

1   *Newspaper advertisements*. Can you afford an 'ad' of sufficient size to attract readers' attention?

2   *Posters*. On buses, trains, advertising hoardings, etc., may be useful for specific localities. The unusualness of this type of 'ad' may make people take notice. The agency which handles the selling of space may even give you special terms.

3   *Radio commercials*. Choose your broadcast time carefully in order to reach your target audience.

4   *Television commercials*. We're now getting close to fantasy unless your budget is exceedingly generous.

Special attractions

So far we have worked on the assumption that telling people about your course is sufficient to attract them along. Perhaps it will be,

but you might have to offer special inducements to encourage their attendance. It is certainly worth increasing the 'attractiveness' of your event, even with people who may have no option but to attend – such as students in schools.

Among possible attractions are the following:

1 *Venue* – Convenience and comfort are essential features and if these can be combined with the opportunity for socialising or fun – such as indoor sports or a bar – all the better.

2 *Features* – Publicise the special attractions that will be included in the course – video, films, visits, etc.

3 *Celebrity endorsement* – You might be able to persuade a local personality to introduce or take part. This is a favourite trick of advertisers for getting people out of their houses and also provides a useful slant to your publicity.

4 *Entertainment* – Certain events could be built around this theme with your information and contact coming as part of the overall programme. Musical items, comedy spots, video films – all could be used as filler/attractions.

5 *Special offers* – The chance of a free gift or discounted prices are the well-established enticements offered by other advertisers and could be used – resources permitting – to encourage attendance. You may be able to have a quantity of small goods donated by companies, or alternatively have a selection of 'prizes' which can be raffled.

6   *Exhibitions/Demonstrations* – The opportunity to see particular products and how they are made, may well appeal to some people. It is especially effective to have disabled people doing the demonstrating.

Putting plans into practice
If a group of people are involved with the community education programme, then it is worthwhile delegating one person to handle all the publicity. This ensures a common and consistent approach to all aspects of the publicity and avoids duplication or missed opportunities. Of course your publicity officer can call on the others to carry out specific tasks but at least he or she knows who is doing what and when.

Firstly, the team should have a brain-storming session and list all the ways whereby they could publicise their course from the traditional to the outrageous, the mundane to the exotic. Vivid imaginations often generate novel and highly effective schemes.

Secondly, a planned sequence of publicity should be devised. For example, you may want posters to be displayed before you start distributing handbills. These should be left to within one week of the event, otherwise people forget. Likewise, agree on the best time for sending out your press release.

Thirdly, recruit as many people as possible to help with the personal contact side – if the worst comes to the worst, they can always bring their best friend along to the meeting.

Using the Media to Increase Public Awareness
Irrespective of whether people respond to your publicity by coming along to the courses, it will have another, less tangible, effect. At the very least, people will have been reminded of disability and at best, you may have changed in a small way some of their preconceptions.

It is this latter effect which we shall be focussing on in this part of the chapter. The aim here is not so much to get across specific information, but rather to try to increase the public's awareness and project a more positive image of people who are disabled than that which is currently portrayed in the media.

When do disabled people make the news?
Two occasions spring immediately to mind. First, in connection with fund-raising events such as marathons, charity appeals or special events and, secondly when services for disabled people make news – opening of new premises; effects of cutbacks or the inadequacies of existing services.

Such publicity may well achieve a vital result – generating money – but it can be at the cost of perpetuating the very stereotypes which your educational programmes are trying to counteract, namely:

1 Disabled people are portrayed as a category – the emphasis is on *the* mentally handicapped, *the* crippled.
2 The focus is exclusively on their disabilities and their dependency on others.
3 The public are distanced into a money-giving role. Indeed if a disabled person asked them to give they might be offended.
4 The need for *specialist* services is emphasised.

Fund-raising groups need to give careful thought to the way they portray disabled people, for unwittingly, they are very potent image-makers. The basis of their appeal to the public must shift from pity and poverty to participation and parity.

Accentuate the positive

As well as changing the nature of existing publicity, some attention should be given to generating a broad spectrum of features about disabled people. As we shall see, there are many different and complementary ways of doing this, but these 'new' approaches will probably be developed around one or more of the following themes:

(a) *Positive achievements* – emphasising the successes of people who are disabled and the extra effort entailed in their achievement.

(b) *Handicapped and non-handicapped mixing together* – fund-raising by teams of disabled and able-bodied people; friendly sporting fixtures of mixed teams; joint holidays for groups of young people and so on. These stories will emphasise the normality of ordinary people joining in activities with disabled people.

(c) *Handicapped people doing ordinary things* – the day when disabled people are seen on television as news readers, entertainers or DJs may still be far off but meanwhile there are many possibilities for creating a 'normal' image of disabled people; for example, stories about a day in the life of a telephone operator who is blind or a teacher who is deaf. Indeed, the British magazine *She* recently used a person in a wheelchair to model clothes on the fashion page.

(d) *Feelings* – stories which emphasise the normality of disabled people's emotions or those of their parents can be a potent counterbalance to the usual emphasis on 'abilities'.

A picture is worth a thousand words – This is especially true in creating images, and some of the features you would want to include in these pictures would be:

(a) Handicapped and non-handicapped people sharing an activity and having fun together.

(b) Disabled people in unexpected situations or activities – rock climbing; canoeing; scoring a goal at football.

(c) disabled people in prestigious contexts – meeting luminaries; taking part on quiz shows.

Television coverage around these themes would be particularly potent.

Methods
Some of the ways whereby you can increase public awareness are:

News coverage of events in which disabled people are participating. Prepare press releases and if you are very keen to have picture coverage, commission your own photographer to take pictures for distribution to the papers.

Articles – suggest articles to newspapers and magazines. Contact the Features Editor and outline some of the possibilities you have in mind. They may well be persuaded to carry an article.

Alternatively you can write, or arrange to have written, an article which you submit to newspapers or magazines with a view to publication. Newspapers may win out on readership but magazines offer greater scope in reaching specific groups and covering a wider range of interests. 'Why we decided to adopt a Down's Syndrome baby' is an ideal topic for a women's magazine – whereas a special interest magazine may well feature an article about the model railway collection of a disabled man or the radio ham who is mentally handicapped. It is quite common for newspapers and magazines to receive unsolicited articles and a proportion of them are published.

Don't be put off if your first attempts are unsuccessful. Take account of comments received and submit the article to another publisher. The bonus is that most publications pay for articles they print.

Radio features Many local radio stations, and indeed some television companies, now offer community groups the opportunity of making their own programmes for broadcasting.

The first step is to decide on suitable themes for your programme and the target audience or audiences you have in mind for each.

Secondly, contact your local radio station and find out the name of the producer responsible for 'open access' broadcasting. If the producer likes your ideas, many of the resources of the station can be put at your disposal: guidance on preparing the script, studios for recordings, tape-recorders for doing interviews on location, etc. They will also help with the editing and production of the programme.

Alternatively, the producer might recommend you to a colleague who may make a programme along the lines you suggest. However, in this case you will have little direct say in the content and style of programme; rather your role becomes more advisory.

Television – Until the advent of cable television, competition for space on existing channels is so intense that the most you can hope for is occasional exposure. Moreover, filmed documentary programmes are such an expensive undertaking that the producer has to be sure of their appeal. Studio interviews are cheaper but less interesting to the viewer. But still, beggars can't be choosers.

Opinion-makers
Finally, there is another avenue outside the media that is develop-

ing. In any community, there are identifiable 'opinion-makers' who can set the tone for new ventures. If you aim your educational inputs directly at these individuals it may set off rippling effects. This strategy relies on making a correct assessment as to who is an opinion-maker. Usually it is personalities, not titles, you are interested in. Among the possibilities are head teachers, local politicians, directors of firms or entertainment personalities. At a more local level there are the 'gang' leaders in youth groups and dominant personalities in community groups and so on. Singling out such people for special attention – invitation to lunch, free tickets for special events you are organising – gives you an opportunity to influence their perceptions in the hope that they, in turn, will live up to their reputation and effect change in others.

Planning for the future
As any marketing executive will tell you, changing a 'product image' is a long-term and uphill job. It needs commitment, determination and imagination. It is all the more significant, then, that in the area of disability it has been handicapped people themselves who have shown the way. The 'self-advocacy' movement that is gaining strength in Western countries with both physically and mentally handicapped people, is the most distinctive challenge to date of existing preconceptions. But the non-handicapped who organise services, and those working in them, must not get left behind. Their commitment to community participation and parity must become more of a reality. Having disabled people living and working within the community remains the most promising way of changing public attitudes. Unless this happens, publicity *per se* will achieve little. To pretend that it will, is an advertisers' dream.

Further Reading
Grapevine information sheets. Obtainable by sending a stamped addressed envelope to *Grapevine*, BBC TV, London W12 8QT. (Especially their sheets on *How to use your local radio station* and *Video*).
Your Independent Local Radio Stations. A leaflet on how local groups can use the station, available from Broadcasting as a Public Service, 5 Tavistock Place, London WC1 9SS.
Using the Media – How to Deal with Press, TV and Radio by Denis McShane. Published by Pluto Press Workers' Handbook. (contains essential information for community activists).

10 CONSUMER REACTIONS

The difficult we do straight away; the impossible takes a little longer.

An ideal motto for community educators, especially when it is re-written as 'educational programmes we construct straight away; making them successful takes a little longer'.

This chapter is about making your educational programme a success. How? The only sure way is by consulting your consumers. They are the only people who can tell you:

- what they already know (or don't know) about disability
- what aspects they would like to know more about
- what they liked (disliked) about your programme
- what they learned from your programme.

If you feel this consultation entails *extra* work, then think again. To us it is not an extra but rather an integral part of programme design and development. Past attempts to educate people about disability have frequently failed because the consumers' reactions to them were ignored. Successful programmes result from inter-actions between designers and consumers. The outcome is new information of interest to the public, presented in an effective and enjoyable way.

Consulting Your Consumers
Like many another task, this can be done in diverse ways, from the simple to the complex, the quick to the laborious, the cheap to the expensive. Market researchers, opinion pollsters and social scientists would have us believe that only they can do the job properly. We disagree. There are many simple, quick and cheap ways of consulting with your consumers. Our aim in this chapter is to show you how to carry out some basic market research through simple questionnaires and how you can use the results to guide the development of your educational programmes.

First, we shall consider how you might do this and the steps involved. Secondly we provide a selection of questions which we have found useful in planning and evaluating our programmes. You could select from these when drawing up your own question-naires. Finally, for those with total faith in us, we provide in

Section 4 sample questionnaires which you can photocopy for distribution to your 'consumer' groups.

Short Self-Completed Questionnaires
There are various approaches to measuring opinions but in a short chapter we have to be selective. We have chosen to concentrate only on:

Questionnaires
A collection of standard questions which people answer orally or more usually in writing. The chief advantage of the latter is that lots of people can complete a questionnaire in a short time. Other methods – notably interviews or group discussions – are more applicable if you want to collect more detailed information (some- times referred to as 'qualitative' data), but you will have to read about these elsewhere (see suggestions for further reading).

Questionnaires with a list of alternative answers
This 'closed' question approach is less time-consuming for respondents – all they have to do is place a tick against the item of their choice – and it is much easier for you (or a computer) to analyse.

As you are probably aware, Government services must be paid for by taxes. For which of these groups of people would you be prepared to pay some extra taxes? Please select one of the following:

Unemployed youth   . . . .
Old people   . . . .
The disabled   . . . .
Children   . . . .
Itinerants   . . . .
None of these   . . . .

However, this type of questionnaire has three disadvantages. It presumes the respondents are good readers (so beware with less able groups eg younger school pupils); secondly, the alternatives listed may mean different things to different people (avoid ambiguity); and thirdly, your list may omit an alternative which people would have selected, consequently respondents' opinions are not accurately tested. Alternative answers have to be chosen carefully and preferably on the basis of past research.

Short questionnaires
There is a great temptation to collect more information than you actually need. It is very important to keep the goodwill of your respondents. They much prefer short questionnaires (don't we all?) and they can become irritated if they cannot see the relevance of the questions.

Brevity can have its dangers. It may yield an unreliable result – at least with longer questionnaires you can check on the consistency of replies – and it may give you an incomplete picture, due to the omission of a topic which you subsequently discover was important. You have to balance the speedy completion and analysis against comprehensive and accurate coverage. But our advice to the inexperienced is to keep it short.

Devising Your Own Questionnaires
In summary, the steps involved are as follows:

1 *Identify your target group* – This will help you to decide on the most relevant questions to ask and on how they should be worded. For example, you have to simplify your questions for primary school children.

2 *Establish the number of people* – Determine the number of people you are likely to be dealing with – is it all the pupils in the school or only the senior classes, or only one fifth year form?

3 *Determine the access you will have* – Will you be able to see them as a group or will you have to contact each person individually? This factor, along with the number of likely participants, will decide how you collect the information – through

interviews, group questionnaires or by posting the questionnaires.

4 *Decide on the questions* – The biggest problem here is curbing your curiosity and omitting questions. Decisions already made – see above points – will help in the selection but the crucial test for each question is: What will I do with the information obtained?' A standard questionnaire for general usage is rarely satisfactory. You end up with answers you don't need and miss out questions you should have asked. However, they are a useful way of gaining expertise in questionnaire design and analysis.

5 *Reproduce the questionnaire* – The questionnaire must be legible, clearly laid out and easily followed – otherwise you run the risk of confusing and alienating your respondents and possibly misrepresenting their replies. It goes without saying that exactly the same questionnaire must be given to all the members of your target group.

6 *Summarise and analyse the results* – Once the questionnaires are completed, it is not sufficient merely to read through the replies you receive, unless you have only four or five respondents. Rather you should summarise for each question the exact number of people who gave or selected a particular answer. This objective summary can easily be shared with other colleagues and even with the people who completed the questionnaire – yes, they might be interested to know the results!

A further stage involves more detailed analysis. For example, you might want to find out if males and females differed in their responses.

7 *Decisions* – Questionnaires are only a means to an end, not, as some researchers are inclined to think, an end in themselves. Hence this step involves using the information you have obtained to make decisions about your programme – what to include/-exclude or what to change.

Of all these steps, arguably the most crucial is that of selecting the right questions to ask. Hence the bulk of the chapter will be given over to selecting suitable questions which will help you to:
 –   plan the content of your programme
 –   evaluate the effectiveness of your programme
 –   improve the presentation of your programme.
The final section will briefly elaborate on some of the other stages noted above.

Questions to Help Plan Your Programme
Once you have identified your target group(s) – see Chapter 4 (P 67) – the next step is to find out more about them, primarily their knowledge of, and previous contact with, disabled people.

You should also carry out some 'market research' into the topics they would be interested in learning more about and possibly the ways in which they would like to receive this information.

The following general guidelines for constructing suitable questions, together with sample questions, may help you to formulate your own questionnaire.

Contact with disabled people – At least one of your questions should cover this area. For instance:

During the past year about how frequently have you been in contact with a mentally handicapped person?
Constantly . . . .
Quite often . . . .
A few times . . . .   Tick one
Seldom . . . .
Never . . . .

Such information is not only interesting in its own right – the extent of community contact in your locality (see Chapter 2) – but past studies have invariably found that people who have had prior contact with disabled persons are more favourably disposed than those with little or no previous exposure. Hence you will need to have some indication of your groups' prior experience in order to put their replies to other questions into perspective.

This data will help you to determine the level at which your programme should be pitched. If they have had little or no previous contact you will have to start from basics. It will also establish the likelihood of having 'resource people' (ie. those with experience of disability) among your participants.

Knowledge of disability – Questioning people about their current knowledge can be revealing both of ignorance and misconceptions. But beware of overdoing these questions – people do not like to be reminded of their inadequacies, and anyway, the results are fairly predictable given your basic premise, viz. the community needs to learn more about disability.

Questions of this type can cover many diverse themes. One useful way of exploring possible confusions between handicapping conditions is to have respondents select alternative names, eg:

What do you feel are other suitable names for the mentally handicapped?

	DON'T KNOW	YES	NO
Mentally Deficient	....	....	....
Slow Learner	....	....	....

Retarded	....	....	....
Mentally Ill	....	....	....
Slow Developer	....	....	....
Mentally Disturbed	....	....	....

A further refinement can be added to this question by the supplementary:

Which one of the above names do you think is the most suitable alternative?. . . . . (Write your answer here).

Other 'knowledge' questions can be included according to your priorities, for example, the causes of disability (especially useful for highlighting ignorance about prevention measures); the financing of services; the various professionals involved in services and what they do; the employment patterns of disabled people. You can select any topic that you feel people should be informed about. Also the information can be quite specific, eg whether or not they know of the special school in their neighbourhood and if so, the type of children who attend.

There are two important points to bear in mind when selecting alternative answers:

1   The wording should not give away the answer. For instance, an item on the causes of deafness, such as 'damaged nerve from ear to brain', would probably be selected by nearly all respondents even though they had little understanding of how people hear.

2   You have to include on your list items which are incorrect but which seem right. These are called distractor items. They force people to think about their replies – rather than ticking every alternative as 'YES'.

What do you think are the main causes of deafness in children?

	DON'T KNOW	YES	NO
Whooping cough*	....	....	....
It runs in families+	....	....	....
Wax in ears*	....	....	....
Jaundice at birth	....	....	....
Mothers smoking during pregnancy*	....	....	....
Meningitis	....	....	....
Lack of oxygen	....	....	....
German measles (rubella) in pregnancy+	....	....	....

(*distractor item; + major causes)

Distractor items also highlight popular misconceptions. For example, we find that the majority of respondents select 'mothers smoking during pregnancy' as a major cause of mental handicap.

What they would like to know – Finally it is worth ascertaining the topics or themes on which your group would be most interested in receiving more information. We have found that a listing of possible topics yields better replies than the open-ended question, 'What information would you like to have about mental handicap?' For example:

What information would you like on mental handicap?

Place a tick in one column	VERY MUCH	MAYBE	NO
The services available to them and their families	....	....	....
What causes it	....	....	....
How they like to be treated	....	....	....
The problems they and their families have	....	....	....
What mental handicap means	....	....	....
How to act with a mentally handicapped person	....	....	....
Voluntary work I could do	....	....	....
How to teach them new things	....	....	....

Likewise you could explore any preferences regarding methods of presenting this information – through books, television, local meetings, etc., or the setting in which this might occur – adult education centre, church hall, local school, and so on.

Questions to Evaluate the Effectiveness of Your Programme

So far the questions have been mainly factual – the best starting point for planning. However, we also need to obtain information about people's 'feelings' towards disabled peers, for example, how willing they would be to meet them. This information can inform your planning, but we have found it to be even more useful in determining the effectiveness of an educational programme. In short, how have their feelings changed?

As you might expect, it is not easy accurately to assess people's feelings. Our difficulties result from human failings. First, respondents desire to give a good impression of themselves; hence they may express more positive attitudes than they actually feel, and secondly, we are asking them to predict their reactions to events which they may never have experienced, and so many a prediction proves inaccurate.

Neither of these hurdles can ever be totally surmounted but there are ways of lessening their effects:

1 *Anonymity*. Respondents are more likely to express their 'true' feelings, rather than give socially acceptable responses, if they are assured that they cannot be identified from the questionnaire, ie. they do not put their name on it, or if they do, that the questionnaire will only be seen by people unknown to them.

The questionnaire should also be presented in a 'neutral' setting and not identified with a group which might bias the responses. For example, a blind interviewer would elicit more favourable responses to the integration of blind people than would a campaigner from 'jobs for the able-bodied'.

2 *Use of rating scales*. Respondents' feelings can be more sensitively measured through rating scales rather than by 'Yes' or 'No' answers. For example:

How would you like to help mentally handicapped people?

	VERY MUCH	MAYBE	NO
Give money on flag days	....	....	....
Do jobs for them	....	....	....
Take them on outings	....	....	....
Work in services for the mentally handicapped	....	....	....
Help to raise money for them	....	....	....
Have one as a paying guest in my home	....	....	....

The three alternative answers, 'Very much like to' 'Maybe' and 'No', help to distinguish between the really eager ('very much') and those who would be inclined to say 'Yes' in case they were thought to be uncaring (the 'maybe' option).

These scales can be extended up to five and even seven points. In these instances, the ends of the scale are labelled and intermediate points on the continuum are merely outlined. For example:

Would you be willing to take a mentally handicapped person on an outing once a month?

| DEFINITELY YES | | | | DEFINITELY NO |

Later a score can be allocated depending on the box ticked – five points for the 'definitely yes', (then four, three, two) down to one for the 'definitely not'.

3 *Personalise the question.* You are more likely to obtain meaningful responses if you confine your questions to specific rather than to vague contexts. For example, you should refer to 'deaf people *I have come across*', rather than the more generic 'deaf people'. Instead of asking how they feel at the prospect of meeting a mentally handicapped person, you should specifiy a scenario such as this one for shop assistants: 'How would you feel if a mentally handicapped customer, of your own age, came to your store tomorrow?'

4 *Comparative responses.* A final technique, which we have found most useful, is to get respondents to rate their reactions to both a mentally handicapped person and to an able-bodied person, viz. 'neighbour', 'stranger of own age', etc. Thus you obtain two sets of answers to the same question – how they feel about a handicapped person and their feeling towards a non-handicapped person. This technique forces people to think about their replies; it gives you a reference point against which to judge their responses to disabled people and finally it is a useful way of determining whether your educational programme brings about specific changes. Their feelings towards the disabled group should change markedly, but not those towards the contrast group.

We have found the following question on people's reactions to meeting a mentally handicapped adult most useful with students.

If a mentally handicapped person of my own age, whom I had never met before, visited my house tomorrow I would. . . .

	YES DEFINITELY		NO, NOT AT ALL		
Know what to say	.....	.....	.....	.....	.....
Feel embarrassed	.....	.....	.....	.....	.....
Find it a good experience	.....	.....	.....	.....	.....

If a stranger of my own age, who I had never met before, visited my house tomorrow I would . . . .

	YES DEFINITELY		NO, NOT AT ALL		
Know what to say	.....	.....	.....	.....	.....
Feel embarrassed	.....	.....	.....	.....	.....
Find it a good experience	.....	.....	.....	.....	.....

Feelings about disabled people and society. Social researchers have frequently used another type of question in their investigations of attitudes to disabled people, namely questions which examine respondents' reactions to their place within society. For example, whether or not disabled children should attend ordinary schools, or whether mentally handicapped adults should be allowed to vote in elections. We have found questions of this type are not particularly useful in the context of community education, since they make two basic assumptions.

First, they presume that all disabled people are equivalent because of a common disability – they refer to *the* blind or a *typical* deaf person – whereas one of the main emphases in any community education programme is their individuality and the avoidance of stereotypes.

Secondly, the questions do not allow for any qualifying conditions. For example, respondents might be in favour of handicapped children attending ordinary schools, but only if additional facilities are made available to the school.

The net result is that it can be extremely difficult to interpret the meaning of people's responses to these questions. People may give the same answer, yet have very different feelings.

But there are occasions when it may be necessary to use questions of this type – for example, if you want to explore the involvement of disabled people in a local community. As you will see from the examples given, they make explicit the conditions under which respondents would be willing to let disabled people use community facilities. For example:

When do you feel mentally handicapped adults should use the public swimming baths?
Please select the one answer which best describes your feelings
. . . . They should be *discouraged* from using it.
. . . . Could use it *occasionally if supervised.*
. . . . Could use it *occasionally without supervision.*
. . . . Could use it *frequently if supervised.*
. . . . Could use if *frequently without supervision.*

Similar questions could be used with other community activities – pubs, cafés, discos.

Questions to Improve Course Presentation

In this case, the focus of the question has altered, for now you want to obtain respondents' reactions to your course and their suggestions for changes.

We find it useful to include some 'open-ended' questions at this stage. Among the most fruitful for us have been

> *'What aspects of the programme did you like best?'*
> *'Were there any parts you did not enjoy or you felt could be improved?'*
> *'What do you feel you got out of taking the course?'*

Questions of this type frequently generate a range of answers – some predictable, others totally unexpected; some may confirm your own impressions; others should force you to think again.

Problems to be overcome

First, people do not like answering a succession of open-ended questions. Blank spaces instead of answers can just as easily mean, 'I'm fed up answering', rather than 'I have no opinion'.

Secondly, you have no way of knowing how much agreement there is among the group for a particular viewpoint. For example, only three out of 50 people may mention a dislike of role-playing during the course. But the remaining participants may also have disliked it and did not think to mention it, or they may even have enjoyed it. The only way to find out is to ask everyone about their reaction to certain aspects of the course. This brings you back to the closed question. For instance:

If this course were to be changed, which of the following changes would you want to see?

	Mark out of 10
More films about children	....
Have a professional talk about his or her work	....
Spend more time explaining what the course will cover	....
Have a parent speak to the group	....
Have more facts and figures	....
Have a mentally handicapped adult address the group	....
Include more information on severely handicapped people	....

The results from this question will let you determine how much support there is among your group for each possible change.

A similar approach can be used to obtain respondents' reactions to the different aspects of the course, eg marks out of ten for each of the teaching techniques employed or the topics covered in the course, or their preference for video-programmes.

A mixture of open and closed questions is a productive way of obtaining reactions and suggestions about your course. For example, after a closed question you can ask respondents to give the reason for their selection: 'What did you most like about your favourite film?'

In addition to having the results from questionnaires, we find it useful to spend 15 minutes or so discussing with the group their impressions of the programme and how it might be improved. You will get more elaborate replies and it will have value for them too. They can assess their own reactions in relation to others – possibly discovering that their fear of meeting a mentally handicapped person was shared by many others and hence that they were not abnormal.

Lastly, there is one important assumption in asking a group to comment on their course – that your next group will have similar interests and come from the same backgrounds. On the whole, this seems a reasonable assumption to make and is preferable to obtaining no reactions at all and relying solely on your own impressions.

Obtaining help. Devising questionnaires or interview schedules can take time. The help of an experienced social researcher (eg from a neighbouring university or college) can be a real bonus. He or she will help you avoid the common pitfalls in measuring people's opinions. But do not under-estimate your own contribution. If the researchers have had no prior experience of disability they will be dependent on you for guidance as to the type of information that is most relevant for your needs. Experienced technicians can do the wrong job in a faultless way.

Asking the Questions
There are basically three ways of getting your questionnaires answered once you have compiled your questionnaire:

(a) *Self-completed in groups.* This is by far the quickest and most efficient way of collecting your information; a roomful of people can work on the questionnaire at the same time. Do ensure, though, that your questionnaire is clearly laid out and that all the necessary instructions are written down on the questionnaire. These should also be repeated verbally. And remember to take along spare pens.

This method is particularly appropriate with groups who come together regularly – schools, youth groups, sports clubs, etc.

(b) *Interviews*. When people have to be contacted individually, it is probably advisable to take them through the questionnaire as an interview – it is speedier, more friendly and less troublesome for them. Nonetheless, it is possible to have them complete it on their own while you wait or call on another person. This method is favoured for door-to-door contacts or in street surveys. A variant is the telephone survey, although this runs the risk of biasing your results, in that more affluent people are the ones with phones.

(c) *Postal surveys*. As a last resort, you may have to post your questionnaires. Unfortunately there is little incentive for people to respond and hence your return rate can be poor; rarely more than 50%. You can increase the likelihood of a reply by a carefully worded explanatory letter which details the importance of the survey; by having the questionnaire as succinct as possible; by enclosing a stamped-addressed envelope and by sending a reminder letter or telephone call. Our advice is to avoid postal surveys if at all possible, although in some circumstances they may be the only option – for instance following up on people who dropped out of your course.

Sampling – This is a much-used way of cutting down on the amount of work involved in measuring people's opinions. Instead of asking everyone for their reactions, you select a sample. For example, in a door-to-door survey you might call on every fourth house or you might take only one class at each level in the school. These samples, if properly chosen, will yield the same outcome as a survey of every person but with much less work.

There is one risk, however. The sample you take may not be typical and you could end up with biased and misleading information. For example, the replies from a postal survey are likely to be biased in that they come from people who were interested enough to complete the questionnaire. So if you do decide to take a sample, make sure it is representative.

Presenting the questionnaire – It is a well known phenomenon that people's responses to questions will vary according to how the question is asked and who asks it. Although more likely to occur in interviews, the danger is still present with questionnaires. Hence, do not declare your interest in disability if you want to obtain a more accurate reflection of their attitudes – opt for a more neutral label, such as, 'I'm from social services'.

Likewise, questions relating to the success of a programme are best put by a stranger rather than by someone involved in the course. Admittedly these refinements emanate from scientific purity, but why shouldn't you set your sights high?

Analysing the Questionnaires

One great advantage of multiple choice questions is that they can be quickly analysed. For small groups, say a class of 30 students, the easiest way is to use a tally system such as the following:

Frequency of contact		Total	%*
Constantly	///	3	11
Quite Often	////// /	6	21 (*Rounded to
A few times	///	3	11 the nearest
Seldom	/	1	4 unit)
Never	//// //// ////	15	54
Spoilt/not answered	//	2 (30−2 = 28)	

Go through each questionnaire one at a time, and on your tally sheet, place a tick against the item selected. Also keep a count of the people who did not answer the question or who selected two alternatives (spoilt).

Once you have summary totals, the findings from different surveys can be compared. In particular, you can determine the results of your educational programme by comparing the percentages and average scores obtained before and after people took part. For instance, has the percentage of people sharing an activity with a disabled person increased? Was there a decrease in the percentage selecting the term, 'mental illness' as an alternative name for mental handicap? This data will help you detect the ways in which your programme was successful and where you failed to bring about change.

Admittedly, these analyses can be time-consuming, routine and ultimately boring, especially if you have a large number of questionnaires to process. Help could be sought from students wanting to undertake a project, eg social science students at a local college. Alternatively explore the possibility of using a micro-computer to help with the analysis.

For the really ambitious, there are 'packages' available on main-frame computers designed specifically for analysing survey data – cg Statistical Package for the Social Sciences: SPSS.

Computer analyses are appropriate when you want to answer detailed questions such as, were there significant differences between males and females, between young and old? If you want to get more involved in measuring the attitudes of your local community, then try to enlist the help of your local University or Polytechnic.

But do not be deterred by this sophistication. As we stated at the outset, the reactions of your consumers can be easily obtained – indeed ready-made questionnaires are provided in Section 4 (p 231). If the basic guidelines in this chapter are followed, the results from the simplest of questionnaires will be just as reliable and valid as those from complex instruments. The important thing is not the quantity of information you obtain, rather is it the opportunity you have given to the consumers to express their views, resulting in programmes that are better planned and evaluated.

Further Reading

Hoinville, G., Jovell, R. and associates, *Survey Research Practice,* Heinemann Educational Books, London, 1978. All the stages of conducting surveys are dealt with, from the initial planning to the production of data.

Oppenheim, A.N., *Questionnaire design and attitude measurement,* Heinemann, London, 1966. Very useful for those who want to know more about the design and pitfalls of attitude scales.

11 WORKING WITH OTHERS

Community education can be a daunting and demanding task. The initial enthusiasm may quickly wane as obstacles arise and problems, apparently unresolvable, are encountered. For one person to initiate and maintain a systematic programme of community education is quite an undertaking, although it is possible. Ultimately it could be counter-productive. There are decided advantages to working in teams – some of the reasons are obvious, others may not be so apparent. For a start, the work load is shared, morale is boosted and a wider range of talents can be drawn upon.

But there are other advantages to team-work. It's an insurance policy; if one person leaves, the programme can still continue. Secondly, the team personifies the message, that community education is not the prerogative of one person; it is a shared responsibility.

In the first part of this chapter, we shall be outlining ways of getting a team together and describing how this group might work to develop community education programmes.

There is a second aspect to working with people – namely encouraging others to make use of the programmes which you and your team have devised. These may be colleagues working in similar settings to yourself in other parts of the country, or they could be 'leaders' of the target group which you want to contact – teachers in local schools, police inspectors, personnel managers and so forth. Having these people using your programmes is the only feasible way of educating large numbers of people in a relatively short time. Hence in the second part of the chapter we shall examine ways of sharing with others the fruits of your labours.

Team-Work

Co-ordinator – Teams have to be created and although there may be a willingness for like-minded people to come together, some one person has to provide the spark. This person may or may not continue to co-ordinate the work of the team, but for simplicity's sake we will assume that he or she does and, furthermore, that you the reader are a potential co-ordinator.

Your job description is simply written – first, to assemble your resource team of people and secondly to co-ordinate their work. The latter is quite an undertaking. Your goal is to avoid ambiguity about who is responsible for each task; to prevent overlap, duplication or, worst of all, contradictions in your approaches and methods; and finally to ensure that the jobs get done by the dates agreed.

We have no preconceived idea as to who the co-ordinator should be. It could be a disabled person, an administrator, a parent, social worker, voluntary helper or care assistant. There is one overriding prerequisite, however: the person should have a direct and on-going involvement with disabled people to the extent that Goffman's appellation, 'the wise', is rightly applicable.

It is also advantageous, although not essential, that the co-ordinator should have some experience of teaching (such as on training courses for staff or parents); of working as a member of a multidisciplinary team; and the confidence to deal with the public and to enjoy doing so.

Assembling the team – The team is going to work together on a specific task. It is not a prestigious committee or an elite social club. Hence no one should be included for appearance's sake, or as a right, or in case they would feel insulted if 'left out'. People are there for the talents they can contribute.

In our experience it is best to limit the team to around four people. Try to have people with complementary skills and experiences. Include, if you can, someone with experience of dealing with the target group you have in mind, for example, a person with experience of teaching in secondary schools if you are working on a school's programme.

First meeting of the team
We are assuming that the members of the team will be available to this community education project only on a part-time basis, and that this work will have to be squeezed in alongside other professional or home commitments. Hence the time available for planning and preparing the programme will be limited and should by used productively, otherwise morale will start to fall.

Some of the items which must appear on the agenda for the first meeting of the team are:

Who is our target group? – We advise you to begin with one specific group.

What form of programme can we undertake? – For example, will it be one evening meeting or an eight-week course?

What are the central messages we want to get across? – It might be overly optimistic to presume that this will be decided at one meeting because you will discover that different people have differing ideas as to what society needs to know, and even of how disabled people should be portrayed. At least that's been our experience. It is important that the team comes to a consensus on the messages they want to convey – ideally these should be simple and unqualified. As Richard Ashmore noted, 'Often mass media programs fail because they aren't comprehended by the audience. This lack of comprehension is sometimes due to educational limitations of the audience and sometimes to the unclarity of the message.'

Measures of success – How will you know whether your programme has been a success? An essential feature of the planning is to determine *beforehand* what measures of success would prove acceptable to you or your team. For instance, would you be content if 100 people turned up to your public meeting? That 10 volunteers were recruited to help with the youth club, or that everyone who attended could cite the two main causes of deafness? The measures of success which the team chooses can be as high or low as you all want them to be. But as you will discover, this is not a new form of parlour game. As you discuss possible criteria of success, you will learn a lot about each other's expectations – some may appear unrealistically high, others pessimistically low. The goal is to arrive at a realistic criterion to which all can work. And note that the criteria should be clearly measurable, not expressed as pious sentiments such as 'people will have more favourable attitudes'.

The biggest dividend of this investment in prediction is gained after the programme has been tried. Now you can measure your achievements against expectations. Aside from the congratulations and commiserations, the discrepancies have to be accounted for: where did your predictions go wrong? How might you do it differently? As you will see, preparation for the next effort is already under way; the experiences gained are not forgotten.

We urge each item to specify clearly the measures which will indicate that their programme has been a success – and good luck!

Assigning tasks – As the foregoing chapters in this section of the book have illustrated, there are many diverse tasks associated with any educational programme. Once the team has clarified its aims and goals, it can begin to consider the jobs which have to be done. We find it useful to list all the tasks – even the most trivial – on a large sheet of paper. This is a constant reminder to everyone of the work ahead.

The next step is to assign responsibility for each task to one person. The background experience of certain team members will ensure that some tasks are automatically theirs; otherwise you will be looking for volunteers – willing or not! Of course, team members need not work alone – they can enlist the help of others, but it remains their responsibility to ensure the work is done. As an indication of this commitment, their name is written on the sheet against each task assigned to them.

Finally, it is worth going through the tasks and ordering them according to those which should be done first, second and so on. This exercise will also help you to determine deadlines for completion of the tasks.

Keeping in touch – Bringing people together to report on progress is an ideal but perhaps impractical way for some teams to operate. However it is essential that some contact be maintained and this will rightly, if inevitably, fall upon the co-ordinator. Telephone calls or, better still, brief visits, will often speed things along and provide opportunities to pass on information about progress in general. The team can come together when new tasks have to be assigned.

Contacting groups of people
In some community education programmes you will be responsible

for recruiting your own group – a topic already covered in Chapter 9. More usually, however, you will be aiming your message at an already existing group. While these may form a captive audience there still remains the daunting challenge of gaining access to them. Some of the lessons which experience has taught us, are as follows:

1   *Personal introduction.* Much as we might like to deny it, it is whom you know, rather than what you are, which often gains you access. Hence a personal introduction – 'Hello, I gather you know John Smith; he suggested I contact you and tell you about . . .' – can open doors that might otherwise remain closed. This is an area in which larger planning teams are a bonus – think of all the friends of friends known to them!

2   *Meet the person-in-charge.* Our goal is to get a meeting with the decision-maker. This gives us an opportunity to explain who we are and what we want. Likewise, it gives our potential ally a chance to assess us – how serious we are, our style of working – and to have their questions or reservations dealt with straight away.

Titles can mislead and similar organisations may operate in different ways, so be prepared to be passed from one person to another. For instance, the Head Teacher of a secondary school gave us a qualified 'yes', but suggested we contact the Head of the RE Department. She rightly wondered what we had to do with religious education and suggested we speak to the civics teacher instead, who was only too ready to accommodate us and took it upon himself to tell the Head Teacher of the new arrangements.

We try to end this meeting with an agreement as to what the next step will be. If the person seems hesitant about giving an immediate commitment, don't force it – instead agree to call in a week's time. Conversely, if he or she is agreeable, you should make arrangements for dates and times before you leave.

Fortunately we have usually found a ready acceptance for our approach, especially from schools and adult education centres. Business and industrial groups require somewhat more persuasion and 'sales' talk – a point to bear in mind when selecting the members of your team.

3   *Specify your requests.* The people you contact will appreciate clear statements of a) what you are planning to do; b) the aspects for which you will be wholly responsible; and c) what, if anything, they will have to do. These facts are best contained in a letter or talked through in a face-to-face meeting – do not attempt to go into details over the telephone.

Keep your demands realistic but unambiguous: 'We should like a one hour meeting with all the sales staff in your clothing department,' 'We should like to take your fifth year pupils for eight class periods, one per week.' From here on, the negotiations can begin.

Improving the course
You have gained access, the programme has been presented and all your tasks, bar one, have been accomplished. It remains for you to review your measures of success and people's reactions to the programme.

First, the team can give their impressions of what they felt went well and what aspects could be improved upon. Secondly, try to get some feedback from people who took part in the programme. This can be done quite casually – chatting to them during a tea-break or before they leave – or more rigorously by including in the programme a short 'reaction' session such as a group discussion, or having each person complete a short questionnaire (see Chapter 10 and examples given in Section 4).

Whatever method you choose, you will find the intelligence gained invaluable.

Repeating the programme
The idea of a 'once-for-all' education programme on disability is naive, not to say impossible. The wish that it could be so is the only thing keeping this myth alive and, sadly, it is still prevalent. Invariably you will be dealing with small numbers of people at a time. But even if you manage to contact all the members of your target group, there will be new people coming along in the future. More significantly, there is evidence from research that the effects of a short community education programme may not be lasting, especially when people do not have regular contact with a disabled person. Their experience and knowledge needs topping up from time-to-time.

For all these reasons, you will have to be prepared to repeat the programme regularly. This need not be an onerous task, especially if you:

1   Document your experiences so that you can be reminded of all you did and so that others can learn from them, eg a brief report outlining the programme, how it was received and suggested changes.
2   'Package' the course; filing all the necessary resource materials – videos, handouts, questionnaires, publicity leaflets, etc. – so that they can be easily found and re-used.

3   Recruit and train others to take on the presenting of the programme. Indeed, work-sharing is our theme for the next part of the chapter.

Sharing with Others

Our assumption now is that you have developed, tested and improved an educational programme on disability for use with a specific group within the community. This in itself is a tremendous achievement, one accomplished by few people to date. Nonetheless you will have reached only a very small proportion of your target audience. An even bigger challenge – albeit of a different nature – now has to be faced: how to achieve widespread and continuing usage of the programme.

Packaging the programme
Other people can be encouraged to use the programme if all the necessary resource materials are available to them – videos, handouts, etc. Having these tangible tools removes much of the work in preparation and any doubts about their adequacies as teachers of others.

As we have explained in earlier chapters, it is quite cheap to produce multiple copies of your materials for distribution or sale to others. Alternatively, you might look to a commercial publisher or, more realistically, a disability organisation, to sponsor these costs and handle the marketing of the materials.

Alongside these materials, you should prepare notes to guide the person presenting the programme. These will explain the aims of the session: what they have to do and how they should do it. Examples of 'tutor guides' are given in Section 3.

Creating a teaching package of resource materials and tutor's notes is an essential but insufficient action to ensure usage of the programme. Many an excellent teacher's kit on health education gathers dust in the staff-room for want of use. Ivan Scheffler talks about the importance of 'personalising knowledge' and it is just as important to do this for potential tutors as it is for participants.

Potential users

There are two distinct though not exclusive categories of users. First, people like yourself with an interest in, and experience of, disability. They may not have the resources or the energy to produce a programme of their own but they might be keen to use yours. This is the most obvious group for you to work alongside.

Secondly, people who by the nature of their job, are in regular contact with the target group you have selected, for instance, school teachers, staff trainers, personnel managers, shop stewards and so on. These people may have had little past experience of handicap but this is more than compensated for, when your programme is accepted as part of their routine work. This not only guarantees regular usage but it embues it with an extra status, namely that learning about disability is important enough to merit inclusion in regular course work.

In our own work to date, we have shared our programmes with secondary school teachers and with adult education organisers. They are now using our programmes on mental handicap. However, it is also our aim to have our other programmes included in the training for new sales staff in city centre stores; in the apprenticeship schemes for staff in the hotel and catering industry and as part of the training for police, priests and other salient groups who provide services to the community. In all these instances, the ideal would be to have the current staff involved in training these people using our packages. But how can other people learn to use your programmes?

Ways of sharing

Apprenticeship – The traditional method of learning, from watching and working alongside a master craftsman, has much to commend it. It is the easiest way, too, for all it entails is having the trainee with you as you present the programme. This one-to-one learning in the real-life setting is probably the most satisfactory way of learning the job, but its one disadvantage is that only a few people can be trained at a time.

Workshops – This drawback can be overcome by bringing groups of people together for a workshop – and the emphasis is on the word 'work'. We suggest that, for part of the time, you should present the programme just as you would with your target audience. This will give your trainees a model of the presenter's role; it will let them get a feel for the programme from the audience's perspective and they will have a chance to preview the resource materials used on the programme.

Other essential elements for these workshops are:

(a) Opportunities to discuss the programme and question-times. This is best done in small groups of around eight people so that everyone has a chance to contribute.

(b) Details of how the programme has been received. For example, with our school's programme, we compiled a 20 minute video-programme of interviews with school pupils, mentally handicapped adults and staff from the training centres. This proved most effective and made compelling viewing.

(c) The workshop should end with each trainee tutor drawing up an action plan showing when and with whom they will use the programme.

Obviously the length of the workshop will vary according to the amount of information you have to impart, but generally one half day should suffice.

Presentations – If the foregoing is beyond your ambitions, then the least you can do is to tell others of your programme, either by writing an article for a professional magazine that potential tutors might read or by giving talks or mounting displays of your materials at conferences or local meetings, etc. Such publicity will create an awareness of your work and may interest some people sufficiently to approach you for more detailed information.

National usage
At the opposite extreme, let us consider how you might set about having your programme – or indeed any programme – used nationally. Some may see this as a pipe-dream but to us it is merely the logical extension of the systematic approach we have propounded.

One approach which we have found effective is the pyramid of training. The originators of the programme train a small number of people who then train others, who in turn use the programme with the public. The number of intermediary levels may vary but the theory – training the trainers – remains the same. There is no doubt that this can be an effective way of reaching large numbers of people.

In Ireland, our approach has been to recruit two or three trainers to cover a designated geographical area. These people have come mainly from disability organisations or Health Boards with some involvement from others who have expressed an interest in using our programmes in their area, for example, teachers in schools. After special workshop training, and having actually used the programme with a target group – in this instance senior pupils in secondary schools – the trainers go on to recruit teachers from the local schools and organise a workshop day in their own area. These teachers then use the programme in their own schools. The advantages of local resource teams for these teachers are many: the greater likelihood of personal contact; immediate help with any difficulties encountered; and easier adaptations of the package to suit local circumstances.

In reality, however, the implementation is far from smooth. A new American religious sect, founded in 1952, expected that within 27 years everyone in the world would be converted if each of the original 12 members gained two converts a year and they in turn brought in another two, and so on. Their calculations were quite correct – check them and see – but some of their assumptions about human nature were not so accurate.

Up to now our biggest difficulty has been the recruiting of local resource teams. There are few people who see this role as fitting their present job-description and there appears to be little interest in changing this – another reflection of attitudes to disability.

The future
Much of what we have just said will seem idealistic to those who have to fit in their community education work alongside many other commitments. We end by questioning if this must always be so. How many disability organisations have appointed full-time personnel to this task – how many have even considered doing so? During the past decade much has been written about integrating disabled people into society. International Years have come and gone and yet the old ways remain largely unchanged. Until organisations have full-time personnel coordinating the efforts of their staff in preparing the able-bodied to live, work and play alongside their disabled neighbours, the task of community education will hardly have begun. This is not to disparage the efforts of the part-timer, but simply a reminder that, as the name suggests, they can only do the work in part, never in full.

SECTION 3: EXAMPLES OF COMMUNITY EDUCATION PROGRAMMES

Introduction

12   A schools programme on mental handicap

13   An adult education course on mental handicap

14   A programme for sales assistants

15   Ready-made packages on disability

INTRODUCTION

This section outlines three very different community education programmes which we developed within the CARA Project – a three year study jointly financed by the Irish Health Education Bureau and St. Michael's House (a large Dublin-based mental handicap service). 'Cara' is the Irish word for friend and is an acronym for Community Attitudes to Retarded Adults.

Based on the approach outlined in Section 2, these programmes are now being widely implemented in Ireland. This wide dissemination has been possible because of the 'package' approach inherent in these programmes, that is:

1 *Resource materials developed for each specific programme*
Some examples of these are given in Section 4 (Fact Sheets, Discussion Sheets) and other materials include video programmes, posters, overhead transparencies, suggestions for group tasks, mini-projects, topic sheets and quiz questions.

2 *Workshop training for prospective course tutors*
One day training workshops were organized to provide tutors with first-hand experience of the approach and the course materials.

3 *Tutor notes detailing the learning techniques and the use of materials*
These are reproduced in this Section.

The School's Programme – is intended for 15 – 17 year-olds and consists of six 40-minute class periods. The topics included are: what are mentally handicapped people like? Relationships among handicapped people; meeting a handicapped person; and basic information about mental handicap. During the programme, mentally handicapped peers *visit the school* for a 'club' type recreation session, and students are offered an opportunity to make a return visit to the special school or centre.

The Adult Education Course – 'Getting to Know Mental Handicap' is a WEA-type evening class consisting of eight weekly sessions, each lasting two hours, and focusses on a particular aspect of the mentally handicapped adult's life style, (eg, work, home-life, leisure activities).

The programme includes a visit by participants, in small groups, to a local club or group home for mentally handicapped adults.

This programme is aimed at the neighbours of mentally handicapped adults living with their families or in community group homes, and those living in the vicinity of local Training Centres and Care Units. It has also attracted those interested in undertaking voluntary work or full time work in the field of mental handicap. The course is tutored mainly by service staff who work with mentally handicapped adults.

Sales Assistants – The purpose of this programme is to facilitate sales staff in identifying and practising the skills most needed when dealing with a customer who is mentally handicapped – in particular, the skills of communication and customer management.

In the second part of the programme, the staff individually meet trainees from the local ATC for lunch in the store's public restaurant and later bring them for a short familiarization tour of the store.

This work-release programme lasts two and a half hours in all, inclusive of the staff's own lunch hour.

Each of these programmes has a number of features in common which we feel have contributed to their effectiveness. These are:

- *participant involvement* in the programme through a variety of techniques – discussion, role-play, group-work, mini-projects, etc.
- *the use of video programmes* to focus on the human implications of handicap and to allow disabled people to speak for themselves.
- the provision of *guidelines* on relating to handicapped people.
- opportunity for *personal contact* with a handicapped person.

There are a growing number of ready-made educational packages available for use in schools and with community groups. Those known to us are listed at the end of the Section and addresses of organizations given in Section 4 may yield others appropriate to your needs.

12   A SCHOOLS PROGRAMME ON MENTAL HANDICAP

CaRa

School Programme

Introduction

The CARA Schools Programme is a short programme on mental handicap for 15 – 17 year old students in second-level schools. The programme consists of *six* 40-minute class periods spread over three to six weeks and forms a suitable module within the Humanities, Pastoral Care, Citizenship or Personal Development curricula.

While factual information is not overlooked, the emphasis in the Programme is on *people*. It explores the interests and life-styles of mentally handicapped people and offers guidelines for relating to them. A central feature is the opportunity for students to meet handicapped peers from a local day centre.

A major aim of the programme is to develop the social skills of students – helping them relate to and feel at ease with mentally handicapped people. Moreover, research has shown that being at ease with one particular handicap increases confidence with all handicaps.

The programme is an initial contribution to the integration into the community of the many mentally handicapped people living with their families or in community hostels. Often they are still socially isolated.

Facilitating the teacher. Teachers understandably are wary of

179

tackling a topic like disability, particularly with senior students, if they lack expertise or first-hand experience. The CARA Programme sets out to provide the teacher with the *approach* and the *resources* needed to present such a topic confidently.

Detailed tutor's notes are given in this booklet and all the materials needed for the six class periods of the programmes are included in the supplied package: videotapes, fact sheets, discussion sheets, transparencies for the overhead projector and a CARA poster.

The CARA approach: Teamwork

Where to start – Try to attend a Workshop Training Day on the CARA Schools Programme. This is designed to introduce teachers to the materials and to offer them the opportunity to experience – and evaluate – the programme at first hand.

The next step for the class teacher is to contact the local service for mentally handicapped adults – a training centre, workshop, care unit or special school. Explain that you are beginning an educational programme, and enquire if any member of staff would be interested in helping out or advising on it.

The staff person is the other half of the team, your willing 'expert' on mental handicap whom you might wish to invite into the classroom to lead a discussion with students or to answer their questions, or to give them guidelines on meeting someone who is mentally handicapped.

Alternatively, this staff person may be invited to take the full programme with the class. The teacher could then take it in other years or with other classes.

In any event, the visit of the mentally handicapped trainees to the school, and of the students to the centre, should be discussed and arranged well in advance. This is the key element in the programme.

An Overview of the Sessions

1   *Introductory Session*
    Improvisation
    Workshop Video

    What students *think* of mentally handicapped people, contrasted with seeing and hearing actual people.

2   *Relationships*
    'Donal and Sally' (TV)
    Arrange Student Session

    Can mentally handicapped people form long-term relationships?

3 *Interaction*
'Donal and Sally' discussed.
How to meet a mentally   Guidelines for interacting with
handicapped person   mentally handicapped people.

4 *'Club' Session*
Visit to school by trainees   Meeting and relating to
                                 mentally handicapped trainees
                                 in a relaxed setting.

5 *Student Session*
Students' reports   Students share their work or
                                 views/reactions with the rest of
                                 the class.

6 *Information Session*
Facts and Figures   Summary of basic information.
Student Feedback   Students' assessment of the
                                 sessions.

SESSION 1: INTRODUCTION – *What are mentally handicapped people like?*

(Resources: Workshop Video I, Student Session Sheet, Discussion Paper I)

(a) *Introduction* – The class teacher briefly introduces the CARA programme and the staff member from the mental handicap service (if present).

(b) *Improvisation* – Students are asked to imagine that they are mentally handicapped and to · visualize themselves in an everyday situation (shop, bus, street) where, because of their handicap, they encounter difficulties.

   Having decided on a situation, they discuss it in detail with a second student.

   They then mime or act out the situation. Tutors divide the class into two discussion groups, and students report on the scene improvised. Stigma-elements in their presentation of mental handicap are noted.

(c) *Workshop Video* – A ten-minute video-tape is shown to students of trainees in workshops talking about themselves, discussing their work and enjoying leisure activities. Students briefly discuss their reactions to the tape and outline the degree of personal contact they have had with mentally handicapped people.

(d) *Next Session – Student Session Sheet* is distributed: listing suggested mini-projects which students report on in Session 5. Students are asked to decide on a topic by next session. Also give out copies of *Discussion Paper 1* – a case-study of a mentally handicapped couple who marry – to be read for the next session.

SESSION 2: Theme – *Handicapped people have feelings too*
(Resources: 'Donal and Sally' Video II, Fact Sheets).

(a) *Student Session Sheet* – Students indicate which topic they
have chosen and whether they are working alone or in groups
of two or three.

(b) *Fact Sheets* – Arrangements are made to have some copies of
the Fact Sheets available in the library for students to
consult during the programme.

(c) *Discussion Paper I* – Students are reminded of its theme by
way of introduction to 'Donal and Sally'

(d) *'Donal and Sally'* – is shown. This is a 30-minute videotape
of an edited version of the BBC *Play for Today*, featuring
a developing relationship between two mentally handicapped
trainees at a Scottish ATC. The video highlights the various
reactions of parents and staff members to this relationship.
Students are asked for their immediate reactions to the video
programme.

(e) Students are asked to write a short, ten-line review of the
play for the next session.

SESSION 3: Theme – *Getting on with a mentally handicapped peer*

(Resources: Students' reviews, Video III)

(a) *Play-reviews* – Three students in each group read their reviews of 'Donal and Sally', followed by comments and discussion with other students.

(b) *Student Projects* – Brief reminder, checking that resource-material is available to those who need it.

(c) *Meeting a mentally handicapped person* – Students who have had contact with mentally handicapped people are asked to recall their impressions of their first meeting.
Three aspects of meeting a mentally handicapped person are then discussed:
  (i)   spontaneous, unconventional behaviour – being over-familiar, breaking social conventions, etc.
  (ii) communication difficulties – why these sometimes arise and how to react to them.
  (iii) personal appearance – why mentally handicapped people may appear different.

(d) *Show Video III* – of people chatting with mentally handicapped trainees.

(e) *Next Session* – The activities/games for the Club Session are discussed briefly and any other necessary arrangements made.

SESSION 4: Theme – *Meeting*

(Resources: Activities/games materials)

(a) *Preparation* – The Session is arranged in a room other than the regular class-room, where tables and chairs and some extra space are available. The group of around 15 trainees should arrive a few minutes before the beginning of the class-period and are met by a few 'host' students who show them to the room.

(b) *Contact Period* – When the rest of the students arrive, they are introduced and grouped on a two-to-one basis with trainees. The groups may become involved in games – snooker, darts, cards, draughts, rings, etc. (See booklet on meeting). The visit might end with refreshments, if these can be arranged, eg a cup of tea.

(c) *Follow Up* – A return visit to the training centre/workshop/care unit might be suggested or arranged at this point. This visit may occur outside school hours so that students are not obligated to attend.

(d) Students are reminded to complete their work for the following week's *Student Session*.

SESSION 5: *Student presentations*

(Resources: As per students' requirements)

(a) *Presentation* – Early on in the programme students were encouraged to choose a topic which they would research and write about and in this session groups or individuals present their work to the class, using notes, diagrams, charts. Each group is allowed about three to five minutes and, after each presentation, students may wish to ask some further questions.

Some students opt for information-based topics – reporting on, for example, the local services, the media coverage of disabled people or causes of mental handicap. Students should be encouraged to *summarize* their information, perhaps using visual aids to emphasise their main points, and end by offering some personal comment on their findings. Personal topics have proved very popular – poetry in particular – but also short-stories and lyrics for a song. Students often focus on their first contact with mentally handicapped people and on the public's attitudes towards disabled people.

SESSION 6: *Information*

(Resources: Transparencies, Commentary Sheet)

(a) *Information* – Review and summary of information in key areas – Causes, Services, History, etc. – see Commentary Sheet and the Fact Sheets. Student presentations may have adequately covered some of these topics already.
Questions and comments taken.

(b) *Evaluation* – Finally students indicate the sessions they found most interesting or useful, and those aspects of the programme they feel could be improved.

Expanding the six sessions – this is a very full programme, although it can be done. For those who want to take more time over topics this can be easily achieved, particularly by spending two class periods on Session 3 and devoting another period discussing students' reactions to their meeting and reports from students who visited the local centre. This makes an eight period module.

The Programme Materials

Teacher's Notes – which you are now reading!

Fact Sheets – basic information on key aspects of mental handicap – causes of mental handicap, historical background, services available, meaning of terms, etc.

Any one sheet can be read in a matter of minutes; *all* the students should be strongly encouraged to read them. They form a starting point for several topics listed for the Student Session.
NB   The Fact Sheets are designed to be easily photocopied to provide extra copies for the class. (Samples given in Section 4).

Student Session Sheet – distributed to students at the end of the first session; it lists suggestions for topics the students might choose to report on in Session 5 and outlines how they could set about doing this. The titles include:
  – A mentally handicapped person I met or know
  – A dialogue
  – Why some people are mentally handicapped
  – Lyrics for a song (name the group/band)
  – Services available to mentally handicapped adults
  – A sketch or painting
  – Names used for mental handicap and what they mean
  – A short story
  – A poem
The most successful reports have been those relating to handicapped people they have met or situations they themselves have experienced (impressions of a visit, a dialogue, or lyrics for a song, etc).
The aim is to encourage the expression of imagination and feeling as far as possible.

Discussion Papers –'Against the Odds' is a case study of a mentally handicapped couple who marry and is linked with the theme of Session 2; 'If Monkeys did the Same Work' is a critical view of Adult Workshops for use in an expanded 8-session programme.
NB   Discussion Papers should be photocopied to provide each student with a copy (samples given in Section 4).

Videotape – Session 1: *Workshop Video* – a locally made ten-minute videotape showing mentally handicapped trainees in a workshop setting discussing their work and leisure activities.

Session 2: *'Donal and Sally'* – A 30–minute edited version of a play; any equivalent programme focussing on relationships between mentally handicapped people would be appropriate.

Session 3: *Video* III – A short, home-made video of trainees inter-acting and talking to visitors or the staff from the workshop.

Transparencies – a summary and revision of basic information on mental handicap, for use in the final Information Session. A commentary sheet accompanies the transparencies and offers guidelines for presenting the summarized information.

The CARA Poster – acts as a visual focal-point for the project period; it depicts the range of facial expressions among handi-capped people, belying the notion of a stereotypic appearance among mentally handicapped adults.

Evaluation Questionnaires (optional) – useful for measuring how effective the package is in changing young people's perceptions of mental handicap. The questionnaire should be completed by the class *prior* to Session 1 and at the end of the final session. It will take students ten minutes at the most to complete. You can then compare their answers before and after taking the programme (sample provided in Section 4).

13 AN ADULT EDUCATION COURSE ON MENTAL HANDICAP

cara

Getting to know mental handicap

This programme is intended as an introduction to mentally handicapped people and is offered as an eight-week evening course, each weekly session lasting two hours and dealing with a separate topic: work, home, alternatives to home, leisure interests, relationships and information about mental handicap. The fifth session allows course participants to meet mentally handicapped people in a local recreation club or group home.

The focus of the programme is mentally handicapped adults and teenagers, *not* children; your publicity should indicate this, otherwise the parents of young mentally handicapped children might assume the course is intended for them.

You, the tutor, will have lived or worked with mentally handicapped adults and will have attended the Workshop Day. It is an advantage if you also have some previous experience of adult education, eg giving courses for parents or other staff, etc.

The programme is aimed at neighbours and acquaintances of families with a mentally handicapped member, those living close to services for mentally handicapped people, those interested in voluntary work or a career in mental handicap services and those whose work brings them into incidental contact with mentally handicapped people (eg postman, milkman . . .).

Enjoyment and variety are the key elements in your presentation; making participants relaxed, getting them involved and maintaining a friendly, open atmosphere. The first evening is particularly important in this respect; meet people as they arrive and introduce participants to yourself and to each other. You should also be aware of their reasons for coming and what they hope to achieve from the course. Finally, you should introduce the programme; the topics that will be covered and the range of materials and activities that are planned; but don't dally on this aspect. Participants will be eager to get started and you will want to encourage their involvement from the beginning.

After the first session, participants will be more relaxed and ready to contribute and, we hope, looking forward to meeting mentally handicapped people.

We begin by reviewing the content of the course; and will then comment briefly on the resource materials.

Synopsis of the Course

1 *Introduction*	Getting to know each other and the course.
At home	What is it like to have a mentally handicapped teen-ager or young adult in the family.
2 *Relationships*	Can those who are mentally handicapped form long-term relationships?
3 *At Work*	The typical Training Centre: what is the real work potential of mentally handicapped adults?
4 *Leisure Activities*	How do mentally handicapped people spend their leisure time?
Meeting a mentally handi-capped person	Guidelines on relating to mentally handicapped people in a leisure setting.
5 *Visit*	Participants meet mentally handicapped adults in a local club, pub or hostel; individually or in small groups.
6 *Alternatives to Home*	Institutions, small units or community homes – where to live?
7 *Facts and Figures*	Basic information on services for children and adults, the role of the professionals involved, and information on causation and prevention, etc.

8   *Review*   The role of the local
                                      community; opportunities to
                                      help. Feedback on the
                                      programme from participants.

SESSION 1: *A mentally handicapped teenager in the family*

(Resources: Discussion Sheet, Video, Topic Sheet, Fact Sheets)

(a) Introduction – Introduce participants to each other and to yourself and present a brief overview of the course.

(b) *Discussion Sheet* – Distribute 'My Brother Michael,' allow reading time and have some comments.

(c) *Group Work* – This is where participants in pairs discuss an everyday situation in which a mentally handicapped person may experience difficulties while among strangers (eg short of bus fare). The two participants discuss this situation and explore how the handicapped person would feel and whether the stranger would identify their handicap.

This introductory exercise avoids the necessity for a formal definition of mental handicap which will have little meaning for them.

Break for Coffee

Video Programme – 'James is our Brother' (BBC Enterprises, 30 mins). James is a Down's Syndrome teenager living with his family; this excellent programme presents the viewpoint of his parents, his brother and of James himself and gives a glimpse of the many aspects of his full life.

Discussion – Comments on programme; and in contrast with their expectations expressed earlier in the Group Work above. (May be done in small groups).

Introduce Topic Spot – The Topic Spot is an opportunity for individual participants to report briefly to the group on an area of expertise or of particular interest; it will be a regular feature of future sessions.

Fact Sheets on mental handicap are now made available and may be of help to those preparing Topic Spots.

SESSION 2: *Mentally handicapped people have feelings, too*

(Resources: Discussion Sheet, Video).

Discussion Sheet – 'Against the Odds': a case-study of two mentally handicapped trainees who marry; participants comment.

Topic Spot – One or two participants give a brief (3 – 5 minutes) review of their chosen topic; ideally the topics chosen for each night should relate to the evening's theme in some respect.

Videoprogramme – 'Donal and Sally' (BBC *Play for Today*, 65 mins) traces a developing relationship between two mentally handicapped trainees and shows the reactions of their parents and members of staff, some favouring its continuance, others feeling Donal and Sally should be separated. The play also gives a good insight into everyday life in the ATC.

Break – We suggest you take a short 'commercial break' for coffee and some comment half way through the play and before participants know how the story ends.

Discussion – Both the play and the Discussion Sheet raise the question: Do mentally handicapped people have the right to marry, to control their own lives; and what other rights must be taken into account?

Those taking next week's Topic Spot should be reminded.

SESSION 3: *Mentally handicapped people at work*

(Resources: Discussion Sheet, Video, Fact Sheets).

Discussion Sheet – 'If monkeys did the same work there would be a national outcry,' a critical look at contract work in ATCs in Britain following the ITV programme 'Working for a Pittance'. Participants comment.

Topic Spot – 1–2 participants reviewing a related topic.

Task Groups – Participants are split up into four groups and given a Task Sheet to work on for 20 minutes, ie.:

Group 1   'You have decided to set up a *Fast Food* business employing mentally handicapped people: decide on your range of products (sandwiches . . .) and work out the details of your training programme for inexperienced mentally handicapped trainees . . . .'

Group 2   'Evaluate what mentally handicapped people have to say about their work (using *Our Lives* Fact Sheet). Are their work-expectations realistic? List the jobs which you consider most trainees might manage. What improvements could *most* easily be made in workshop employment . . .?'

Group 3   Examine whether it would be viable to set up a launderette, café or contract cleaning service employing mentally handicapped people. (Choose *one*). What skills would be essential (list)?

Group 4   'Look at the range of abilities among mentally handicapped people and try to list the skills each grouping (high ability, mixed ability, low ability) has or could acquire in the area of work.' (see Fact Sheet 3)

Groups Report Back – (one person reports for each group) followed by discussion.

Break for Coffee

Video Programme – 'Labels Disable': case studies of mentally handicapped people in open employment filmed by third level students on a Communications Course in Dublin.

Discussion – participants' reaction to the programme; these are contrasted with handicapped trainees' work expectations (see Task Group II).

SESSION 4: *Leisure activities and meeting handicapped people*

(Resources: Discussion Sheet, Video, Tutor's own notes on local leisure opportunities).

Discussion Sheet – 'The Loneliness of 15,000': a survey article which highlights the social isolation of mentally handicapped people in Ireland.

Topic Spot – One or two participants review a related topic.

Videoprogramme – 'Let me Win': an RTE-produced film of the Special Olympics which focusses on one girl's attempt to win the gymnastics competition.

Break for comments and coffee

Tutor Input – The Tutor presents an overview of the leisure opportunities for mentally handicapped people in the area.

Next Week's Arrangements – Confirm arrangements for next week's visit to local recreation club, pub, community hostel, bowling alley, etc. Give some background to the people chosen – number of members, their abilities, usual activities and interests, etc.

Guidelines – Discuss with the group how to overcome any communication problems with mentally handicapped people and how to accept spontaneous behaviour, etc. Participants should be reassured that these difficulties are generally minor and are easily overcome.

SESSION 5: *Contact with handicapped people*

There is no formal session in the centre; the group are split up and may be visiting a club for handicapped people, invited to a local hostel, or arranging a get-together in the local pub or leisure centre . . . and some participants may suggest and arrange new ways of getting together. These meetings will take place during the fortnight between the fourth and sixth sessions and the role of the Tutor is that of facilitator, helping arrange introductions, contacting the local club or hostel, etc. The mentally handicapped adults taking part should have the opportunity to suggest venues and activities which they would enjoy. Local contacts should be encouraged, eg between a mentally handicapped adult and course participants who are neighbours.

SESSION 6: *Alternatives to home*

(Resources: Video, Flip-Chart or Blackboard)

Discussion on Contact Session – Feed-back on impressions of visit to club, hostel, etc. . . . surprises, difficulties, good experiences. . .

Topic Spot – 1–2 participants review their chosen topic.

Videoprogramme – Recent RTE Current Affairs programme on residential choices in the West of Ireland, focussing on the controversy concerning the proposed building of a residential 'village' complex in a small town. (alternatively: excerpts from the BBC 'Silent Minority' film)

Discussion – Current trends in residential choices: where should more severely handicapped people live – institutions or houses? The problems of ageing parents, etc. How good neighbours help integration . . . .

Information Wanted – Preparation for next week's Information Session. Using the blackboard/flipchart, have participants suggest the areas of most interest to them as a group. This will help you decide the content for next week.

Fact Sheets will be available for sale next week – price: £2.00. (Reminder for those taking Topic Spot for Session Eight – you should suggest that the Topic be a creative or personal one, eg poem/story/personal experience. (No Topic Spot *next* week)

SESSION 7: *Information session*

(Resources: Video, Blank Charts and Markers, Fact Sheets)

Task Groups – Participants are split into small groups, supplied with a large sheet of paper and felt marker, relevant Fact Sheets and other resource material and assigned a task. Below are some common areas which arise, but the tutor should incorporate the participants' suggestions from last week:

Group 1   Make out a simple chart on *Causes and Prevention of Mental Handicap*, using headings, diagrams, etc. (see Fact Sheet 9).

Group 2   Chart on *Services* – listing or illustrating (preferably) the kinds of services that are or should be available (see Fact Sheet 4).*

Group 3   *The Role of Professionals* in helping handicapped people – how and what each profession can contribute towards the development of the handicapped person (see Fact Sheet 5).

Group 4   How *People are Misinformed* about mental handicap – the common mistakes of the 'man/woman in the street' (see Fact Sheet 11); illustrating these, if possible with sketch/mime/headings.

Group 5   *What does Mental Handicap Mean?* an attempt to explain simply in words/illustrations (Fact Sheet 1).

Information Presentation – Each group makes a presentation using chart/role playing, etc., with brief discussion following each.

* After Group 2 presentation show *Team Work* Video, a 15-minute 'home-made' programme illustrating the role of professionals with mentally handicapped people.

Next Week – Announce Quiz for next week: *'So You Think You Know about Mental Handicap'* and make arrangements for *refreshments* if feasible. Give reminder for next week's creative *Topic Spot*.

SESSION 8: Review

(Resources: Quiz Sheets, Evaluation Sheet, Course Certificates)

Topic Spot – Participants' reactions to their experiences on the course through any artistic medium: cartoon, poem, short story, dialogue, etc.

Quiz – 'So You Think You Know About Mental Handicap?' Participants are grouped into teams and allowed to confer before answering questions. The quiz is an opportunity to revise course content in an enjoyable way.

How you can help – Tutor's and participants' suggestions on ways of helping people who are mentally handicapped, ranging from being friendly neighbours to volunteer involvement in summer workcamps; 'buddy' schemes; respite care for handicapped children; having a handicapped adult as a paying guest for a weekend break.

Break for refreshments: discussion and course evaluation.

For the course evaluation, participants complete the short *Evaluation Sheet* in their own time and deposit them on the table when they leave.

Participants receive their *Course Certificates* on completion of the programme.

Programme Materials

1   *Videoprogrammes* – Almost four hours of video-material is used in the programme, both to inform and as trigger material for discussion on various topics. These programmes offer the handicapped individual the opportunity to give his or her views, while allowing course participants to see handicapped people close-up, to hear them and to see what they can achieve. Do ensure that the Centre has a TV and video recorder and you know how to use it.

2   *Discussion Sheets* – These are used mainly to introduce the evening's topic, 'setting the scene'. They are chosen to complement closely the video material, offering a different and sometimes contrasting perception. They also provide participants who arrive early with appropriate reading (sample provided in Section 4).

3   *Fact Sheets* – Form a resource for those preparing a 'factual' Topic Spot; for the Task Groups on employment in Session 4; and for the Group Work in the Information Session. The range of topics covered is considerable: from Causes and Prevention to Community Attitudes and Helping Handicapped Adults (see Section 4).

Other Written Material

Task Sheets – for the Group Work on employment in Session 4.
Quiz Questions – for the final session.
Topic Sheet – listing suggestions for the Topic Spot at the beginning of each session.

Evaluation Sheet – (optional) useful for measuring how effective the package is in changing participants' perceptions of mental handicap. The questionnaire should be completed by the group *prior* to Session 1 and at the end of the final Session. It will take 10 minutes at the most to complete. You can compare their answers before and after taking the programme (sample provided in Section 4).

Alternatively it can be used to record participants' comments at the end of the programme.

Course Certificate – Those who complete the programme receive a certificate signed by the course tutor.

The Information Session (Session 7) requires the use of *large sheets* of paper (for charts) and *felt markers* which the tutor should supply on the night.

Recommended Reading
Jennifer Rogers, *Adults Learning* (2nd Edition), Milton-Keynes, Open University, 1977.
An excellent pocket-book for adult educators, full of practical suggestions.

14 A PROGRAMME FOR SALES ASSISTANTS

HELPING
CUSTOMERS

Introduction

This is a short programme (duration two and a half hours) to facilitate sales assistants in serving customers who are mentally handicapped. The approach used in the programme is to use the staff's existing sales skills and experience as the central resource; while the tutor's role is to identify with them the likely problem areas and to suggest the appropriate sales techniques in overcoming any difficulties.

The programme is intended for use by either service staff who are involved in social skills training with mentally handicapped adults (on the invitation of the store's management and training departments), or the store's own training personnel (once they have been fully introduced to the programme) with support from the local mental handicap service.

Outline of the Programme

Activity	Aim/Purpose
A Identifying Sales Techniques	
1 Introduction	Describing the mentally handicapped customer
2 Video viewing	Mentally handicapped customers managing well
3 Role-play	The difficulties that can arise

4 Flip-Chart Analysis   Identifying the problems and
                                      techniques

5 Participant role-play   Practising techniques

B Meeting the Customers

6 Shared Lunch   Getting to know a mentally
                                     handicapped person

7 Tour of Store   Explaining layout, exploring
                                     preferences, difficulties

8 Question and Answer   Reactions to experience
   Session

9 Leaflet Distributed   Summarizing main points

A Identifying Sales Techniques

This section of the programme will focus on the following broad areas:

(i)   Initial contact with customer
(ii)   Effective communication
(iii) Effective situation management

The initial stages in the session are intended to alert participants to possible difficulties in these areas. Before beginning, the tutor should enlist the help of a participant as accomplice in the role-play Point 3 below.

1 *Introduction*. The tutor introduces him/herself (if not already known to the staff); the purpose of the programme is made clear (ie. to help staff help mentally handicapped customers) and the approach is stressed: the tutor is working with the staff in identifying the appropriate skills. This active involvement by the staff is essential to the programme's success.

2 *Video-viewing*. A six-minute video, consisting of excerpts from other programmes, shows mentally handicapped people successfully purchasing a range of goods. Equally, it is an opportunity for participants to see and hear mentally handicapped people.

3 *Tutor's role-play*. With the help of an accomplice, the tutor role-plays a shopping situation (buying a jacket) where things go wrong; the sales assistant eventually discovers that the jackets being tried on are not what the customer has in mind at all and are beyond what he can afford.

4 *Flip-chart analysis:* Participants identify the problem areas and

suggest how they might be more effectively dealt with. The analysis and discussion may result in something like this:

(a) *Initial contact:*
  – eye contact, facial expression, stance, introductory remarks.

(b) *Effective communication*
  – establishing what the customer wants (showing examples. . .)
  – confirming the price range (how much has she or he to spend?)
  – coping with language difficulties (ask to repeat, to point to it, speaking simply, avoiding jargon).

(c) *Effective situation management*
  – pacing the interaction (not rushing the customer, leaving stranded, being aware of difficulties)
  – giving clear directions (where the mirror/cash desk/fitting rooms are; where assistant will be)
  – anticipating difficulties (with zips, buttons, fasteners, belts, or laces . . .)

5 *Participant role-play.* The participants, in pairs, role-play another situation as it might arise in their department (eg buying footwear, toiletries . . .), thus applying the techniques to their particular situation.

B. Meeting the Customers

6 *Shared lunch.* Sales staff are then introduced on a one-to-one basis to trainees from the local Training Centre, who are on a familiarization visit to the store. The trainee joins the staff member for lunch in the store's public restaurant.

7 *Tour of store.* The trainee is then shown around the store by the staff member; it is an opportunity for the sales assistant to learn something of the trainee's preferences and difficulties when shopping in the store.

8 *Question-and-answer session.* Allows for staff questions and comments on their lunch hour experience and to talk about application of techniques in practice.

9 *Summary leaflet.* This 'fact sheet' is intended as a programme summary and offers suggestions on 'Helping Customers who are Mentally Handicapped'.

SUGGESTIONS

Often you will be able to treat a mentally handicapped customer, just as you would any other customer. Indeed, you may be unaware that they are handicapped. Sometimes though, you will come across people who will need extra help. Here are some suggestions –

* OFFER TO HELP
  Rarely will you be refused!

* IDENTIFY WHAT THEY ARE LOOKING FOR
  Take nothing for granted; they could be in the wrong part of the store

* CLARIFY THE TYPE OF ARTICLE THEY HAVE IN MIND
  Their preference for colour, style

* CHECK THE PRICE THEY CAN AFFORD
  Like the rest of us, they might be a bit short

* SHOW THEM ALTERN-ATIVES
  Pick out some possibilities for them to examine

* POINT OUT AIDS LIKE MIRRORS
  They may not spot them as readily as other shoppers

* LEAVE THEM TIME TO DECIDE
  Some will take longer than others

* SHOW THEM TO FITTING ROOMS, CASH DESK
  This lessens the risk of them getting lost in the store

* REMIND THEM OF PRICE BEFORE FINAL CHOICE IS MADE
  Give the bad news early on!

IF

* YOU CAN'T UNDERSTAND WHAT THEY SAY
  – Ask them to repeat themselves
  – Have them point out what they want

* YOU FEEL THEY HAVE MADE A WRONG DECISION
  (for example, wrong size, style)
  – Offer them a more suitable alternative
  – Point out the improvements

* THEY DO NOT WANT ANY HELP
  – React as you would with any other customer; but keep an eye open – they may change their mind.

Programme Materials

1 *Video programme* of mentally handicapped people successfully purchasing a range of goods. You may need to take along video equipment.
2 *Summary Leaflet*
3 *Flip-chart:* Not supplied with the programme! Available in most Staff Training Centres.

You may also require 'props' for your improvisation, but these will be minimal.

15 READY-MADE PACKAGES ON DISABILITY

Physical and Sensory Handicap
The first three kits are available from Community Service Volunteers (CSV), 237 Pentonville Road, London N1 (Tel: 01–278 6601); and are designed for use in schools and colleges.

1 *Physical Handicap.* Contains basic information, leaflets, case studies, project work and simulation; deals with deafness, blindness, epilepsy and spinal injury. Designed to increase understanding and discourage patronizing attitudes. From CSV, price £3.00.

2 *Who Are You Staring At?* Includes 36 photo-posters, audio cassette (interviews), teacher's notes and resources; presenting six young people with various handicaps and how they experience life. (Produced in association with the Mental Health Film Council, 1980). From CSV, price £8.00.

3 *Design with Disabled People.* Contains extensive teacher's notes, 24 colour slides showing examples of student-made aids; 5 posters providing information on arthritis, multiple sclerosis, spina bifida and stroke and the stages in designing aids. The approach involves students working closely with disabled individuals in identifying, designing and evaluating an aid (eg large knob for TV switch) which students construct during craft classes (eg metalwork, woodwork). Developed by the Salford School Concern Project Team, 1981. From CSV, price £5.00.

4 *Communication '81.* Contains posters, teacher's notes, work cards and an audio cassette; explores the nature of communication disorders and special educational methods and therapy. Designed for 14–17 year olds. Available from Association for All Speech Impaired Children, Central Markets, Smithfield, London EC1A 9NH.

5 *Don't Shout, I'm Deaf.* Contains a 25-minute film, 30 slides, audio cassette and student's and tutor's notes. Designed for all those whose work brings them into contact with the hearing-impaired. Produced by the Department of Health and the Welsh Office, and available from: Central Film Library,

Government Buildings, Bromyard Avenue, Acton, London W3.

6 *Understanding Others.* A set of 20 broadsheets outlining, with text and photographs, scenarios depicting aspects of relationships. Designed for use with 12–16 year olds. Published by TACADE, 2 Mount Street, Manchester, M2 5NG, England (Catalogue available on request).

7 *John Groom's Association. Schools Information Packet on Disability.*Contains posters and film strip focussing on access for wheelchair-bound people, illustrated through practical examples. Available from John Groom's Association for the Disabled, 10 Gloucester Drive, London N4 2LP (Tel: 01–802 7272).

8 *Action Research for the Crippled Child. School's Information Package.* Consists of eight class project leaflets, teacher's handbook, wallchart and project book. Intended for use with 14+ age groups, although the project book is suitable for younger students. (A series of 12 film-strips to complement this material is available through EFVA – address below). The pack is published by the National Fund for Research in Crippling Diseases, Vincent House, 1 North Parade, Horsham, Sussex, RH12 2DA.

9 *The Handicapped in the Neighbourhood.* Contains filmstrip and teacher's notes; designed to make young people aware of the difficulties encountered by handicapped people in their everyday lives. Available from: EFVA, Film Library, Paxton Place, London SE27. (Tel: 01–670 4247).

10 *People You'd Like to Know.* Part of this series includes *Harold*, a ten-minute American film (16 mm) on a fourteen year old blind boy. Teacher's notes accompany film. Suitable for young teenagers. Available from Fergus Davidson Associates, 376 London Road, West Croydon, Surrey, CR9 2SU. (Tel: 01–689 6824).

Mental Illness

11 *Mental Health Kit.* currently being developed by Community Service Volunteers (CSV) to replace the 'With Us in Mind' kit which it now out of stock. The new kit should be available in 1983. See address above.

12 *Look Behind the Label.* Contains 30-minute video, posters

and pamphlets. The video focusses on social attitudes towards mental illness and is intended as trigger material for a guided discussion. Produced by the Scottish Health Education Groups (see address p.248).

Mental Handicap

13 *We Belong.* Resource materials for public education on mental handicap; includes a Speaker's Kit (speeches and press releases on Community Living, Employment, Retardation and Integration in Schools); handbook on lobbying politicians; a general booklet on handicap; and specific leaflets on employment, group homes, and prevention of mental handicap. A half-hour 16 mm film or videocassette, 'Exploding the Myth', looks at misconceptions about mental handicap; the film's theme song 'Give me a Chance' is available on record. Produced by the OAMR and available from: Distribution Centre, 36 Overlea Blvd., Toronto, Ontario M4H 9Z9, Canada.

14 *Happy Birthday!* A classroom resource kit on the *causes and prevention* of mental handicap. Developed in association with OAMR; includes 13-minute slide-tape presentation, two Teacher's Guides (introduction and topics for further study). and 30 'masters' for reproduction on slides or transparencies (for the overhead projector). Intended for second-level students, the material can offer a single-class overview or a series of lessons on different aspects of prevention. Available from Belsten Publishing Ltd., 25 Planchit Road, Unit 7, Maple, Ontario L0J 1E0, Canada; (price $125.00).

15 *Listen Please.* Public education kits containing six brochures on ways to become involved with handicapped people, two booklets and prices for TV and Radio Spots. Available from National Institute on Mental Retardation, Kinsmen Building, York University Campus, 4700 Keele Street, Downsview, Ontario M3J 1P3, Canada. Kits $1.25 each.

16 *Law Enforcement and Handicapped Persons: An Instructor's Training and Reference Manual:* A practical 65-page handbook for police training in relating to people with mental handicap and other disabilities. Available from NIMR, Canada (see above) Price $3.50.

17 *Police Training in the Recognition and Handling of Retarded Citizens:* A short tutor's manual offering guidelines in setting

up a police-training programme; and details of a two-hour training session. Prepared by Dolores Norley for the American National Association for Retarded Citizens (NARC), Box 6109, Arlington, Texas 76011, USA.

NARC have also produced a wide range of leaflets including some on employment and leisure-involvement with retarded people.

Campaign for Mentally Handicapped People have 'Meeting Mentally Handicapped People' and 'Who are these People Anyway' – useful supplementary leaflets to short presentations to adult groups. Available from 16 Fitzroy Square, London, W1P 5HQ (Tel: 01–387 9571).

This listing is by no means complete, but is mainly intended as a starting point. Section 4 will yield further resource material (films, leaflets, booklets, posters), which might form the basis for a complete package. As we mentioned earlier, preview films before using and especially before purchasing; and do check how suitable the materials are for your particular target groups.

SECTION 4: RESOURCES

Introduction

1 *Sample Materials*
Fact-sheets
Discussion leaflets
Questionnaires

2 *Information*
Directories
Audio-visual materials
Books
Magazines and Journals
Courses

3 *Organisations*

4 *References used in compiling the book*

INTRODUCTION

Community educators are traders in information. You need to be informed so that you can pass on knowledge to others. In this section of the book we shall attempt to make your job a little easier by providing various sources of information about disability.

First, we present samples of the materials we have used in our community education programmes on mental handicap – fact sheets, discussion leaflets and questionnaires. You can either use these as examples when it comes to drawing up your own materials, or you are most welcome to make photocopies for use in your programmes.

Secondly, we shall list other published materials which you might find helpful. Some of these – such as films and videos – you will be able to use in your programmes, whereas others like books and journal articles will provide you and your colleagues with background information. These should prove useful when compiling your own fact-sheets or discussion leaflets.

Obviously our listings are not exhaustive and they will become quickly out-dated. Hence, we provide the names and addresses of the main publishers of books and films. You could contact them for up-to-date information.

Finally, we give the names and addresses of the main organisations for disabled people in Britain and Ireland. Often they can provide you with a great deal of information, both about their services and about disabilities in general. As most of their materials are aimed at the general public, you should find some which could be distributed during your programme.

1 SAMPLE MATERIALS

Community Attitudes to Retarded Adults

Fact Sheets
Developed within the CARA programme, these Fact Sheets give essential information about mentally handicapped people in Irish Society. Each sheet focusses on a particular topic – there are eleven in all – and the facts are summarised in a clear and straightforward way. They form a unique reference source, designed to be used in community education programmes, the preparation of volunteer workers and in training courses for new staff.

Contents
1   What is Mental Handicap
2   Names given to Mentally Handicapped People
3   Mental Handicap through the Ages
4   Mentally Handicapped Adults – characteristics of those living in the community
5   Mental Handicap Services
6   Working with Mentally Handicapped People – jobs, careers, professions
7   Helping Mentally Handicapped People
8   Our Lives – mentally handicapped people's comments on the quality of their lives.
9   Reducing Handicaps – through teaching new skills and helping children and families 'at risk'
10 Preventing Mental Handicap from causes known to damage the developing child
11 Community Attitudes to Mental Handicap
    © Health Education Bureau and St Michael's House Research, 1982

Copies of the complete Fact Sheets can be purchased from St Michael's House, Upper Kilmacud Road, Stillorgan, Co. Dublin, Ireland.

What is
Mental Handicap

Mentally handicapped people are those who have
1 **Low scores on tests of intelligence** – scores on these tests are reported in terms of intelligence quotients (IQ). Average people have scores between 85 and 115. More intelligent people will score higher; for example two people in every 100 will have IQs over 130. Likewise, some people score low. If their IQ falls below 70, they may be considered mentally handicapped.

However these tests are not always reliable. Different IQs can result from different types of tests; from different people giving the test and from the mood of the person on the day they were tested. Hence IQ scores are best given as a range rather than a single figure, eg IQ is between 65 and 75. Also IQ scores do change over time; people may score markedly higher or lower when tested one year later. Thus these tests are not a foolproof way of identifying mentally handicapped people. Nevertheless, they are the most commonly used way, especially in childhood.

2 **Poor social competence** – they are unable to look after their everyday needs such as preparing food for themselves, keeping house, looking after their clothes, shopping or working and so on. They need other people to look after their basic needs and to protect them from common dangers.

A person's social competence can be assessed using special rating scales. However, these scales only reflect present performance; they cannot predict the person's *ability to learn*. Some people score low because their parents do everything for them and never give them a chance of learning to look after themselves. But given the opportunity, they may quickly learn. Indeed, nearly all mentally handicapped people can be successfully taught social skills to some degree. Hence social competence is a reflection of learning opportunities as well as of abilities.

Both conditions – low IQ *and* poor social competence, have to be fulfilled before a person is considered mentally handicapped. If a person scores below 70 on an intelligence test and yet is capable of looking after herself and her family, then she is *not* mentally handicapped. Equally, some people (elderly, physically handicapped and mentally ill) are unable to look after themselves yet they are intellectually normal. They too are *not* mentally handicapped. But sometimes such people are wrongly classed as mentally handicapped.

No clear-cut division – exists between normal people and mentally handicapped people. Children may be classed as mentally handicapped but once they leave school, get a job and start their own home, it is obvious that they are no longer handicapped. Their handicap was only apparent in educational subjects such as reading and number work.

Mentally handicapped people can look normal – unlike physical disabilities, a mentally handicapped person can look perfectly normal. The definitions given earlier said nothing about appearance, only abilities. Some mentally handicapped people do look different but this is because their whole body is affected, as in Down's Syndrome (mongolism). Past experience has shown that such people *usually* are mentally handicapped. However there are some Down's Syndrome people who learn to look after themselves and who score close to the average range on intelligence tests. Hence they are no longer mentally handicapped, even though they still have Down's Syndrome.

Mental handicap is NOT a physical condition – as would be the case with deafness, and although it can be associated with some abnormality of brain or body this need not be so. Rather mental handicap is descriptive of a person's abilities and capacity to learn. But mentally handicapped people can learn, although it takes them longer than it does a normal person. If they master the basic skills of living, albeit at 20 or 30 years of age instead of 15 years, then they are no longer handicapped.

Degrees of handicap: Some people can be more handicapped than others. In Ireland, three main subdivisions are now used –

Mild mental handicap: there is usually nothing physically wrong with these people. Their handicap is most apparent during schooling and they attend special schools or special classes but the majority end up working in ordinary jobs. However these people are not handicapped in the usual sense of the word and in other countries they are referred to as slow learners or educationally retarded.

Moderate mental handicap: This group usually has some identifiable physical abnormality, such as Down's Syndrome or brain damage. They attend special National schools and the majority go on to work in sheltered workshops or training centres. Only a small proportion at present find ordinary jobs.

Severe mental handicap: As the name suggests, these people are much less able to look after themselves and frequently they have additional handicaps. Children ascertained as severely mentally handicapped are not allowed to attend schools. Instead they may go to special care units where they are looked after by nursing or other staff.

Finally, some people are referred to as *profoundly* mentally handicapped. These are the least able and invariably have other pronounced handicaps – deformities of legs and arms, deafness, blindness or epilepsy. Frequently these people will be in residential care although a proportion are cared for at home by their families.

No clear-cut divisions: These categories should be thought of as rough divisions. There are no accurate and reliable ways of allocating people to one group or the other. Indeed, if anything, these divisions should not refer to people but rather should describe the type of services available, so that individuals can receive the services best suited to their needs. For every one person considered to be profoundly mentally handicapped, there are five severely mentally handicapped, twenty moderately mentally handicapped and one hundred mildly mentally handicapped.

Helping
Mentally Handicapped People

● There are very many ways of helping. But you need to get to know someone before you can start. Perhaps there is a mentally handicapped person living in your neighbourhood whom you meet in the local shop or at the bus-stop? Have a chat with them. Everyone likes having *friendly neighbours*.

● If the mentally handicapped person is about your own age or a little older, they might like the chance to join in on what you're doing (see the suggestions under *Leisure Activities* below).

● When parents have a young handicapped child, they often don't get much opportunity to go out. An offer to *baby-sit* might be appreciated, especially if you've got to know the child and the family.

There are also a small number of severely handicapped adults who can't be left alone in the house. You might offer to look after them, to give the parents a break.

● You might decide to call to a local *mental handicap centre*. It is a good idea to start by 'phoning, saying you'd like to drop down, and asking them to suggest a good time to call. (You might already know someone who works there). When you call, don't just look around; do try to meet and to talk to the trainees or adults who work there. You might join in on something they're doing. If you feel a little awkward at first, don't worry. Once you get to know some *people*, you will begin to feel at home. It helps if you remember *first names* – and don't forget to give your own.

Clubs and Organizations

Many local centres run some kind of a *club* or occasional *disco* for those attending. You might like to help out. Remember that you can often help most by just joining in and enjoying yourself.

Also, the local workshop or care centre may organize a *summer camp* or weekend away. They are usually grateful for extra help at that time. It is an opportunity to get to know handicapped people very well while doing some hard work!

There are often difficulties in getting from home to the club – an offer of *transport* is always appreciated, especially if there isn't a direct bus service, or if it involves travelling late at night.

Many mentally handicapped adults, living at home, spend their evenings passively watching television. Their friends in the workshop may not live nearby. And so some mental handicap services encourage older volunteers (18+ age groups) to befriend a mentally handicapped person who needs to be encouraged to get involved in ordinary activities. The Friendship Scheme in Dublin is one example of this.

There are a number of organisations which you can join. The *ARCH clubs* in Dublin, Cork, Drogheda and Dundalk organize leisure-time activities for mentally handicapped children and adults. Some mental handicap services have set up their own *Volunteer Corps* (eg St Michael's House in Dublin) which give some basic training in how to help, arranging specific work-tasks, as well as giving the volunteers a chance to get to know each other. The corps is usually run by a committee chosen by the volunteers themselves. The *VSI* also help run holidays for handicapped and disadvantaged people.

Leisure Activities

There are many *ordinary activities* which mentally handicapped people enjoy. These include going to a football match, going swimming, going into town, going to a roller-disco or film; even just calling into someone else's house can be enjoyable.

These, and many others, are activities that any individual can decide to try on their own, or they may be part of a scheme, organized by the local service.

A class or group of students might decide to undertake a *project* that involves either mentally handicapped children or adults. The local children's care unit or pre-school would certainly appreciate some equipment. If you can saw plywood and use a paint-brush, then there are lots of ideas for you in *Lets Make Toys* – a handbook that tells you exactly what to do. The staff in a local centre may have other suggestions also.

Does your class or school organize a *disco* at the end of term? Perhaps you could invite trainees along from the local training centre or workshop. There may be other activities which you organize as a class where trainees could also participate.

Finally, there are ways in which a family can help. **Being neighbourly** is important. It's nice to feel welcome in a neighbour's house – whether you are handicapped or not. **Baby-sitting** was mentioned earlier – parents of a handicapped child need a break now and again; why not have the handicapped child come down to your house while the parents are out? Indeed, some parents will have got out of the habit of going out, and may need some encouragement to do so!

Most of us like a holiday some time. **Break Away** is a scheme which gives parents of the more handicapped child a holiday break, while another family minds their handicapped child. The social worker at the local mental handicap service will have the details. It sometimes happens that the parents of a newly-born handicapped child are unable to keep the child. In such cases, it is much better for the child to grow up in another family (a foster family), than be institutionalized. Arrangements for *fostering* are usually made through the local social worker.

Our Lives

Are mentally handicapped people happy with their way of life? The committee for the International Year of Disabled People sponsored a survey of mentally handicapped adults in Dublin to get their views.

Fifty-four people were interviewed, nearly all in workshops or a training centre. The workshops are involved in simple assembly-type work, eg assembling window-cleaners and ear-phones, putting mail in envelopes, re-labelling music tapes, sewing and weaving, and making pottery in moulds. No single workshop does all these tasks, however. The training centre offers instruction in basic work-skills.

More than half of those interviewed live in hostels in different parts of the city. Those who took part were 17 years of age or older, and there was an equal number of men and women.

This Fact Sheet presents some of their comments on their present life-style – their work and leisure activities, their friendships and relationships with others. It also highlights some of the frustrations of being handicapped.

Work

People call it work, but I would classify it as occupational therapy.

I love it. I like all the staff. I'm quite happy.

I just feel as if we were left out; I feel we are not noticed here.

I'd like to see more pottery – different designs, not all the same; different colours.

I think it's a good idea to learn (sewing) now; it saves an awful lot of money on your clothes, 'cause clothes are really dear now.

Coming in here hurts – I don't know what it is, the work, the fellas I work with, or what.

I like it. I think they are doing a great job.

I have an ambition to become the head of this place. . . see what it is like to actually run a workshop; do things (the manager) does from day to day, and see what it's like.

I used to want to be a guard or a barber. . . but I just grew up and forgot about it.

Other Jobs

I'd like to have outside work and more money. I'd like a bigger variety of work. It can become boring – it's the same in the outside world, but there you always have a choice.

I'd like to work in a hotel, in catering or a kitchen porter or a hall porter – something in that line. It's very interesting bringing cases into places.

I was in outside employment for a while. I didn't really like it. I felt some people did not know what I was. . . If they knew I was 'mildly'. they would not have touched me at all – I don't think they realized it at all. In my last job, people realized it and thought I was a human being like they were, and they weren't doing anything stupid and ridiculous.

Outside employment is a challenge – it's very important to me, very important. It gives me a sense of responsibility for myself and the people around.

Friendships and Relationships

THE FRUSTRATIONS OF BEING HANDICAPPED

I had friends when I was small, friends down the road. They are grown up, now, they are working.

If they are playing games, they say 'no' and I go in the next block. . . and I say 'play with me' – 'no', they say 'no'; I get sad and then it gets dark and I say 'play with me' and they say 'no'.

My schoolfriends are all married. . . they have families and are gone out of my life.

I love my mum. . . Sometimes I hate the rest. . . the rest always go out for drinks and dances (sigh), I hate the rest.

I would like to have friends. My mammy wouldn't like friends coming in all the time.

I have loads of friends. I wish I could get to know a lot more people.

I never get lonely. I used to when I came here first. I think it was because I hadn't much friends – I didn't know them. I said what's the use of worrying and sitting inside.

Ah no, I've no friends at home – no way – I stay in the house every night.

SOMEONE SPECIAL

I need a friendship; I wish I had a companion, a boy I could have as a companion, that I could go out with and chat to. I have nobody and it hurts me.

I'd like someone to go around with, like girls in the club. They have their own friends and they go around with each other.

CLUBS

I like the club the way it is. It has billiard tables and records and reading and all.

I'd go to dances but I've such a long way to come, it would be half-eleven again I got home.

Well, I'd go to (the club) but I felt it wasn't worth it. . . they hadn't got the games that I like. . . they had only Ludo, Snakes and Ladders, and it wasn't up to my taste.

They are good in a sense and very boring in another; you might get the same record over and over again.

The club I'm in has very good facilities.

It's always the same face, like only having one last snap in the camera. . . you keep looking at that one and you can remember all the other times in the past you have done this.

Hostel Life

I don't call it a hostel, I call it a house really, because it's more homely than a hostel.

It's good living in a hostel. It's the same as if you were living with your own family. You just get along with one another, or fight like cats and dogs – we have our ups and downs like everybody else.

I'm not keen on (the hostel). They have everything set up for you. . . you are going here this day, and there the next day. . . Nobody is trying to force you, but mentally they are doing it, not physically.

I'd like to see the whole place (a hostel) with less doors because I think there's far too many doors in the house completely.

I like quietness. (The hostel) is too noisy. They are always making noise with the records and radio. They leave it on.

Two of my friends are coming here (the hostel) tomorrow for dinner and then there's another one coming down at half-seven.

There's too much messing every weekend. When a few of them gets up, they start fighting and I'm just sick and tired of seeing them, and I'm trying my best to stop everyone from fighting.

Sometimes my girlfriend comes over to the house.

Everyone should have a mirror in their bedroom and a few shelves.

Being Handicapped

When I go to the shop for the paper, small children – they kind of look at me.

I'm a bit backward and I take my time doing work.

Sometimes I say "group home" . . .sometimes they might say "Oh you are living in a hostel" and they just take it for granted. I think some people find it upsetting.

I do half it; then I have a brother and he knows, he's quicker; he'd have it done by the time you'd start yourself.

I wish I could play the piano and do the delph myself.

My intelligence was not high enough to get into AnCO.

I can read and write and all.

I'd like to bring hope to my mother.

● *I'd like to go home and let everything start all over again. Start my life all over again.*

(*All quotations are from Our Lives* by Francesca Lundström-Roche, International Year Committee, July 1981)

Discussion Leaflets
As the name suggests, the main purpose of these leaflets is to provoke discussion. Of the examples included here, one has been taken from a magazine, the other is a compilation of newspaper and magazine cuttings.

'If monkeys did the same work there would be a national outcry'

Peter Beresford and Patience Tuckwell examine the work done in Adult Workshops in Britain, following a critical ITV 'World in Action' Programme: 'Working for a Pittance'.

ANYONE WHO has ever visited an adult training centre and hopefully, that includes all directors of social services, knows the accuracy of the picture of menial work and appalling pay in most of them painted by Granada TV's *World in Action* "Working for a pittance" on February 20 recently. What seems to have caused the controversy is that whereas those responsible for ATCs and other sheltered workshops have grown accustomed to judging them by the comfortable and complacent criteria of charity and paternalistic welfare, *World in Action* used the more appropriate standards of the shop floor.

World in Action documented a depressing catalogue of conditions. It showed mentally handicapped workers paid £2 and £3 and sometimes less for a 27 or 30 hour working week. This is a world where snapping wheels on to toy tractors all day is described as "of great therapeutic value" and where trainees have to sift one by one through a mountain of drawing pins to check each tip. If monkeys were made to do the same work, there would be a national outcry. We saw British Airways try to hide the fact that gift sets for Concorde passengers were packed in a sheltered workshop, feeling it was "inappropriate to link Concorde with disabled people".

Nine out of 10 ATCs rely on such contract work – contracts from local companies, large household names, nationalised industries and the local authorities themselves. The British Airways representative spoke for all of them when he said, "we're not a charity, we're a business". Contractors save on pensions, national insurance, welfare and redundancy payments, heating, lighting and the rest. They use ATCs against homeworkers, other sheltered workshops in prisons and elsewhere and against each other, knowing their dependence on their contracts.

Doing them a favour

Beneath the present complacency about ATCs, there seems to be more than a hint of a smug assumption that we are really doing the mentally handicapped a favour by providing ATCs at all. With ATCs we give them self-respect. If it wasn't for ATCs they would either be sitting at home vegetating or have to be in a subnormality hospital. Putting to one side for the moment the fact that this kind of negative approach to social policy would have us still thanking God for the workhouse, it is a gross misrepresentation of the capabilities of mentally handicapped people. They are a hetrogeneous group with a wide range of aptitudes and abilities. The tradition of low expectations of the mentally handicapped arises from the unstimulating regimes of the old subnormality hospitals, rather than from any inherent incapacity of their own.

Ability to work well

One thing that is beyond dispute is their ability to work and to work well. They may be slower than some other workers, but they still get the job done, as is amply testified by the continued interest of eminently unsentimental contractors. As for ATCs offering the mentally handicapped an alternative to hospital, at least two school leavers we knew were considered unsuitable by ATCs and ended up in subnormality hospitals, not least because it was the demands of the contract rather than the needs of the mentally handicapped that took precedence. Another girl was considered "too wilful" for the dreary routine.

May I speak?

While *World in Action* asked other handicapped workers their opinions, it seemed to feel that the mentally handicapped could not speak for themselves. A pity, because given the chance they can, and they would have added weight to the programme's arguments. This is what some recent school-leavers said to us about being in an ATC:

- "It's boring."
- "You get told off if you can't work fast enough."
- "I hate it. I work all day with old men, sorting screws."

Workers exploited?

Those who say ATCs give the mentally handicapped a chance to work like other people, deny the fact that they bear little relation to outside employment, not least because of their token wages. Mentally handicapped people are not unaware of this, like the boy we knew who had looked forward to the day when he left school and would be a working man like his brother but who quickly realised that working and the ATC were not the same thing, both from the way he was treated and when he had not the money to buy clothes or go out like others of his age.

Intentionally or otherwise, ATCs exploit their workers. Few authorities even pay the maximum £4 a week. In one we know, trainees got docked for "cheek" and "laziness" as well as for poor work. Some pay some trainees as little as 50p a week. In Oxfordshire, for example, in 1975 when the wage limit was raised from £2 to £4, the social services committee recommended that the council keep the £2 limit and its advice was taken, although one Oxfordshire unit alone had made a £13,000 profit that year. The argument was that the profits were ploughed back into the service.

THE SCANDAL OF ADULT TRAINING CENTRES

Many ATCs do try to continue the education of their workers. They may have a trained teacher on the staff whose job it is to help those who might be able to learn to read and write, to recognise a few key words, to improve their manners, dress sense and understanding of hygiene and so on. But all this is of secondary importance. ATCs' two aims, of work and education, are often incompatible. Their dependence on outside contracts dictates this.

Treated as children

This social education is also made an excuse for the appalling rates of pay. But what other apprentices or trainees in Britain are expected to work the hours they do for a maximum of £4 a week? It is another of the ways in which mentally handicapped people are still treated as children. If it were really training, one might expect that they would be getting student grants or something similar which would expire when their period of training ended and they got jobs on the open market. The pitiful pay is also excused on the grounds that they are receiving social security or other benefits anyway. This is no excuse for contractors to pay them a pittance. If they are working they should receive the proper rate for the job like other employees, instead of having to depend so much on state benefits. Given the chance, it is difficult to believe they would not opt for a fair wage instead of benefits, or at least more earnings and less benefits.

For the most part ATCs do not offer training in any real sense. If they are to be called *training* centres, then they must provide proper work training that equips people for outside employment and offers them a real chance of getting it. Training should be for a specific time and with specific aims, or else it should not be called training.

Training?

It is difficult to see how the kind of low-grade contract work in most ATCs can be described as training. It would be hard to think of anything less suitable for a group like the mentally handicapped, whose development is likely to be slower and to continue longer than that of the rest of us and who have a particular need for stimulation.

Only a very small number of "trainees" ever go on to outside employment from ATCs. Most are there for life. It is hardly surprising they do not get work. What employer is likely to see this kind of "training" as any kind of qualification?

Community Care (Supplement) 2nd August, 1978, pp 20–21

You, the Jury, ...

If a newly-born *severely* handicapped infant needs an operation to maintain life, then the parents and doctors are faced with a difficult decision.
Recently, Public Bodies and the Courts have also become involved in making the final decision.
Consider this recent Court Case and, acting as the Jury, give *your* verdict.

The Background

THE RECENT COURT CASE in England involving the decision by the Appeal Court to overrule the wishes of the parents of *a baby with Down's Syndrome* and order an operation.
In brief, the baby was *born with an intestinal obstruction* which was incompatible with life. *The parents* wished to let the baby die. *Hammersmith Council* wanted the operation to take place and after the rescinding of a wardship order in favour of Hammersmith Council the operation took place and was successful.
   The publicity given to this situation might suggest that we are dealing with a rare phenomenon. In fact, the problem involved in such decision taking is a very common one both for parents and doctors.

The Facts
   These extracts are by courtesy of Sunday Times Ltd. and written by Marjorie Wallace and Linda Melvern and published August 16th.
The battle over Alexandra's life began on July 28th, the day she was born at Queen Charlotte's Hospital, London.

Day One, Dr. R. Dinwiddie, paediatric consultant, informed Alexandra's parents that their baby was doubly handicapped with a blockage of the duodenum which meant that without an operation she would soon die. She also had Down's Syndrome. The parents refused consent for the operation which would save baby's life.
Day two: Dr Dinwiddie discussed same with the social worker.
Day three: After meetings with the doctor and social workers the parents still refused their consent. The Ast. Dir. of Social Services Richard Jeffries and his team from Hammersmith local council referred the decision to their director David Plank (wife works for Campaign for the Mentally Handicapped). Unanimous advice that baby's life should be saved.
Day four. Hammersmith made Alexandra a Ward of Court, and Plank signed the consent form for the life-saving operation.
Alexandra transferred to Great Ormond St. Children's Hospital, but doctors refused to operate against parents' decision.

Day eight: David Plank hears this and acts.

Day nine: Hammersmith applied to High Court for a judge to authorise the operation. Justice Ewbank hears representation from both sides and rescinds the wardship order and Alexandra is back in the hands of the parents. That afternoon Hammersmith appeals against morning's judgement and wins. The wardship order was reinstated and Alexandra is once again under the legal control of Hammersmith.

Day twelve: the operation takes place and to date the baby is progressing well.

The Issues

The rights of the child in question; wishes of parents or others; the impaired quality of life for the handicapped; legal aspects; judicial opinion.

The operation was to remove a suspected duodenal obstruction. Without the operation the child would have died within a week.

The baby's parents had decided to let the child die.

Different Views

THE PARENTS

It had been argued for the parents that nature had made its own arrangements to terminate a life which could not be fruitful, and that the parents' decision to let the child die should be respected. It is *always* a great shock for parents to find their child is severely handicapped. What they expect to be a very happy occasion has suddenly become heart-breaking. Their decision at this moment is extremely difficult, and they will often ask the doctor to advise them.

THE DOCTORS

The doctor said that mongol foetuses were routinely aborted when spotted before birth, adding that natural abortions very often took place in such cases.

One leading doctor said that 'high-grade' mongols – amounting to about a quarter of the category – could often do useful work of a simple repetitive nature.

"It was a medical decision made in the utmost good faith and it was totally provisional and dependent on the parents still retaining their express wish that the baby should not survive".

The first defence witness was Professor Alexander Campbell, head of the child health department at Aberdeen University and a fellow of the Royal College of Physicians. He said the vast majority of paediatricians did not believe or accept that the responsibility to preserve life was absolute.

"There must be occasions, rare but in the world of paediatricians relatively common, when in consultation with the parents it seems prudent, thinking of the future of the infant and the family, to allow the baby to die."

THE COUNCIL

A report that caring for the child until the age of eighteen would cost Hammersmith Council £100,000.

The Council decided it would take care of the infant and applied to the Courts for control of the child.

The High Court decided in favour of the parents, and Hammersmith Council took the case to the Appeal Court.

THE COURT

In the Appeal Court judgement Lord Justice Templeman said that if the operation was a success the baby's life expectancy would be twenty to thirty years, and the court had to decide whether her life would be so awful that she must be condemned to die.

He added: "The choice before the court is this: whether to allow the operation to take place, which may result in the child living for 20 to 30 years as a mongol. or whether to terminate the life because she is mongol with an intestinal complaint.

YOUR DECISION ? ....

THE DECISION OF THE HIGH COURT

The original decision of the parents to refuse permission for the operation was supported by a High Court judge, but Hammersmith Council referred the case to the Appeal Court.

THE DECISION OF THE APPEAL COURT:

'Faced with that choice, I have no doubt that it is the duty of this court to decide that the child must live. It is not for the court to say that a life of that description ought to be extinguished.'

The judge said there might be a case where the child was likely to be in pain so that the court would be driven to a different conclusion, but in this case the child should live.

THE RESULT

Doctors successfully operated at the weekend on the two-week-old mongol baby girl who was last week at the centre of a legal battle concerning whether or not she should be allowed to live.

The child is now a ward of court, with Hammersmith Borough holding parental rights.

Last night the parents, who live in Cheshire but have not been publicly named, said they still felt the child should have been allowed to die. They said they felt they had made the right choice and they still wanted her to die. They would not say whether they wanted to have the child back.

Extracts from *Irish Times*

Questionnaires

Two sample questionnaires are included. The first is a general purpose one which can be used in surveys of people's knowledge of, and attitudes to, mentally handicapped adults. It can also be used to monitor changes in their opinions resulting from educational programmes.

This questionnaire can be used as it stands, if your interest is in mental handicap. For other disabilities it will need minor adjustments, eg changing the term 'mental handicap', and for some questions, changing the alternative answers listed.

Of course, you can easily delete questions or add others which are more relevant to your needs.

The second questionnaire, is a simple way of ascertaining participants' reactions to your course on disability.

Guidance on the use and analysis of questionnaires is given in Chapter 10.

cara

THANK YOU FOR AGREEING TO FILL IN THIS QUESTIONNAIRE
DO NOT SPEND TOO MUCH TIME OVER EACH QUESTION
WE ARE MAINLY INTERESTED IN YOUR FIRST REACTION
PLEASE ANSWER EVERY QUESTION AS YOU COME TO IT

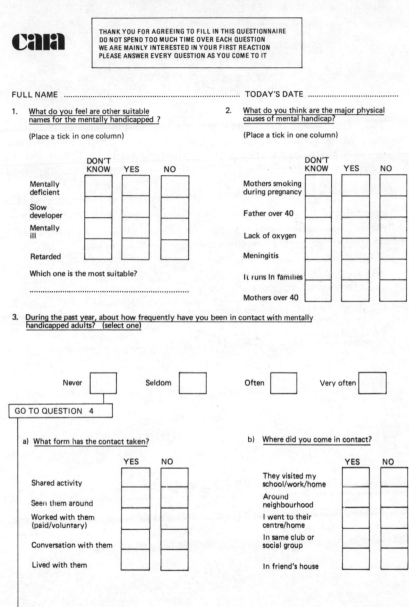

FULL NAME .... TODAY'S DATE ....

1. What do you feel are other suitable names for the mentally handicapped ?

   (Place a tick in one column)

	DON'T KNOW	YES	NO
Mentally deficient			
Slow developer			
Mentally ill			
Retarded			

   Which one is the most suitable?

   ....

2. What do you think are the major physical causes of mental handicap?

   (Place a tick in one column)

	DON'T KNOW	YES	NO
Mothers smoking during pregnancy			
Father over 40			
Lack of oxygen			
Meningitis			
It runs in families			
Mothers over 40			

3. During the past year, about how frequently have you been in contact with mentally handicapped adults? (select one)

   Never [ ]   Seldom [ ]   Often [ ]   Very often [ ]

   GO TO QUESTION 4

   a) What form has the contact taken?

	YES	NO
Shared activity		
Seen them around		
Worked with them (paid/voluntary)		
Conversation with them		
Lived with them		

   b) Where did you come in contact?

	YES	NO
They visited my school/work/home		
Around neighbourhood		
I went to their centre/home		
In same club or social group		
In friend's house		

On the following page you will come across a layout like this.

                                    AGREE   DISAGREE
"are always happy"   [✔] [ ] [ ] [ ] [ ] [ ] [ ]

If you <u>agree very strongly</u> with the sentence, place a tick in the first space beside the sentence, as above —

[ ] [ ] [ ] [ ] [ ] [ ] [✔]

If you <u>do not agree at all</u> with the sentence, place a tick in the very last space, as above —

[ ] [ ] [✔] [ ] [ ] [ ] [ ]

If your feelings are <u>in between</u> use the other spaces, as above

4. DO YOU AGREE OR DISAGREE WITH THESE STATEMENTS?

    The mentally handicapped adults whom I have come across . . .

                                    AGREE   DISAGREE

    are always happy . . . .   [ ] [ ] [ ] [ ] [ ] [ ] [ ]

    have problems in
    talking clearly . . . . . . [ ] [ ] [ ] [ ] [ ] [ ] [ ]

    are unfriendly . . . . . . [ ] [ ] [ ] [ ] [ ] [ ] [ ]

    always need to
    be supervised . . . . . . [ ] [ ] [ ] [ ] [ ] [ ] [ ]

    can be violent . . . . . . [ ] [ ] [ ] [ ] [ ] [ ] [ ]

    have physical
    deformities . . . . . .   [ ] [ ] [ ] [ ] [ ] [ ] [ ]

    are lonely
    and isolated . . . . [ ] [ ] [ ] [ ] [ ] [ ] [ ]

    will always be
    like children . . . . . . [ ] [ ] [ ] [ ] [ ] [ ] [ ]

5. <u>If a MENTALLY HANDICAPPED PERSON of my own age, whom I had never met before visited my house
    tomorrow, I would . . .</u>

                                    YES Definitely . . . . not at all: NO

    know what to say . . . .   [ ] [ ] [ ] [ ] [ ] [ ] [ ]

    feel embarrassed . . . . [ ] [ ] [ ] [ ] [ ] [ ] [ ]

    find it a good experience . . . . . . [ ] [ ] [ ] [ ] [ ] [ ] [ ]

    <u>If a STRANGER of my own age visited my house tomorrow, I would</u>

    know what to say . . . .   [ ] [ ] [ ] [ ] [ ] [ ] [ ]

    feel embarrassed . . . . [ ] [ ] [ ] [ ] [ ] [ ] [ ]

    find it a good experience . . . . . . [ ] [ ] [ ] [ ] [ ] [ ] [ ]

6. In daily life we are often forced to meet people. How would you feel if a mentally handicapped adult . . .

	I'd encourage it	It would be o.k.	Unsure	I prefer they didn't	I wouldn't allow it
. . . talked to you in the street					
. . . sat beside you on a bus/train/café					
. . . moved into the house beside yours					
. . . wanted to become your friend					
. . . wanted to live in the same house as you					

7. What information would you like to have on mental handicap?

(Place a tick in one column)

	VERY MUCH	MAYBE	NO
What causes it			
The problems they and their families have			
What mental handicap means			
How to act with a mentally handicapped person			
Voluntary work I could do			

8. How would you like to help mentally handicapped people?

(Place a tick in one column)

	VERY MUCH	MAYBE	NO
Give money on flag days			
Do jobs for them			
Help to raise money for them			
Take them on outings			
Work in services for mentally handicapped people			

9. Could you please give us the following information about yourself? —

SEX: Male [ ]   Female [ ]   ARE YOU: Single [ ]   Married [ ]

AGE: Under 15 [ ]   15-24 [ ]   25-34 [ ]   35-54 [ ]   55+ [ ]

Thank you very much for completing this questionnaire

We would like to have your reactions to our course on disability. This information will enable us to improve the course for others. Thank you for your help.

WHAT DO YOU FEEL YOU GOT OUT OF TAKING THE COURSE?

WHAT ASPECTS OF THE COURSE DID YOU LIKE BEST?

WERE THERE ANY PARTS YOU DID NOT ENJOY OR YOU FELT COULD BE IMPROVED?

ANY SUGGESTIONS FOR IMPROVEMENTS

ANY OTHER COMMENTS?

2 INFORMATION

In the following pages we have listed useful resource material which you might include in your educational packages on disability, or sources which will provide you with background information when compiling your programmes. We have grouped these into three main sections dealing with audio-visual materials, books, journals and magazines, but we begin with directories which you should find particularly helpful.

Directories
Health Education Index (1980) published by B. Edsall and Co. Ltd., 6 Eccles Square, London SW1V 1PF (New edition expected in 1983). Over 9,000 aids to health education are listed in the directory: titles of books, leaflets, films, slides, posters, video-cassettes – along with addresses of suppliers. The materials are grouped by disabilities.

Information published 6 times a year, this journal lists newly published books, teaching and learning materials, films, posters etc. for use in health and medical education. It is obtainable on subscription from BLAT Centre, BMA House, Tavistock Square, London WC1H 9JP.

Directory for the Disabled, compiled by Ann Darnborough and Derek Kinrade, published by Woodhead-Faulkner in association with RADAR, (3rd edition, 1981).
Although aimed at disabled people themselves, it contains a wealth of information for the community educator to draw upon; highly recommended.

Yearbook of Adult Education published by National Institute of Adult Education, 193 deMontfort Street, Leicester, LE1 7GE.

National Directory of Adult and Community Education Agencies, published by AONTAS, National Association of Adult Education, 14 Fitzwilliam Place, Dublin 2.
Both these directories list possible contexts in which courses on disability could be included.

Willing's Press Guide (1982) published by Thomas Skinner Directories, Windsor Court, East Grinstead House, East Grinstead, West Sussex, RH19 1XE (most libraries have a copy).
A guide to the newspapers and periodicals of the United Kingdom and the principle publications of Europe, USA and

Australia. Useful for advertising, press releases or finding a source for publications about disability.

Audio-Visual Material

(a) *Organisations hiring or selling films, videos and slide/tape programmes.*
Most of these organisations will send you their catalogues on request. However, it is worth mentioning your interest in disability and asking them for specific information about suitable materials.

Recommended

Concord Films Council Ltd, 201 Felixstowe Road, Ipswich, Suffolk IP3 9BJ (Irish agents: Glencree Film Library, 1 Belgrave Square, Dublin 6). They have over 100 films dealing with physical and mental disabilities and will send you a free brochure giving brief details of each one. Many are now available as video-cassettes.

BBC Enterprises, Film Hire, Woodston House, Oundle Road, Peterborough PR2 9PZ.
Purchases + Catalogue: Room 503 Villiers House, The Broadway, London, W5 2PA.
They have a growing collection of programmes dealing with disability, all available on video-cassettes. These have all been broadcast on BBC Television.

Graves Medical Audiovisual Library, Holly House, P.O. Box 99, 220 New London Road, Chelmsford, Essex CM2 9BJ.
They have a large stock of slide/tape programmes available for hire.

Mental Health Film Council, 22 Harley Street, London W1N 2ED
Their catalogue is an excellent compilation of films and videos on autism, mental handicap and mental illness.

OTHER SOURCES
Camera Talks, 31 North Row, Park Lane, London W1. (Slide-tape productions)
Central Film Library, Government Building, Bromyard Avenue, Acton, London W3.
Darvill Associates, 280 Chartridge Lane, Chesham, Bucks. HP5 2SG.
Granada Television, Film Library, Manchester M3.
Guild Sound and Vision Ltd, Woodston House, Oundle Road, Peterborough PE2 9PZ.
Irish Film Institute, 65 Harcourt Street, Dublin 2, Ireland.
National Audio-visual Aids Library, Paxton Place, Gipsy Road, London SE27 9SS.

Scottish Central Film Library, Gowanhill, 74 Victoria Crescent Road, Glasgow G12 8JN.

Town and Country Productions Ltd., 21 Cheyne Row, Chelsea, London SW3 5HP.

Welsh Office Film Library, Oxford House, Hill St., Cardiff CF1 2XG.

In addition associations and organisations concerned with various disabilities (see p246) have their own collections of films and programmes some of which will be available for hire.

(b) *Film and video-programmes*

Recommended

James is our Brother (25 mins., colour: BBC Enterprises)
An award-winning film of a sixteen year-old Down's Syndrome man in a large supportive family. The film ends with an up-date on his life, five years later.

Joey (70 mins., colour, BBC Enterprises)
Based on the extraordinary autobiography of Joey Deacon, who was born in 1920 with brain damage, grew up severely spastic, unable to walk and talk, but with the help of two handicapped friends wrote his life story in the book *Tongue Tied*, which was published in 1974.

Transitions (30 mins., colour, Concord)
Shows how three young adults, two physically handicapped and one mentally handicapped, work towards living independently. An American production.

A Different Approach (27 mins., colour, Concord)
A humorous and highly effective look at employers' prejudices against disabled workers.

How to Survive in an Occupied Country (30 mins., colour, Concord)
Focusses on mentally handicapped people working in open employment and living in the community.

We're Outsiders Now (26 mins., colour, Concord)
Four mentally handicapped adults leave an institution to live in an ordinary housing estate. This film shows them organising the house, getting to know the neighbours and trying to get a job.

The Right to Work (25 mins., colour, Concord)
Produced by the Spastics Society, this film illustrates the practical difficulties encountered by physically handicapped people, both in securing employment and obtaining suitable working conditions.

Not Just a Spectator (35 mins., colour, Town & Country)
Illustrates a wide range of physical activities which disabled

people can and do participate in, including basketball, climbing and canoeing.

Like Other People (37 mins., colour, Concord)
The story of two severely disabled spastic people living in a residential centre who want to establish for themselves a normal life. More suitable for adult audiences.

A Hidden World (21 mins., National Audio-Visual Aids Library)
A description of various physical disabilities with scenes of children and young adults working to overcome their handicaps.

The Rubella Problem (20 mins., Colour, Irish Film Institute)
An Irish film on the need for teenage girls to be vaccinated against German measles, in order to prevent the birth of deaf, blind and mentally handicapped babies.

Deaf in a Hearing World (25 mins., colour, Guild Audio-Visual)
Eight adults who are hard of hearing perform four role-plays about various relationship problems encountered by deaf people. A useful introduction to improvisation techniques.

Out of Mind (30 mins., colour, Granada)
Shows the efforts which are being made to find homes for people living in mental hospitals but who do not need to be there. Focusses on the lives and hopes of a few typical patients.

It All Depends On You (30 mins., colour, MS Society of Ireland)
Introduces multiple sclerosis and its effects on people's life-styles. It stresses that people do learn to cope. A good positive introduction to this disability. The film was made in Ireland.

Breaking Ice (50 mins., black and white, Darvill)
An account of mentally handicapped adults living independently in flats and apartments in Sweden. Much of the commentary is by a handicapped woman with a speech defect and so the sub-titles are a bonus.

Day in the Death of Joe Egg (25 mins., colour, Guild Audio-Visual)
An Open University production of scenes from Peter Nichol's play in which actors role-play the situations faced by parents of a handicapped child. Excellent trigger material for discussion on parents' feelings.

They Can All Work (28 mins, colour, Concord)
A Canadian film about mentally and physically handicapped people employed in a factory where they are treated as any other workers.

Ready, Willing and Disabled (25 mins., colour, Granada)
A report from the '*World in Action*' series on the employment prospects of disabled people.

The Swedish Fokus (25 mins., colour, Guild Audio-Visual)

Specially designed apartments in Sweden for handicapped people are featured, illustrating the freedom which residents enjoy there. An Open University production which should stimulate debate.

(c) *Broadcast programmes*
Another source of video-material is off-the-air recordings of programmes broadcast on national television. Unfortunately you do not get much advance notice of when these programmes will appear and frequently you cannot purchase copies of them from the broadcast organisations. However, we mention one programme which is broadcast regularly on British Television and the names of several programmes which we have found particularly useful, in the hope that you might be able to track down a copy through friends, etc., or that they will be re-shown.

Link (Produced by Central Television, and networked by Independent Television. Usually broadcast on Sundays)
  A magazine programme aimed at disabled people but carrying many informative items which could be incorporated into community education programmes. (A similar programme, *Does He Take Sugar?*, is broadcast on BBC Radio 4).
Donal and Sally (BBC 'Play for Today', First broadcast 1979)
  The story of two Scottish teenagers attending a Training Centre for the mentally handicapped, who develop a close friendship, and the concern of the staff and parents that they might have intercourse. (Now available from Concord Films Council.)
John David (BBC 'Play for Today', First broadcast 1982)
  A mother and father's reaction to the birth of a Down's Syndrome baby.
Walter (Channel 4, First broadcast 1982)
  The story of a mentally handicapped man and his family, told at two points in his life: when he is in his twenties and then in his fifties.
Best Boy (Channel 4, First broadcast 1982)
  An award-winning, American documentary film about three years in the life of a fifty year-old mentally handicapped man living with his ageing parents, covering his move from home to a day centre and finally to a group home nearby. (Available from Concord.
Let Me Win (RTE Television, First broadcast 1981)
  A documentary on the Irish Special Olympics for mentally handicapped people.
The Silent Minority (BBC documentary, First broadcast 1981)
  Portrays life in various residential centres for mentally handi-

capped people, including a mental subnormality hospital. Caused controversy when first broadcast. (Now available from Concord.)

Books

In recent years there has been a wealth of books published about disability. It would be impossible and indeed unnecessary to list them all here. Your local librarian or bookseller will help you track down possible titles once you specify your topic. Alternatively, publishing houses will happily supply their catalogues on request. We begin by giving the names and addresses of publishers who have a reputation for books on rehabilitation and disability. We then go on to recommend specific books which should be of use to community educators.

(a) *Publishers*

Associated Book Publishers (Methuen, Tavistock), North Way, Andover, Hants.

Croom Helm, St John's Chambers, 2–10 St John's Road, London, SW11 1PN.

George Allen & Unwin, PO Box 18, Park Lane, Hemel Hempstead, Hertfordshire, HP2 4TE.

Heinemann, 15 Queen Street, London W1.

Hodder and Stoughton Educational, Mill Road, Dunton Green, Sevenoaks, Kent.

NFER – Nelson, Darville House, 2 Oxford Road East, Windsor, Berks SL4 1BW.

Penguin Books, Bath Road, Harmondsworth, Middlesex, England.

Routledge & Kegan Paul, Broadway House, Reading Road, Henley-on-Thames, Oxfordshire RG9 1EN.

Souvenir Press – Human Horizons Series, 43 Great Russell Street, London WC1B 3PA.

Woodhead-Faulkner, 17 Market Street, Cambridge CB2 3PA

(b) *Selected Books*

More than Sympathy: The everyday needs of sick and handicapped children and their families, by Richard Lansdown, Tavistock Press, 1979.

Very readable and informative overview of all the different types of handicap. A chapter is devoted to each: outlining the causes, treatments and services.

People like us: Disability – the people and the facts by Anne Dempsey, Union of Voluntary Organisations for the Handicapped in association with the Health Education Bureau, Dublin, 1982.

Clearly and succinctly outlines the main features of each disability with plentiful references to case studies. In addition there are six profiles of disabled people.

Disability – whose handicap? by Anne Shearer, Blackwell, London 1981.

Explores the significance of disability and society's attitudes through a series of personal accounts from people with different impairments.

The Disabled Child and Adult by Brian M. Meredith, London, Baillierc Tindall, 1982.

Written mainly for professionals in training, it gives a good overview of the various people employed in services for disabled people.

Handicap in a Social World edited by Anne Brechin, Penny Liddiard and John Swain, London, Hodder and Stoughton/- Open University Press, 1981.

Look at it This Way: New perspectives in rehabilitation by Anne Brechin and Penny Liddiard, London, Hodder and Stoughton/- Open University Press, 1981.

Two excellent resource books of articles covering many different facets of disabled people living in the community.

Down's Syndrome: an introduction for parents by Cliff Cunningham, London, Souvenir Press, 1982.

People not Patients: Problems and policies in Mental Handicap by Peter Mittler, London, Methuen, 1979.

Visually Handicapped Children and Young People by Elizabeth Chapman, London, Routledge & Kegan Paul, 1978.

The Hearing Impaired Child and the Family by Michael Nolan and Ivan Tucker, London, Souvenir Press, 1981.

The views of disabled people or their families

A boy called Alan, by Ray Rivlin, Mercier Press, Dublin 1974.

The account of an Irish mother's experiences in bringing up a mentally handicapped son.

Tongue Tied by Joey Deacon, the Royal Society for Mentally Handicapped Children and Adults, London, 1974.

Written by a man who was resident for 30 years in a mental handicap institution. it is a fascinating account of life from the inside.

Disabled We Stand by Allan T. Sutherland, Souvenir Press, London, 1981.

Looks at the practical difficulties facing people with disabilities.

Where's there a Will by Mike Brace, Sphere paperbacks, London, 1982.
The author, blinded when 10 years old, tells how he adjusted and built himself a fulfilling life. He gives frank opinions on the facilities for disabled people.

Deafness: A personal account by David Wright, Allen Lane, 1969.

For the Love of Ann by James Copeland, Arrow Books, 1973. A father's account of his daughter's autism and gradual improvement.

Another door Opens by Margaret and Jack Wymer, Souvenir Press, London, 1980.
A wheelchair-bound married couple tell of their experiences of living on their own.

I Can't See what You're Saying by Elizabeth Browning, Elek, 1972. A highly readable account of a mother's life with a son who had a severe language disorder.

Images of ourselves: Women with disabilities talking edited by J. Campling, Routledge and Kegan Paul, London, 1981.

We can Speak for Ourselves: Self-advocacy by mentally handicapped people by Paul Williams and Bonnie Shoultz, Souvenir Press, London, 1982.

A Disjointed Life by Corbet Woodall, Heinemann, London, 1980.
A television personality describes his struggle against arthritis and his determination to improve the public's attitude towards the disabled.

Services

Guide for the Disabled by Richard Mooney, Ward River Press, Dublin, 1982.

Directory for the Disabled by Ann Darnborough and Derek Kinrade, Woodhead-Faulkner in association with RADAR, Cambs, 3rd edition, 1981.

The Politics of Mental Handicap by Joanna Ryan with Frank Thomas, Penguin Books, 1980.

Normalization: The principle of normalization in human services, by Wolf Wolfensberger, National Institute on Mental Retardation, 1972.

A Life Together: The distribution of attitudes around the disabled by Tim Dartington, Eric Miller and Geraldine Gwynne, by Tavistock, London, 1981.

Major issues in planning services for mentally and physically handicapped persons by Pauline Faughnan and Sile O'Connor, National Economic and Social Council, Government Publications, Dublin, 1980.

A Handbook for Parents with a Handicapped Child by Judith Stone and Felicity Taylor, Arrow Books, London, 1977.

Rehabilitation Today edited by Stephen Mattingly, Update Publications 33–34 Alfred Place, London WC1, 1980.

Physical Handicap: A guide for staff of social services departments and voluntary agencies by Leslie Bell and Astrid Klemz, Woodhead-Faulkner, Cambridge, 1981.

Getting Together: A study of members of PHAB Clubs by Rosalind Lain, NFER – Nelson, Windsor, 1982.

Mental Retardation: The Leading Edge – Service Programs That Work US Department of Health, Education and Welfare, Washington, 1979 (available from US Government Printing Office, Washington DC 20402).

Magazines and Journals

(a)   General interest articles about disability are carried from time to time in the following magazines, which can be ordered through newsagents or on subscription direct from the publishers:

New Society
New Science Publications, Commonwealth House, 1–19 Oxford Street, London WC1.

Health and Social Service Journal
Therapy (aimed mainly at therapists) 4 Little Essex Street, London WC2R 3LF.

Community Care
IPC Building and Contract Journals Ltd., Surrey House, 1 Throwley Way, Sutton, Surrey.

Rehabilitation World
American magazine for disabled people. Available on subscription from: Circulation Department, 20 West 40th Street, New York, NY 10018, USA.

NB Organisations concerned with different disabilities also produce regular newsletters or magazines (see p246). These often contain informative articles, with special features on individuals.

(b)   *Research Studies*
There have been many research studies into community education, some of which we have referenced (see p250). However, it is impossible to give a comprehensive listing and this would become quickly out-of-date. We have chosen instead to list those journals which are most likely to publish pertinent articles. Often these are obtainable only in

specialist libraries, but most universities or polytechnics do allow outside readers to consult their journal collections.

Listings of Journal Articles

Current Contents: Social and Behavioural Sciences
Institute for Scientific Information, 3501 Market Street, University City Science Centre, Philadelphia, Pennsylvania, 19104, USA.
A weekly listing of articles published in journals along with authors' names and the address to write to for copies of the articles.

Current Awareness Service
British Institute for Mental Handicap, Wolverhampton Road, Kidderminster. Worcestershire, DY10 3PP.
A monthly listing of recently published articles on mental handicap arranged under themes.

Rehabilitation Literature
2023 W. Ogden Avenue, Chicago, Illinois 60612, USA.
Abstracts of articles published in journals.

Journals

American Journal of Mental Deficiency
Amer. Assn. Mental Deficiency, 5101 Wisconsin Ave., NW, Washington DC, 20016.

Education and Training of the Mentally Retarded
Council for the Exceptional Child, Division on Mental Retardation, 1920 Association Dr., Reston., Va. 22091.

Exceptional Children
Council for the Exceptional Child, Division on Mental Retardation, 1920 Association Dr., Reston, Va. 22091.

Focus on Exceptional Children
Love Public. Co., 1777 South Bellaire St., Denver, Colorado 80222.

International Journal of Rehabilitation Research
G. Schindele Verlag. Hugo-Stotz-Str 14, D–6900, Heidelberg 1, Fed. Rep. Germany.

Journal of Mental Deficiency Research
Blackwell Scientific Association Ltd., PO Box 88, Oxford OX2 0E1, England.

Journal of Rehabilitation
National Rehabilitation Association, 633 S. Washington Street, Alexandra, Va. 22314.

Journal of Rehabilitation of the Deaf
Prof. Rehab. Workers Adult Deaf, 814 Thayer Ave., Silver

Spring MD 20910, USA.
Mental Retardation
Amer Assn Mental Deficiency, 5101 Wisconsin Ave. NW Washington DC 20016, USA.
Public Health
Academic Press Inc. Ltd., 24–28 Oval Road, London NW1 7DX, England.
Rehabilitation Counselling Bulletin
Amer. Personnel Guidance Assn. 2 Skyline Place-Suite, 400 5203 Leesburg Pike, Falls Church, Va 22041, USA.
Rehabilitation Literature
National Easter. Seal. Soc., 2023 W. Ogden Ave., Chicago, Il. 60612, USA.
Rehabilitation Psychology
Springer Publ. Co. 200 Park Ave South, New York, NY 10003, USA.

Courses

Open University – 'The Handicapped Person in the Community'
This is a one-year course open to anyone on application and it can also be taken by students studying for a degree with the Open University.

It consists of 16 units of specially written text along with accompanying television and radio programmes and regular tutorials held in local centres. All the studying is done at home. This forms a most comprehensive and unique course on handicap. All the materials for the course have recently been updated. Highly recommended for those who wish to make an in-depth study of disability.

Further information from: Open University, Walton Hall, Milton Keynes MK7 6AT.

British Institute of Mental Handicap
Details of their educational programme can be had from the Conference-Course Organiser, BIMH, Wolverhampton Road, Kidderminster, Worcs. DY10 3PP.

Castle Priory College (The Spastics Society) Thames Street, Wallingford, Oxfordshire, OX10 0HE.

3 ORGANISATIONS

Most of the organisations listed here produce information leaflets about disability, publish a regular newsletter or magazine with articles on many aspects of disability, including human interest stories, and keep listings of relevant films, etc. Some will have produced educational packages, but all should be able to direct you to other sources of information.

England and Wales
Action Research for the Crippled Child
  (National Fund for Research into Crippling Diseases),
  Vincent House, North Parade, Horsham, West Sussex RH12 2DA.
ARMS (Action for Research into Multiple Sclerosis),
  71 Gray's Inn Road, London WC1X 8TR.
Association for all Speech Impaired Children,
  347 Central Markets, London EC14 9NH.
Association for Spina Bifida and Hydrocephalus,
  Tavistock House North, Tavistock Square, London WC1H 9HJ.
British Association of the Hard of Hearing,
  6 Great James Street, London WC1N 3DA.
British Council for the Rehabilitation of the Disabled,
  Tavistock House South, Tavistock Square, London WC1 9LB.
British Epilepsy Association,
  Crowthorne House, New Wokingham Road, Wokingham, Berkshire RG11 3AY.
British Institute of Mental Handicap,
  Wolverhampton Road, Kidderminster, Worcestershire, DY10 3PP.
Campaign for Mentally Handicapped People *and* Community and Mental Handicap Educational and Research Association,
  16 Fitzroy Square, London W1P 5HQ.
Disabled Living Foundation,
  346 Kensington High Street, London W14 8NS.
Down's Children's Association,
  Quinbourne Centre, Ridgeacre Road, Quinton, Birmingham, B32 3TW.
Health Education Council,
  78 New Oxford Street, London WC1.

L'Arche UK,
  14 London Road, Beccles, Suffolk, NR4 9NH.
Mencap – The Royal Society for Mentally Handicapped Children
  and Adults,
  123 Golden Lane, London EC1Y 0RT.
MIND – National Association for Mental Health,
  22 Harley Street, London W1N 2ED.
Multiple Sclerosis Society,
  286 Munster Road, London SW6 6AP.
National Association for the Deaf-Blind and Rubella Handicapped,
  164 Cromwell Road, Coventry, CV4 8AP.
National Children's Bureau,
  8 Wakley Street, Islington, London EC15 7QE.
National Federation of the Blind of the United Kingdom,
  c/o Jill Allen, 59 Silversea Drive, Southend, Essex.
National Autistic Society,
  276 Willesden Lane, London WC2 5RB.
Network for the Handicapped,
  Bedford House, 35 Emerald Street, London WC1N 3QL.
PHAB – Physically Handicapped and Able-Bodied,
  42 Devonshire Street, London W1N 1LN.
RADAR – The Royal Association for Disability and Rehabili-
  tation,
  25 Mortimer Street, London W1N 8AB.
Royal National Institute for the Blind,
  224–8 Great Portland Street, London W1N 6AA.
Royal National Institute for the Deaf,
  105 Gower Street, London WC1E 6AH.
The Spastics Society,
  12 Park Crescent, London W1N 4EQ.
Spinal Injuries Association,
  5 Crowndale Road, London NW1 1TU.
Wales Council for the Disabled,
  Llys Ifor, Crescent Road, Caerphilly, Mid-Glamorgan CF81
  1XL.

Scotland
Multiple Sclerosis Society – Association of Scottish Branches,
  27 Castle Street, Edinburgh, EH2 3HT.
Scottish Council on Disability,
  18–19 Claremont Crescent, Edinburgh EG7 4QD.
Scottish Epilepsy Association,
  48 Govan Road, Glasgow G51 1JL.

Scottish Health Education Group,
  Woodburn House, Canaan Lane, Edinburgh EH10 4SG.
Scottish Society for the Mentally Handicapped,
  13 Elmbank Street, Glasgow G2 4QA.
Scottish Spina Bifida Association,
  190 Queensferry Road, Edinburgh EH4 2BW.
Scottish Trust for the Physically Disabled,
  32 Inglis Green Road, Edinburgh EG14 2ER.

Northern Ireland
Association for Spina Bifida and Hydrocephalus – Northern
  Ireland Association,
  132 Orangefield Crescent, Belfast 6.
MENCAP – Northern Ireland Region,
  Segal House, 4 Annadale Avenue, Belfast BT7 3JH.
Multiple Sclerosis Society – Northern Ireland Branch,
  34 Annadale Avenue, Belfast BT7 3HT.
National Society for Autistic Children – Northern Ireland Society,
  13a Seahill Drive, Craigavad, Holywood, Co. Down.
Northern Ireland Council for the Handicapped,
  2 Annadale Avenue, Belfast BT7 3JH.
Royal National Institute for the Blind – Northern Ireland Branch,
  Bryson House, 28 Bedford Street, Belfast BT2 7FE.

Republic of Ireland
The Arthritis Foundation of Ireland,
  12 Herbert Street, Dublin 2.
Camphill Village Community,
  Duffcarrig, Ballymoney, Co. Wexford.
Central Remedial Clinic,
  Vernon Avenue, Clontarf, Dublin 3.
The Downs Syndrome Association of Ireland,
  P.O. Box 1045, Ballsbridge, Dublin 4.
Health Education Bureau,
  34 Upper Mount Street, Dublin 2.
Irish Association for Spina Bifida and Hydrocephalus,
  Ground Floor, Joseph Plunkett Tower, Ballymun, Dublin 11.
Irish Epilepsy Association,
  249 Crumlin Road, Dublin 12.
Irish Wheelchair Association,
  'Aras Cuchulain', Blackheath Drive, Clontarf, Dublin 3.
The Mental Health Association of Ireland,
  2 Herbert Avenue, Merrion Road, Dublin 4.

National Association for the Deaf,
  25 Lower Leeson Street, Dublin 2.
National Association for the Mentally Handicapped of Ireland
  (NAMHI),
  5 Fitzwilliam Place, Dublin 2.
National Council for the Blind of Ireland,
  Armitage House, 10 Lower Hatch Street, Dublin 2.
National Rehabilitation Board,
  25 Clyde Road, Dublin 4.
National Social Service Board,
  71 Lower Leeson Street, Dublin 2.
Rehabilitation Institute,
  30 Leeson Park, Dublin 6.
The Union of Voluntary Organisations for the Handicapped,
  29 Eaton Square, Monkstown, Co. Dublin.

Selected Addresses in North America
American Academy for Cerebral Palsy,
  1255 New Hampshire Avenue NW, Washington, DC 20036.
American Association on Mental Deficiency,
  5101 Wisconsin Avenue NW, Washington, DC 20016.
American Council of the Blind,
  1211 Connecticut Avenue NW, Suite 506, Washington DC
  20036.
Association for Retarded Citizens,
  2501 Avenue J, P.P. Box 6109 Arlington, Texas 76011.
Council for Exceptional Children,
  Information Services, 1920 Association Drive, Reston, Va
  22091.
Epilepsy Foundation of America,
  1828 L Street NW, Washington, DC 20036.
International Exchange of Information in Rehabilitation,
  400 East 34th Street, New York, NY 10016.
National Association of the Deaf,
  814 Thayer Avenue, Silver Spring, MD 20910.
National Institute on Mental Retardation,
  University Campus, 4700 Keele Street, Downsview, Toronto,
  Canada.
National Paraplegia Foundation,
  333 N. Michigan Avenue, Chicago, IL 60601.
National Society for Autistic Children,
  306 31st Street, Huntingdon, WV 25702.

4 REFERENCES USED IN COMPILING THE BOOK

Introduction to Section 1
1 Robert A. Scott (1969), *The Making of Blind Men,* New York, Russell Sage Foundation.
2 Ivan Scheffler (1967), 'Philosophical Models of Teaching,' in *Concepts of Education*, edited by R.S. Peters, London, Routledge and Kegan Paul.
3 Peter Moore (1982), profiled in *People Like Us*, by Anne Dempsey, Dublin, U.V.O.H.
4 Erving Goffman (1963), *Stigma, Notes on the management of spoiled identity*, Middlesex, Penguin.

Chapter 1
1 Christy Brown (1974), *My Left Foot: The childhood story of Christy Brown*, London, Pan Books.
2 *Integrating the disabled: Report of the Snowdon Working Party*, (1976) Horsham, National Fund for Research into Crippling Diseases.
3 Home Office, Department of Education and Science, Ministry of Housing and Local Government, Ministry of Health (1968), *Report of the Committee on Local Authority and Allied Personal Social Services* (The Seebohm Report). Cmnd 3703, London, HMSO.
4 Michael Bayley (1973), *Mental Handicap and Community Care: A study of mentally handicapped people in Sheffield*, London, Routledge and Kegan Paul.
5 David Thomas (1978), *The Social Psychology of Childhood Disability,* London, Methuen.
6 *People Like Us: Disability – the people and the facts* (1982), Dublin, Union of Voluntary Organisations for the Handicapped.
7 Peter Townsend, (1973) *The Social Minority*, London, Allen Lane.
8 Amelia Harris *et al* (1971), *Handicapped and Impaired in Great Britain, Vol. 1.* London, Office of Population Censuses and Surveys, HMSO.
9 Department of Health and Social Security, *Priorities for Health and Personal Social Services in England*, Consultative Document, London, HMSO.

10   Michael Mulcahy *et al* (1983), 'Census of the Mentally Handicapped in the Republic of Ireland 1981,' *Irish Medical Journal*, 76, No. 1.

11   Roy McConkey *et al* (1981), 'The recreational pursuits of mentally handicapped adults,' *International Journal of Rehabilitation Research*, 1981, 4, 493–499.

12   Health Education Bureau. (1979). *Leisure, Health and Fitness: A survey of Irish adults*, Dublin, Unpublished report

13   T. Dowling et al (1971), *Urban community survey*, Dublin, Unpublished report.

14   Sally Cheseldine and Dorothy Jeffree (1981), 'Mentally Handicapped Adolescents: Their use of leisure,' *Journal of Mental Deficiency Research*, 25, 49–59

15   Shunit Reiter and Avraham Levi (1981), 'Leisure Activities of Mentally Retarded Adults,' *American Journal of Mental Deficiency*. 86, 201–203.

16   V. Beck Ford *et al* (1979), 'Recreation and leisure time as an integral part of rehabilitation programming for the mentally handicapped adult,' *REAP (Research exchange and practice in mental retardation)*. 3, 153–168.

17   Francesca Lundström-Roche (1981), *Our Lives*, Dublin, Irish National Committee for the International Year of Disabled People.

18   In *Youth Service*, 1974, Vol 14 no. 3.

19   Gillian S. Johnson and Ralph Johnson (1973) 'Paraplegics in Scotland: a survey of employment and facilities,' *British Journal of Social Work*, 18, 19–38.

20   Pauline Faughnan (1977) *Dimensions of Need*, Dublin, Irish Wheelchair Association.

Chapter 2

1   Louis Batty, (1966) 'The Chatterly Syndrome,' in *Stigma: The experience of disability,* edited by Paul Hunt, London, Geoffrey Chapman.

2   'Our image of the disabled and how ready we are to help' (1981), *New Society*, January 1.

3   'Has the International Year helped disabled people?' (1981), *New Society*, December 24.

4   Norman Webb and Robert Wybrow, *The Gallup Report: Your opinions in 1981*; London, Sphere.

5   Reaction of the general public to physically disabled, and mentally handicapped and ill people (1981), Unpublished report, Dublin, Health Education Bureau.

6   Public attitudes towards the mentally handicapped – a research study conducted by Market and Opinion Research International for Mencap in 1982.

7 Roy McConkey *et al* (1983), 'A National Survey of Young People's Perceptions of Mental Handicap,' *Journal of Mental Deficiency Research* (in the press).
8 Milton Rokeach (1973), *The Nature of Human Values,* New York, Free Press.

Chapter 3
1 Snowdon Working Party (op. cit.).
2 J. Donaldson (1980), 'Changing attitudes to handicapped persons: a review and analysis of research,' *Exceptional Children,* 46, 504–514.
3 A. Sandler and R. Robinson (1981), 'Public attitudes and community acceptance of mentally retarded persons: A review,' *Education and Training of the Mentally Retarded,* 16, 97–103.
4 B. Kutner (1971), cited by J. Donaldson (op. cit.).
5 J. Gottlieb (1975), 'Public, peer and professional attitudes towards disabled and mentally retarded persons,' in M.J. Begad and S.A. Richardson (eds.), *The Mentally Retarded in Society: A Social Science Perspective*, Baltimore, University Park Press.
6 R. Ashmore (1975), 'Background considerations in developing strategies for changing attitudes and behaviour towards the mentally retarded,' in M.J. Begad and S.A. Richardson (op. cit.).
7 G. Siperstein and A. Chatilion (1982), 'Importance of perceived similarity in improving children's attitudes toward mentally retarded peers,' *American Journal of Mental Deficiency,* 86, 453–458.
8 R. McConkey *et al* (1983), 'Changing young people's perceptions of mentally handicapped adults,' *Journal of Mental Deficiency Research* (submitted).
9 J. Shotel *et al* (1972), 'Teacher attitudes associated with the integration of handicapped children,' *Exceptional Children,* 38, 677–683.
10 B. Wallston, *et al* (1972), cited by J. Donaldson (op. cit.).
11 J.H. Evans (1976), 'Changing attitudes toward disabled persons: An experimental study,' *Rehabilitation Counseling Bulletin,* 19, 572–579.
12 R. McConkey *et al* (1983), 'Changing attitudes to mental handicap through an adult education course, *Public Health* (in the press).
13 J. Donaldson and M. Martinson (1977), 'Modifying attitudes toward physically disabled persons,' *Exceptional Children,* 43, 337–341.
14 S. Salend (1981), 'Cooperative games promote positive

student interactions,' *Teaching Exceptional Children*, 13, 76–78.

15 M. Ballard *et al* (1977), 'Improving the social status of main-streamed retarded children,' *Journal of Educational Psychology*, 69, 605–611.

16 G. Siperstein *et al* (1977), 'Effects of group discussion on children's attitudes toward handicapped peers,' *Journal of Educational Research*, 70, 131–134.

17 T. Jones, *et al* (1981), 'Changing children's perceptions of handicapped people,' *Exceptional Children*, 47, 365–368.

18 A. LeUnes *et al* (1975), 'Institutional tour effects on attitudes related to mental retardation,' *American Journal of Mental Deficiency*, 79, 732–735.

19 E. Langer *et al* (1976), 'Stigma, staring and discomfort: A novel stimulus hypothesis,' *Journal of Experimental Social Psychology*, 12, 451–463.

20 B. Tones (1977), *Effectiveness and Efficiency in Health Education*, Edinburgh, Scottish Health Education Unit.

21 J. Donaldson (1976), 'Channel variations and effects on attitudes toward disabled persons,' *Audio-visual Communication Review*, 17, 315–321.

22 J. Freedman and D. Sears (1965), 'Selective Exposure,' in L. Berkowitz (ed.), *Advances in Experimental Social Psychology: Vol. 2.* New York, Academic Press.

23 J. McGuire (1969), 'The nature of attitudes and attitude change,' in G. Lindzey and E. Aronson (eds), *The Handbook of Social Psychology* (2nd Ed.), Massachusetts, Addison-Wesley.

24 J. Rogers (1977), *Adults Learning* (2nd Edition), Milton-Keynes, Open University.

25 M. Sedlick and J. Penta (1975), 'Changing nurse attitudes toward quadriplegics through use of television,' *Rehabilitation Literature*, 36, 274–278, 288.

26 A. Forader (1970), cited by J. Donaldson (1980).

27 V. Westervelt and J. McKinney (1980), 'Effects of a film on nonhandicapped children's attitudes toward handicapped children,' *Exceptional Children*, 46, 294–296.

28 E. Wilson and D. Alcorn (1969), 'Disability simulation and development of attitudes toward the exceptional,' *Journal of Special Education*, 3, 303–307.

29 G. Clore and K. Jeffrey (1972), 'Emotional role playing, attitude change and attraction toward a disabled person,' *Journal of Personality and Social Psychology*, 23, 105–111.

30 A. Lazar *et al* (1971), 'Changing attitudes of young mentally gifted children toward their handicapped peers,' *Exceptional Children*, 37, 600–602.

31 A. Handlers and K. Austin (1980), 'Improving attitudes of high school students toward their handicapped peers,' *Exceptional Children*, 47, 228–229.

32 D. Myers and H. Lamm (1975), 'The polarizing effect of group discussion,' *American Scientist*, 63, 297–303.

33 M. Rokeach, op cit.

Chapter 4

1 E Miller and G. Ğwynne (1972), *A Life Apart: A pilot study of residential institutions for the physically handicapped and the young chronic sick*, London, Tavistock.

2 P. Morris (1969), *Put away: A sociological study of institutions for the mentally retarded*, London, Routledge and Kegan Paul.

3 P. Williams and B. Shoultz (1981), *We Can Speak for Ourselves: Self-advocacy for mentally handicapped people*, London, Souvenir Press.

4 W. Meyer (1979), 'Breaking down prejudices about the handicapped in the Federal Republic of Germany' in *Factors promoting or hindering Health Education*, proceedings of 4th International Seminar on Health Education, Cologne, Federal Centre for Health Education.

5 R. McConkey *et al* (1983), 'Have we met? Community contacts of adults who are mentally handicapped,' *Mental Handicap* (in the press).

6 'Has the International Year helped disabled people?' (1981) *New Society*, December 24th.

7 J. Donaldson (1981), 'The visibility and image of handicapped people on television,' *Exceptional Children*, 47, 413–416.

8 President's Committee on Mental Retardation (1979), *Mental Retardation: The Leading Edge – Service programs that work*, Washington, Department of Health, Education and Welfare.

9 *Our Life. A report on the first conference held in England for mentally handicapped*, London, Campaign for Mentally Handicapped People, 1972.

10 *Rights Now: A learning programme on rights and responsibilities;* Toronto, National Institute for Mental Retardation.

Chapter 5

1 J. Ryan and F. Thomas (1980), *The Politics of Mental Handicap*, Middlesex, Pelican.

2 DHSS (1979), In-patient statistics from the *Mental Health Enquiry for England, 1976*, London, HMSO.

3 A. LeUnes, op. cit.

INDEX